Signifying bodies

Corporealities: Discourses of Disability

David T. Mitchell and Sharon L. Snyder, editors

Books available in the series:

"Defects": Engendering the Modern Body
edited by Helen Deutsch and Felicity Nussbaum

Revels in Madness: Insanity in Medicine and Literature
by Allen Thiher

Points of Contact: Disability, Art, and Culture
edited by Susan Crutchfield and Marcy Epstein

A History of Disability
by Henri-Jacques Stiker

Disabled Veterans in History
edited by David A. Gerber

Narrative Prosthesis: Disability and the Dependencies of Discourse
by David T. Mitchell and Sharon L. Snyder

Backlash Against the ADA: Reinterpreting Disability Rights
edited by Linda Hamilton Krieger

The Staff of Oedipus: Transforming Disability in Ancient Greece
by Martha L. Rose

Fictions of Affliction: Physical Disability in Victorian Culture
by Martha Stoddard Holmes

Foucault and the Government of Disability
edited by Shelley Tremain

Bodies in Commotion: Disability and Performance
edited by Carrie Sandahl and Philip Auslander

*Moving Beyond Prozac, DSM, and the New Psychiatry:
The Birth of Postpsychiatry*
by Bradley Lewis

Disability in Twentieth-Century German Culture
by Carol Poore

Concerto for the Left Hand: Disability and the Defamiliar Body
by Michael Davidson

Disability Theory
by Tobin Siebers

*The Songs of Blind Folk: African American Musicians and the
Cultures of Blindness*
by Terry Rowden

Signifying Bodies: Disability in Contemporary Life Writing
by G. Thomas Couser

SIGNIFYING BODIES

§

Disability in Contemporary Life Writing

G. Thomas Couser

THE UNIVERSITY OF MICHIGAN PRESS
Ann Arbor

Published in the United States of America by
The University of Michigan Press
Manufactured in the United States of America
♾ Printed on acid-free paper

2012   2011   2010   2009   4   3   2   1

A CIP catalog record for this book is available from the British Library.

Library of Congress Cataloging-in-Publication Data

Couser, G. Thomas.
  Signifying bodies : disability in contemporary life writing /
G. Thomas Couser.
    p. cm. — (Corporealities: discourses of disability)
  Includes index.
  ISBN 978-0-472-07069-5 (cloth : alk. paper) — ISBN 978-0-472-05069-7
(pbk. : alk. paper)
    1. People with disabilities—United States—Biography—History
and criticism.   2. People with disabilities, Writings of, American.
3. People with disabilities in literature.   4. Autobiography.   I. Title.
PS153.P48C68   2009
810.9'92087—dc22   2009018643

§

In memory of

Lucy Grealy (1963–2002)

and

Harriet McBryde Johnson (1957–2008)

Acknowledgments

This book represents the culmination of work that began with *Recovering Bodies: Illness, Disability, and Life Writing* (Wisconsin, 1997) and continued with *Vulnerable Subjects: Ethics and Life Writing* (Cornell, 2004). In this long project my interest in life writing brought me into the field of disability studies. Over the course of my involvement in disability studies, I have incurred debts beyond those I can do justice to here. But I want to thank Rosemarie Garland-Thomson, who first welcomed me into the field—before I knew it existed, much less that I was in it.

I am also indebted to editors of journals and special issues in which earlier versions of some chapters appeared: Rita Charon, editor of *Literature and Medicine,* for soliciting chapter 2 (under a different title), "Paradigms Cost: Disability and Cultural Representation"; Charles M. Anderson for permission to reprint it; James C. Wilson and Cynthia Lewiecki-Wilson for editing the volume, *Embodied Rhetorics,* in which chapter 3, "Rhetoric and Self-Representation in Disability Memoir," first appeared (under a different title); Southern Illinois University Press for permission to reprint it; Craig Howes, editor of *Biography* (and running companion in Melbourne, Beijing, and Honolulu), for permission to reprint chapter 5, "Identity, Identicality, and Life Writing: Telling (the Silent) Twins Apart"; Monica Casper for editing the special issue of *Journal of Contemporary Ethnography* in which chapter 6, "Autoethnography and Developmental Disability: *Riding the Bus with My Sister,*" appeared; Scott A. Hunt, editor of *JCE* for permission to reprint it here; Brenda Brueggemann and Marian Lupo for editing the special issue of *Prose Studies* in which chapter 7, "Disability as Metaphor: What's Wrong with *Lying,*" appeared; Ronald Corthell, editor of *Prose Studies,* for permission to reprint it; Andrew Sparkes, editor of *Auto/Biography,* for permission to reprint (under a new title) chapter 8, "Lucy Grealy and the Some Body Obituary," and for introducing me to real ale in Exeter, UK; Brenda Brueggemann, again, for not taking no for an answer when she invited me to write and deliver the paper that became chapter 9, "Life Writing and Disability Law: Undoing Hardship"; James Phelan, editor of *Narrative,* for permission to reprint it. In addition, I thank Robert Polito of the New School for the invitation that led to the talk that provided the kernel of "The Some Body Memoir."

The manuscript benefitted from generous, thoughtful, and helpful comments by Susannah Mintz and an anonymous reader. I am also indebted to Sharon Snyder and David T. Mitchell for initiating the Michigan series in which this volume takes its place—as well as for their seminal work in the field. And I am grateful to LeAnn Fields, senior editor at the University of Michigan Press, for her generous reception of my manuscript; to Scott Ham and Marcia LaBrenz, for expeditious handling of it; and to Janice Brill for eagle-eyed copyediting.

Julia Watson, longtime friend, colleague, and e-penpal, first put the idea for this book into my head. Without her thoughtful nudge, it might well not exist.

As my teaching career draws toward its end, I am increasingly grateful for the intellectual stimulation and companionship of colleagues in my two areas of specialization, life writing studies and disability studies. They are too many to name, but in life writing, let me single out John Eakin, whose work has been a model of clarity and cogency and who has enlivened many conference venues. In disability studies, I owe a particular debt to Michael Bérubé for an opportunity to present some of the contents of this book at Pennsylvania State University and for his generous response to my earlier work.

On the home front, my daily life, corporeal and otherwise, continues to be enriched by the presence of my wife and peerless kayaking companion, Barbara Zabel.

Contents

1 ❧ Introduction

The Some Body Memoir

In April 2002, in a lively review-essay entitled "Almost Famous: The Rise of the 'Nobody' Memoir" in the *Washington Monthly,* Lorraine Adams distinguished, usefully but also invidiously, between the "somebody memoir" and the "nobody memoir," according to whether the author is known before its publication or becomes known only through its publication. Thus, Hillary Clinton's *Living History* is a somebody memoir while Lucy Grealy's *Autobiography of a Face* is a nobody memoir. This difference entails another, of course: somebody memoirs have preexisting audiences created by the eminence of their authors, whereas nobody memoirs have to create their readership from scratch by means of marketing, reviews, and word of mouth. One could say, then, that although nobody memoirs may be new, they earn their readership the old-fashioned way—on their merits.

Based on a sample of more than 200 recent memoirs, Adams drew up a taxonomy of the nobody memoir; according to her, the most popular types are "in order of popularity" "the childhood memoir—incestuous, abusive, alcoholic, impoverished, minority, 'normal,' and the occasional privileged . . . [;] the memoir of physical catastrophe—violence, quadriplegia, amputation, disease, death[;] . . . and [the memoir of] mental catastrophe—madness, addiction, alcoholism, anorexia, brain damage" (para. 8). Note the emphasis on dysfunction in the first type of memoir, with normal and privileged childhoods trailing traumatic ones, and the fact that the other two types are characterized as narrating distinct kinds of catastrophe. If you're not somebody, it seems, your claim to public attention as a memoirist is strongest if you have had a tragic childhood or a past visited by traumatic injury, impairment, or illness.

The demographics of the nobody memoir shed a good deal of light on the memoir boom and the backlash against it. For these new, nobody memoirists are often young, female, and highly educated; many have earned MFAs in creative writing. It has become possible, even trendy, for women to produce memoirs before they reach the age of forty (or even thirty). Lucy Grealy is typical: after graduating from Sarah Lawrence, she was trained at the Iowa Writers' Workshop, and her first book was a memoir, *Autobiography of a Face.* Lauren Slater represents an extreme instance of this phenomenon: as we'll see in chapter 7, before turning forty, she had written *four* memoirs.

Another, less obvious demographic dimension of the nobody memoirist, however, may be more significant than these: two of Adams's three categories—what she terms physical and mental catastrophe—are, in effect, *constituted* by disability. Indeed, I would argue that those two are really one: while it may make intuitive sense, Adams's distinction between physical and mental "catastrophe" is difficult to maintain at a time when mental illness is increasingly seen as primarily a function of biochemistry. While Adams's distinction between the somebody and the nobody memoir helpfully illuminates the memoir boom, I wish to point out that, ironically but significantly, the new nobody memoir is also often the memoir of *some body.* Far more than the somebody memoir, the nobody memoir is often about what it's like to have or to *be,* to live in or *as,* a particular body—indeed, a body that is usually odd or anomalous. Less often, it's about living *with,* loving, or knowing intimately someone with such a body. (I will refer to the latter as somatography, the former as autosomatography, and the two together as auto/somatography.) And that means that the much-ballyhooed "memoir boom" has also been a boom in disability life writing, although publishers and reviewers rarely, if ever, acknowledge it as such.

In this regard as well, Lucy Grealy personified—literally embodied—the nobody/some body memoirist. From its title on, *Autobiography of a Face* is concerned with what it was like to live with a particular bodily configuration. Grealy had cancer of the jaw as a child; the initial treatment was significantly disfiguring, and over the course of her too-short life—she died in her late thirties—she had dozens of reconstructive surgeries. Her condition thus demonstrated both the potential and the limitations of contemporary medicine, which could save her from a cancer with a very high mortality rate but could never fully repair the damage to her face. Indeed, her facial disfigurement was largely iatrogenic, caused not so much by her cancer as by the medical treatment for it; moreover, cosmetic surgery on her face scarred other parts of her body, from which it scavenged tissue. So while biomedicine saved her life, it exacted a price literally in pieces of flesh.

Before the memoir boom, memoirs that foregrounded the life of the body were written mostly by movie stars (about their sex lives) or by sports stars (about their athletic feats), often with the help of collaborators. In the case of movie stars, the memoirists typically embody ideals of physical beauty; in the case of professional athletes, ideals of physical fitness or athletic skill—in short, the very sorts that people with disabilities (PWDs) sometimes refer to as "severely able-bodied." Such memoirs serve not merely to associate success and celebrity with outstanding beauty or coordination but also to suggest that exceeding physical norms is a reliable route to iconic cultural status. More to the point here, both sets of memoirs are by definition *somebody* memoirs, not *some body* memoirs. Only in the last quarter of a century or so have memoirs by anonymous individuals with anomalous bodies been widely read and critically acclaimed. This development powerfully contravenes the implicit message of the somebody memoir and of our popular culture generally.

Thus, the rise of the nobody/some body memoir represents a subtle but significant shift in the demographics and body politics of American life writing. Indeed, I consider the emergence of the some body memoir the most important development in American life writing in the last three decades or so and thus a cultural and historical phenomenon of great significance. Although it is not often recognized as such, eluding most critics' radar, disability has become one of the pervasive topics of contemporary life writing. This is especially true if we look for "life writing" beyond the most obvious site, literary memoir—for example, in that most ubiquitous and overlooked life-writing genre, the obituary (see chapter 8), and in documentary film (see chapter 4). Largely unheralded, auto/somatography has become one of the primary venues through which disability authorship has spread through North American public culture at the turn of the century. Its dissemination presents a new opportunity for enhancing disability literacy in the body politic.

This phenomenon of the some body memoir has two major dimensions, which are distinct but complementary. The first is that a few conditions—diseases or disabilities—have generated large numbers of narratives, in effect, literatures of their own. In *Recovering Bodies: Illness, Disability, and Life Writing*, I surveyed four such conditions— breast cancer, HIV/AIDS, deafness, and paralysis. I could easily have added three more: blindness, depression, and autism—four, if you consider addiction a medical condition or disability. (It qualifies as a disability under the Americans with Disabilities Act; that is, people with a history of substance abuse are part of the class protected against discrimination by the law.)

This surge in auto/somatography should be understood in the context of the civil rights movements of the last quarter of the twentieth century. Just as what we sometimes call *the* civil rights movement was paralleled by the proliferation and prominence of African American autobiography (e.g., by Claude Brown, Angela Davis, Eldridge Cleaver, and Malcolm X), the women's rights movement was accompanied by the emergence of breast cancer narratives. When my mother had breast cancer in the early 1960s, not a single published narrative was available to give her comfort, support, or guidance, but narratives of breast cancer proliferated in the 1980s (in the wake of Betty Rollin's 1976 book *First, You Cry*)—a function not of advances in the medical treatment of breast cancer, alas, but of women's assertion of control over their own bodies. Such control may not protect women from cancer, but their authorship of cancer narratives is related to their claiming autonomy as patients in determining their own treatment (and as citizens more generally).

Similarly, HIV/AIDS, a disease that simultaneously killed and outed so many gay men in the United States, inevitably manifested itself in life writing as well as in more overtly political arenas. The currency of AIDS narratives (and memoirs of gay lives generally) obviously benefitted, and benefitted from, the gay rights movement.

Accounts of deafness are clearly related to the assertion of Deaf Pride and Deaf Power by people who are Deaf with a capital D—that is, those whose primary language is American Sign Language and who consider themselves not disabled but culturally distinct from those who communicate primarily through spoken language. Accounts of paralysis are similarly related to the disability rights movement, whose major legal manifestation in the United States was the passage of the Americans with Disabilities Act in 1990, a civil rights law that made it illegal to discriminate against people with disabilities on the basis of those disabilities; in fact, the law requires public facilities to be accessible to PWDs and requires employers to accommodate their special needs. As PWDs have become more visible in the public sphere, public-ation of their *lives* is an apt, perhaps inevitable, cultural corollary. (Chapter 9, "Life Writing and Disability Law: Undoing Hardship," explores the complex and reflexive relations between the ADA and disability life writing.) The larger point, however, is that disability life writing has not sprung up in a cultural or legal vacuum but rather responded to, and helped to create, greater opportunity and access to public life.

Narratives of blindness, depression, and autism are less closely linked to particular minorities with distinct political agendas. But depression has become the paradigmatic mental illness of the postmodern period, and autism has become the paradigmatic developmental disability. All three conditions have been the focus of substantial numbers of narratives. Although initially autism was more often narrated by a parent (or sibling) than by the person with autism him- or herself, there have been so many recent first-person narratives by people with autism that they have been granted, or have claimed, their own generic term: *autie-biography*.

The other major aspect of the rise of the some body memoir is complementary to the first: many conditions—again, diseases, disabilities, or minor anomalies—have produced small numbers of memoirs. Some of these conditions are of relatively recent vintage, as modern biomedicine continues to proliferate diagnostic labels and to pathologize human variation; others, though long known, have never before been represented in nonscientific nonfiction, in particular in life writing. In this latter category of conditions are amputation (Andre Dubus), amyotrophic lateral sclerosis, or Lou Gehrig's disease (Albert B. Robillard), anorexia and other eating disorders (Marya Hornbacher), Asperger's syndrome (Liane Holliday Willey), asthma (Timothy Brookes), bipolar illness (Terri Cheney), borderline personality disorder (Susanna Kaysen), cerebral palsy (Ruth Sienkiewicz-Mercer), chronic fatigue syndrome (Floyd Skloot), cystic fibrosis (Laura Rothenberg), deformity (Kenny Fries), diabetes (Lisa Roney), disfigurement (Lucy Grealy), epilepsy (Teresa McLean), locked-in syndrome (Jean-Dominique Bauby), multiple sclerosis (Nancy Mairs), Munchausen syndrome by proxy (Julie Gregory), obesity (Judith Moore), obsessive-compulsive disorder (Amy Wilensky), Parkinson's (Michael J. Fox), stuttering (Marty Jezer), stroke (Robert McCrum, May Sarton), and Tourette's syndrome (Lowell Handler).[1]

More remarkable, conditions that might seem to preclude verbal self-representation have recently been given autobiographical expression: for example, aphasia (lack of speech, Helen Harker Wolf), Down syndrome (Jason Kingsley and Mitchell Levitz), and even early-stage Alzheimer's (Thomas DeBaggio, Diane Friel McGowin).

Auto/somatography also responds to recent scientific developments. In particular, the decoding of the human genome has made possible more definitive testing for risks of hereditary conditions. Thus, following the example of Alice Wexler's pioneering *Mapping Fate: A Memoir of Family, Risk, and Genetic Research,* which chronicles her mother's decline and demise from Huntington's disease and explores the questions that her lineage raises for her and her sister, others have explored these same issues with regard to other genetic conditions, including some types of breast and ovarian cancer (e.g., Jessica Queller). Such life writing, which we may call auto/genography, is notable for the way in which it inscribes a particular kind of biological relationality, exploring the way certain somatic conditions may be passed along from generation to generation—or not: such memoirs are often spurred by the hope that the genetic transmission can be arrested.

What links these books is the fundamental endeavor to destigmatize various anomalous bodily conditions. Disability memoir should

---

1. Not all some body memoirs have to do with disease or disability. I would also include under this heading narratives of minor anomalies. One such narrative would be Susan Seligson's *Stacked: A 32DDD Reports from the Front.* I would also include erotic memoirs, more and more of which are being published by women other than sex workers, under their own names. See, for example, Jane Juska's *A Round-Heeled Woman.*

be seen, therefore, not as spontaneous self-expression but as a re-sponse—indeed a retort—to the traditional misrepresentation of dis-ability in Western culture generally. One can see why autosomatogra-phy is a particularly important form of life writing about disability: written from inside the experience in question, it involves *self*-repre-sentation by definition and thus offers an opportunity for personal revaluation of that condition. Disability autobiographers typically be-gin from a position of marginalization, belatedness, and pre-inscrip-tion. Long the objects of others' classification and examination, dis-abled people have only recently assumed the initiative in representing themselves; in disability autobiography particularly, disabled people counter their historical objectification (or even abjection) by occupy-ing the subject position. The representation of disability in such nar-ratives is thus a political as well as a mimetic act—a matter of speaking *for* as well as speaking *about*.

Not everyone welcomes the rise of the auto/somatography. In a re-view of my *Recovering Bodies,* a physician, A. M. Daniels, attributed the recent proliferation of narratives of illness and disability to "the death of humility as a social virtue"; he went on, "at one time, after all, only people of great or exceptional achievement, or with an extraordinary or exemplary tale to tell, would have written an autobiography." (The latter point may sound plausible, but it certainly has not been the case for the last couple of hundred years that only those of exceptional ac-complishment have written autobiography; from its origins, modern memoir has always attracted scoundrels as well as paragons.) Daniels unapologetically favors the somebody memoir over the some body memoir. Notice, however, that Daniels does not frame his judgment in literary terms. In fact, he hadn't read the books in question; he just knew that he didn't want to. To Dr. Daniels, sick and disabled people are to be seen—preferably in the clinic—and not heard, and certainly not read. Conservative cultural critics like him may be quite outspo-ken in their efforts to perpetuate the silence of people with aberrant bodies. But autobiography can be an especially powerful medium in which disabled people can demonstrate that they have lives, in defiance of others' commonsense perceptions of them.

Indeed, disability autobiography may be regarded as a postcolonial—indeed, an anticolonial—phenomenon, a form of autoethnography, as

Mary Louise Pratt has defined it: "instances in which colonized subjects undertake to represent themselves in ways that *engage with* [read: contest] the colonizer's own terms" (7). A text that demonstrates this particularly well is Susanna Kaysen's *Girl, Interrupted,* an account of her sojourn in a mental hospital. Kaysen astutely avoids ready-made narrative formulas and plots; instead of offering a linear account of her experience, she produces a collage of short chapters of distinct and very disparate types. Some are brief vignettes of herself or other patients; others are meditations on the inadequacy of medical terminology and hence the diagnosis of mental illness. (In her riff on her diagnosis of "borderline personality disorder," she makes the point that, as defined by the *Diagnostic and Statistical Manual of Mental Disorders* [DSM], many of its symptoms are features of adolescence as experienced by many young women, and I have found that reading the DSM definition aloud in class invariably stimulates nervous laughter.) Still others incorporate and interrogate the actual documents that effected her diagnosis, supervision, and discharge. Taken together, they challenge medical discourse and destabilize the commonsense distinction between the mad and the sane. Similarly, in chapter 6, I discuss Rachel Simon's *Riding the Bus with My Sister,* a memoir that, among other things, performs an act of autoethnographic advocacy for people with developmental disabilities.

I don't necessarily like, admire, or endorse all of these books; I would readily acknowledge that many of the memoirs I have read in the course of my research are not very good. But I very much welcome the phenomenon of which they are a part. For me, such books are welcome because of the way they help us to face the fact of our embodiment. I much prefer the locution "facing the body" to phrases like "thinking through the body" or "conceptualizing the body," because its use of the dead metaphor *face* for *confront* reminds us that most of the terms we use for processes of intellection are themselves derived from our embodiment.[2] In this sense, the phrase *does* what it asks us to do. (At least, it does if we revive the dead metaphor.)

---

2. I like very much Nancy Mairs's account, in *Waist-High in the World,* of balking when instructed to "conceptualize the body" at a conference, "as though I myself—my thinking self— were no body, as though this disembodied self could speak not only for the body that it is not but for bodies in general. ... The effect of the assignment seemed to me to divorce the speaking subject from her own corporal existence while permitting her to make free ... with the bodies of others" (40).

The abstraction and generality of its other term, *the body*, however, remind us of the difficulty, if not the impossibility, of ever fully confronting our embodiment. It's important to theorize our embodiment, but our quick resort to terms like *the body* reminds us how difficult it is to think effectively about embodiment without in some ways obscuring or eliding it. The brain, so highly developed in humans, the very organ that enables us to contemplate our bodies, also enables us to repudiate them. So the phrase "face the body" nicely encapsulates the problems and paradoxes involved in the project it describes.[3]

Facing our bodies is important in part because it is difficult, and it is difficult because so many forces in Western culture—Christian theology and Cartesian dualism, to name just two—operate to devalue and thus *efface* the body. Furthermore, as part of its pervasive and persistent tendency to efface embodiment, Western culture has tended to *deface* some bodies; that is to say, it has marked, marginalized, and muted whole sets of people on the basis of bodily difference—along lines of gender, race, ethnicity, and sexuality, of course, but more generally along the lines of those somatic conditions we call illness and disability.

This latter form of devaluation affects all of us because all of us may, and probably will, become ill or disabled. Unlike racial and gender minority status, disability is a minority status that anyone may assume unexpectedly at any time. Like race and gender, however, it also affects everyone in that *all* bodies are defined by the same standards and norms: just as we are all raced and we are all gendered, we are all embodied. As is the case with the parallel binaries of race, gender, ethnicity, and sexuality, the privileged position depends on its definition of the marginalized position; the notions of health and illness, normality and disability, we might say, are "co-dependent."

---

3. Our modes of communication may exacerbate this tendency. In oral cultures, the body provides the medium of communication in a fairly direct way; people speak literally face-to-face. Communication is always "live" and always transmitted bodily (the same is true of Deaf communities, that is, those that use sign language). As a medium, print effaces the body: handwriting, with its distinctive personal signature, gives way to typefaces that reflect not a book's author but its designer. With radio, the body is also absent or invisible. With the advent of television and its eventual saturation of the broader culture, the body returns to prominence, but less as the medium of communication than as its subject or subtext. Bodies are constantly and continuously on display. To sense the implications of this, we need only to consider how different the bodily parameters are for writers or radio personalities, in comparison to television news anchors.

Evidence that the policing of the borders between illness and health, abnormality and normality, is an anxious and pervasive activity is found in the fervent attempts made by many healthy, nondisabled people to reshape their bodies by means of diet, exercise, liposuction, and plastic surgery.[4] It may be worth noting in this connection that in the field of plastic surgery, what was once the paradigmatic operation, rhinoplasty, has greatly declined in popularity while other plastic surgeries have increased dramatically. The surgeries that are increasing in frequency serve not to efface ethnicity—as the nose job historically has done—but to forestall or reverse the effects of ageing; rather than disguising our different origins, plastic surgery today tends to deny our common destiny. It does this by quite literally re-facing the body—either altering the entire face by lifting it or giving the whole body a new appearance by remodeling the torso. All of this I cite as evidence of powerful impulses in modern Western culture to perfect, control, or even to transcend the body—rather than to face it as it is.

One of the late Henny Youngman's better-known one-liners was, "Death is nature's way of telling you to slow down." Similarly, we might say: illness and disability are nature's way of making us face our bodies. The moments in which we are perhaps most aware of our embodiment, then, may be those times when our bodies ail or fail, when they deviate from some more-or-less comfortable stasis or some norm that allows us to take them for granted, to put them out of mind. Until quite recently, life writing has participated in the general evasion or effacement of the body. In capsule form, the problem has been this: what Western culture (and life writing) valorize—that which makes the individual different—is, in the case of the diseased or disabled body, what Western culture devalues. Thus, the body, that which most fundamentally endows us with existence—that which most obviously individuates us—has been kept largely in the background.[5]

To me, precisely because their bodies demand to be reckoned with,

---

4. Tattooing and body piercing may be a countertrend, in that they do not attempt to efface stigmatized deviations, to make bodies conform to cultural norms, but rather to customize and individualize bodies by aesthetic alteration; they may be seen as attempts to design and "sign" one's own body, as though it were not already individual enough.

5. This is true, I think, of life writing. In dramatic and fictional literature, however, disabled bodies are often in the foreground; think of the tradition of crippled or maimed protagonists from Oedipus on through Richard III, Ahab, and the Hunchback of Notre Dame.

people with odd or problematic bodies are in a position to remind us all of our embodiment, a fundamental dimension of the human condition. In writing their lives, they advance the ongoing process by which memoir realizes its potential as what William Dean Howells famously referred to as "the most democratic province of the republic of letters" (798). By putting so many disabled lives in print, the some body memoir both reflects and advances the progress of civil rights, broadly conceived. The presence of such books in bookstores (especially if they are integrated into the "biography" section, rather than ghettoized under "health"), in public libraries, in classrooms, and in readers' homes and hands is an analogue of the higher profile of anomalous bodies in the public sphere. Bodies have always signified in Western culture, too often to the disadvantage of those with bodies that differ from some ideal or norm—racial, ethnic, and so on. Perhaps what most distinguishes life writing in contemporary America is that individuals with such bodies are choosing to signify *on* their own bodies, rather than to allow their signification to be determined by others.

Of course, some conditions do impede or prevent self-representation, autosomatography. Under such circumstances, however, proximate others often step into the gap to produce a different sort of some body memoir. *Memoir* is an odd (and confusing) generic term in that it can be used to refer both to *self*-biography (in this sense, often with the first-person pronoun and sometimes in the plural: my memoirs) *and* to the informal, memory-based *bio*graphy of someone else whom the author knows well (in this sense, often followed by the preposition *of*: a memoir of my father or mother, e.g.). As noted earlier, the first memoirs of autism were written by the parents of autistic children. Similarly, most of the first HIV/AIDS memoirs were written by relatives of men who had died of the complications of the condition. And now, at the dawn of the new millennium, as baby boomers' parents are entering senescence and sometimes senility, memoirs of parents with Alzheimer's are rapidly proliferating. Insofar as the nature of dementia, especially Alzheimer's, is to strip away the memories and cognitive abilities that create and maintain one's personal identity, memoir ventures here into the realm of the postpersonal.

All these may be considered under the umbrella of auto/somatography because they are memoirs provoked by and focusing on living in and as a particular body, even if the person inhabiting that body is not telling the tale him- or herself. No matter who is doing the telling, certain traps and pitfalls present themselves; those will be the subject of chapters 2 and 3, which discuss ethical, political, and rhetorical issues that are raised by disability memoir specifically and cultural representation of disability more generally. Chapter 2 should also serve to place the contemporary upsurge in disability life writing in long historical perspective, showing what contemporary life writers are up against as they seek to represent their own bodies on their own terms.

Contemporary life writing should be seen not just against the background of related civil rights movements; it also needs to seen in the context of a vast expansion in the venues (genres, media, and "platforms") available to life writers and the consequent diversity of contemporary life writing practices. When I emerged from graduate school in the mid-1970s, what is now called "life writing studies" focused primarily on autobiography, a genre privileged because of its self-authorship and distinguished tradition in Western culture, from St. Augustine onward. But the field soon recognized that autobiography was far from a gender-neutral genre; it depended on and valorized a kind of autonomous (and even atomistic) individualism more available to men than to women. Thus, many scholars' attention turned to forms of life writing more accessible to women and other marginalized groups: letters, diaries, journals, *testimonio* and other forms of witnessing, and "relational" life writing (i.e., narratives whose primary subject is not the writer but a proximate other, such as a blood relative or a partner, or the relationship between the author and that other). The term *life writing* came into use as an umbrella term to cover a wide range of not necessarily literary discursive practices devoted to representing the lives of real individuals.

The coming of the digital age has made possible new postprint forms of representation, such as the blog and the online diary. Online life writing (like self-published books) escapes the winnowing traditionally done by the gatekeepers of publishing. It may be sidestream rather than mainstream, not advertised or promoted. But it can also be live-streamed, and thus quickly and directly available: more im-mediate, in more than one sense. In this way, the digital age has had a powerfully democratizing effect on life writing. So has the availability of small, cheap, user-friendly digital cameras, which make documentary film less expensive and less difficult to produce.

At the same time that new digital media were facilitating unprecedented forms of life writing, an old medium, radio, became newly welcoming to life narrative. *This American Life,* which has been broadcast on many American public radio stations for about ten years (and made the transition to television in 2007), is essentially an on-air life-writing magazine. This weekly one-hour show typically assembles several thematically related personal narratives, sometimes elicited in interviews by the host, Ira Glass. A similar, larger-scale project is StoryCorps. Founded in 2003, StoryCorps is modeled on an important oral history project carried out in the 1930s under one of the New Deal's cultural programs, the Works Progress Administration (WPA). Underwritten by nonprofit organizations and foundations, Story Corps offers virtually free access to recording facilities in which Americans nationwide are invited to interview friends or family members for forty minutes; the recorded interviews are given to the participants on CDs, and, more important, archived in the American Folklife Center at the Library of Congress; brief excerpts from some are broadcast on National Public Radio programs. StoryCorps episodes are thus a dialogical form of "relational" life writing.

Ironically, of course, these new media, individually and collectively, threaten to make the term *life writing* obsolete, at least if *writing* is taken literally. But they have greatly expanded the repertoire of life narrative. Today the computer literate, at least, may present themselves relatively directly and freely, with little or no screening, to a mass audience in new electronic venues: the blog, a personal page on MySpace, or a personal video uploaded to YouTube (which really ought to be called MeTube). Of course, the very openness of access here militates against reaching a large audience, since easy access permits so many to compete for attention. Still, surely there is something significant in the fact that more and more otherwise anonymous people (nobodies) can place themselves, by themselves, before the public.

Not surprisingly, these media too have been explored by nobodies with odd bodies. In a recent survey of YouTube, the *New York Times* cultural reporter Virginia Heffernan selected for comment what she called "five tribes" of YouTube—that is, five clusters of related videos. Of particular interest here is cluster Heffernan refers to as "Fat Rants." In "Fat Rants," individuals comment on obesity, usually their own, often unapologetically or even proudly. This cluster in effect consists of manifestos. Although the manifesto is not a new form of life writing, it may be one to which YouTube is particularly conducive. The Internet seems to discourage extended linear narrative because, as is generally acknowledged, the attention span of the Web surfer is quite short.

A remarkable and often viewed example of a some body manifesto is "In My Language." This eight-minute video begins with startling footage (apparently shot by the subject herself) of a young woman engaged in telltale autistic behaviors. She sways back and forth, humming and flapping her hands; she bangs household objects together rhythmically; she moves her hand back and forth under running tap water; she holds a book open in front of her, but instead of reading it, she rubs her face in it over and over. (I found this particularly transgressive.) After a while, one hears a synthesized voice reading a text typed by the subject.

Autistic people are often characterized as absorbed in worlds of their own; after all, the term *autism,* like *autobiography,* comes from the Greek root for self. Contrary to this stereotype, the author of this manifesto, A. M. Baggs, a disability activist, proclaims that she interacts with her environment more fully than most "neurotypicals," who pay attention only to each other and not to the sights, sounds, and textures of their immediate surroundings. What looks deficient, she claims, is in fact excessive, not sub- but supra-normal. I cite her not to endorse her view of autism but rather to suggest that such a direct and unedited form of self-representation was hardly possible before the confluence of a number of factors, among which the technological are only the most obvious. At the beginning of a new millennium, the potential of these new media is only beginning to be tapped.

Whatever their media or platform, both autosomatography and somatography can be thought of as *quality-of-life* writing because they address questions discussed under that rubric in philosophy, ethics, and especially biomedical ethics. As such, they should be required reading for citizens in a world with underfunded, often inadequate, health care, with enormous technological capability to sustain life and repair bodies in the case of acute illness and injury but with very little commitment to accommodate and support chronic illness or disability. People with disabilities are increasingly visible in public spaces and open about their disabilities. But their physical presence in public life represents only a rather limited kind of access. Properly conceived and carried out—admittedly, a large qualifier—auto/somatography can play a crucial role by providing the reading public with mediated access to lives that would otherwise remain opaque and exotic to them. In a culture such as ours, which is at once fixated on and dismissive of bodies, narratives of anomalous somatic conditions offer an important, if not unique, point of entry for inquiry into the responsibilities of contemporary citizenship.

2 § Paradigms Cost

Disability and Cultural Representation

In chapter 1 I argued that the some body memoir is something of a special genre insofar as it speaks from the standpoint of disability (in the case of autosomatography) or from the vantage of a proximate other (in the case of somatography). Here I wish to explore the conventional cultural representation of disability more generally in order to explore its past, present, and possible future impact on a historically marginalized population. (In the subsequent chapter, I will return my attention to disability memoir.)

We may begin with the simple observation that narrative of any kind demands difference for its genesis and momentum: no complication (deviation from the status quo), no plot; no plot, no story. In short, narrative of any sort depends for its very existence on some deviation from the usual course of events. Enter disability, for as David T. Mitchell and Sharon L. Snyder have observed in *Narrative Prosthesis: Disability and the Dependencies of Discourse,* disability is called upon to accommodate narrative's dependence on anomaly with a frequency that has been generally underestimated and underanalyzed (49).

In everyday life, for example, the unmarked case—the "normal" body—can pass without narration; the marked case—the limp, the scar, the wheelchair, the missing limb—calls for a narrative. Thus, entering new situations, or reentering old ones, people with anomalous bodies are often called upon, sometimes quite explicitly, to account for them: they are often asked, without preamble, "What happened to *you?*" (Testimony to this effect can be found in a collection of narratives entitled exactly that: *What Happened to You? Writing by Disabled Women* [ed. Lois Keith].) One of the social burdens of disability, then, is that it exposes affected individuals to inspection, interrogation, and violation of privacy. The more visible the difference, the more this is the case.

In effect, people with extraordinary bodies are held responsible for them, in two senses. First, they are required to account for them—often to complete strangers; second, the expectation is that their accounts will serve to relieve their auditors' discomfort. Although the request for narration may seem impromptu, often the answer to the question, what happened to you? is in effect pre-determined: the elicited narrative is expected to conform to, and thus confirm, a cultural script. For example, people with conditions as different as lung cancer and HIV/AIDS are expected to admit to behaviors that have induced the condition in question—to acknowledge having brought it upon themselves. Thus, one fundamental connection between life writing and somatic anomaly is that to have certain conditions is to have one's life written *for* one.

Cultural representation mirrors daily life. Thus, people with disabilities are also vulnerable to involuntary and prejudicial representation in diverse media. As is demonstrated in Mitchell and Snyder's *Narrative Prosthesis,* Western culture has persistently deployed disability in literary and subliterary texts not only as a prompt for narrative but also as a trope that conflates narrative and character. Even when disability does not generate narrative, then, it may imply a back story: a crippled or scarred character, for example, may be assumed to have been traumatized and embittered, in the manner of Melville's Ahab. Scarred, maimed, and mutilated movie villains are too numerous to list; such characterization is a trite filmic convention, especially in genres like horror and film noir. Indeed, the notion of the scar as a sign of bad character sometimes even provides the *name* of the title character, as in *Scarface,* whose protagonist was played by Paul Muni in the 1932 original and by Al Pacino in the 1983 remake, or of the archvillain, as in Disney's *Lion King,* whose antagonist is called simply Scar. (Not incidentally, such characters are often put to death by the plot, lending force to the impression that deformed or disfigured people are doomed, as well as cursed.) Disabled people may be unique among marginalized populations in having been overrepresented in various media, such as the novel, drama, and film. Merely to *have* certain conditions is in some sense to be pre-represented: Western culture, both high and low, often pre-inscribes narratives on the bodies of people with aberrant somatic conditions, willy-nilly.

As I pointed out in the Introduction, however, in the last quarter of the twentieth century, a new genre has come to the fore, the some body memoir. And in the United States, at least, it has become increasingly common for ill and disabled people to represent themselves in life writing.[1] Those who represent their own experiences with disability are often consciously countering ignorance about or stigmatization of their conditions. In any case, insofar as they initiate and control their own representation, they become less vulnerable subjects. Indeed, their narratives may seek to *reduce* their vulnerability to pre-inscribed narrative. But this is still a relatively new and unappreciated cultural phenomenon, and it takes place against a background of representation in popular and literary media that often thoughtlessly perpetuates negative stereotypes.

I wish to address here, then, the situation when the portrayal of aberrant somatic states is *not* autobiographical. Such representation poses ethical problems, especially when the conditions in question render the subjects unable to represent themselves or even to collaborate in an informed way with others who undertake to represent them. Individuals with disabilities that preclude or interfere with self-representation are thus doubly vulnerable subjects.[2] Often, narratives about them are produced by people in preexisting intimate relations with them: parents, siblings, spouses, and now, with the advent of Alzheimer's narratives, adult children.[3] Less frequently, they are writ-

---

1. "Life writing" need not literally be written; documentary films and videos would be included.

2. I focus on disability here, but of course not all people with disabilities are vulnerable in this way. Further, disability is not the only condition that creates such vulnerability: so can illness, extreme age, youth, poverty or economic disadvantage, illiteracy, or lack of intellectual sophistication.

3. Parental narratives of disabled children constitute a significant body of literature; indeed, autism alone has generated a literature of its own. Clara Claiborne Park's maternal narrative, *The Siege,* is the mother of this genre; an example of a sibling narrative is Paul and Judy Karasik's *The Ride Together.* John Bayley's *Elegy for Iris* is a spousal narrative of a partner, the novelist and philosopher Iris Murdoch, who was unable to consent to her representation because of her dementia. Narratives of demented or otherwise incompetent parents have been written by Sue Miller and Elizabeth Cohen.

ten by people in professional relationships with the subjects: physicians (like Oliver Sacks in *The Man Who Mistook His Wife for a Hat*) or therapists (like Lauren Slater in *Welcome to My Country*). All such narratives involve great risk of invasion of privacy.

Considered as a whole, this enterprise involves an ethical dilemma. On the one hand, it is desirable for disability to be represented as it is actually experienced by particular human beings. When those individuals cannot or will not represent themselves, it can be of value to have their lives represented by others. So when autobiographical representation is not possible, there is great potential benefit in nonautobiographical representation. On the other hand, portraying people not able to speak for themselves (and, in some cases, not clearly able to grant meaningful consent) entails the risk of *mis*representing them, speaking about them without speaking for them (that is, advocating for them) or even speaking with them (that is, consulting them to learn their desires).

In *Vulnerable Subjects: Ethics and Life Writing,* I argued that both the creators and consumers of this kind of life writing might seek guidance from two fields in which similar issues arise: biomedical ethics and the ethics of anthropology, especially of ethnography. Specifically, I suggested that the bioethical approach known as principlism may be adapted to the ethical problems raised by these life writing scenarios.[4] In addressing such cases, it is useful to distinguish between subjects' *rights* and their *interests.* Respect for their autonomy concerns their right to self-determination. Concern about harming them involves consideration of their interests. In *Vulnerable Subjects,* my emphasis was on the dangers of exploitation and harm, which I sought to illustrate through discussion of particular texts and cases. Here I would like to pursue another tack: how can we guarantee, or at least try to ensure, that representation serves the best interests of vulnerable subjects generally?

A global approach would involve considering the interests of vulnerable individuals as linked to the interests of communities to which they belong. In the case of disability, it is not necessarily useful, how-

---

4. The standard text is *Principles of Biomedical Ethics* by Tom L. Beauchamp and James F. Childress.

ever, to think in terms of "a" or "the" disability community. Furthermore, because of the way the disabled minority is constituted, it is arguably more heterogeneous than those of race, ethnicity, gender, class, and sexual orientation.

Although respect for communities of vulnerable subjects is an important ethical consideration (a key disability principle is "nothing about us without us"),[5] it raises some difficult procedural questions in practice. First, some conditions, such as cognitive impairments, may interfere with consultation with subjects or compromise the standard of informed consent. Even when that is not the case, the constitution of the community may not always be clear. How is membership determined and by whom? Is mere possession of a particular impairment enough, or does membership involve conscious affiliation—identifying as "X"? Further, even if one could be sure of the boundaries of a particular disability community, how would one negotiate with it? Are some parties authorized to speak for the group? If so, who? (Distinct disabilities have their own organizations and lobbying groups, and these may be a place to start, but these are not elected bodies, like tribal governments, which are authorized to speak for their members.) Finally, the term *community* may be misleading here; in ethnography it is used to refer to groups of people who share a culture and who typically live together or at least interact with one another; this is not often the case with people who share an impairment. Not, that is, unless they are institutionalized, but in that case, too often the very fact of their institutionalization serves to reflect and reinforce their marginalization and disenfranchisement; they may be a community, but they are a community of clients or patients whose lives are not often in their own control. As with individuals, then, negotiating consent with a group, though desirable, may be impractical, if not impossible. But that is not to say that the interests of the group can safely—ethically—be ignored. The principle of respect for the community recognizes that groups, and not just individuals, may have interests, if not rights, and those interests may be harmed by representation.

Where consultation is not possible or practical, one might gauge the potential impact of any representation of disabled individuals with

---

5. I take this phrase from the title of a book by James I. Charlton, *Nothing About Us Without Us.*

reference to which of three available paradigms of disability is deployed. Is it the *symbolic* (or metaphorical) paradigm, under which a particular impairment serves as a trope for a moral or spiritual condition? Is it the *medical* (or individual) paradigm, under which a particular impairment is seen solely as a dysfunction of a particular body, which biomedicine may cure, fix, or rehabilitate? Or is it the *social* or *cultural* paradigm, according to which disability is located at the interface of particular bodies with particular environments—physical, social, attitudinal, legal, and broadly cultural?

The origins of the symbolic paradigm are ancient and thus indistinct. But its key feature is clear enough: disability—some irregularity, defect, dysfunction, or anomaly in the body—is seen as a stable, legible, and reliable sign of a moral condition or divine disfavor. The outer appearance of the body is understood to reveal the inner character of the person. This paradigm thus maps the supernatural onto the natural, the metaphysical onto the physical, the intangible onto the tangible. This paradigm is present in key Judeo-Christian scriptures and thus deeply embedded in Western culture from very early on. A mild version of it is detectable in the book of Leviticus, in which people (actually, only men, and only "the sons of Aaron") who have various physical defects—"he that hath a blemish, . . . a blind man, or a lame, or he that hath a flat nose, . . . or a man that is broken-footed, or broken-handed, or crookbacked, or a dwarf, or that hath a blemish in his eye, or be scurvy, or scabbed, or hath his stones [i.e., testicles] broken"— are excluded from certain ceremonial functions of the priesthood, on the grounds that only those who are undefiled should serve in close proximity to the most holy (21:18–20 [King James]). Like the beasts to be sacrificed, the priests who perform the sacred rituals must be unblemished. The implication is that not just cleanliness but physical wholeness is next to holiness.

The stakes are raised in the New Testament as the disciples distinguish the teaching of Jesus from that of the scribes and Pharisees. In the Gospels, Jesus is at pains to disassociate holiness from strict observance of the Law and to associate it with being in a right relation to God (i.e., in a state of grace). Unfortunately, the way in which Jesus establishes his authority is to heal people whom we would regard today as diseased or disabled. This is most dramatic in the cases of those who are explicitly described as being possessed by evil spirits and thus in need of spiritual cleansing or salvation. (Here we witness the origins of the Christian practice of faith healing, which persists in some pockets of modern American culture.) The cost of this is obvious: it adds insult, literally, to what may be physical injury. What should be remarked is that insofar as Christ demonstrates his spiritual power by healing, Christianity is founded on the bodies of disabled people.

That paradigm persists to this day in various manifestations. It may undergird what Sander Gilman and others have characterized as a contemporary "moral panic" over obesity in North America (quoted in Kolata). Obesity does entail significant health risks, but some recent research suggests that those risks may have been exaggerated, at least as regards longevity (Kolata). Thus the widespread public concern over the "epidemic" of obesity seems to reflect not only a legitimate public health issue but also a moralistic concern about overconsumption and self-control. Evidence for this (anecdotal, but ample) is that people who are conspicuously overweight are sometimes urged to diet by utter strangers. Even when this is couched as advice, rather than criticism, the implication is that obesity is largely, if not entirely, a function of poor self-control or personality defect—in effect, a moral failing.

While the value ascribed to particular conditions under the symbolic paradigm is not always negative—consider the notion of the blind as having second sight—this paradigm always generalizes, stereotypes, essentializes. A particular condition or trait is regarded as a more or less transparent sign of the moral or spiritual status of an affected individual. One cost of this paradigm, then, even when it is not obviously prejudicial, is that it erases individual differences within the group marked off as different. It makes a particular trait—say, deformity or blindness—the master status of all those who possess it, reducing their complex humanity to a single (usually visible) attribute. The use of this code (the tangible trait for an intangible quality) to represent a single character—even a fictional one—serves to characterize all those who share the selected trait.

In contrast to the obscure origins of the symbolic paradigm, the advent of the medical paradigm is associated with the birth of the clinic in the eighteenth century. But insofar as this paradigm adopts a naturalistic and increasingly empirical view of disability, it is adumbrated during the Renaissance. For example, we can detect it in Michel de Montaigne's late sixteenth-century essay "On a Monster-child." Here the French essayist contemplates a child out of whose chest seems to grow another child—in effect, two bodies with one head. As Montaigne was well aware, the term *monster* derives from the Latin *monstrum* (portent), and in the Middle Ages, such anomalies were conventionally viewed as revelations of divine will. While Montaigne retains the term and treats the child as an omen, of sorts, his reading of the sign is not explicitly religious, and it is surprisingly (perhaps shockingly) optimistic.

> This double body and these sundry limbs all depending on one single head could well provide us with a favourable omen that our king will maintain the sundry parties and factions of our State in unity under his laws.

Moreover, he immediately undercuts this interpretation with a joke about prognostication: "For fear lest the outcome should belie it we should let that happen first, for there is no divining like divining about the past!"

Further, and more remarkably, he concludes his essay with the assertion that nothing in creation is, or can be, un-natural.

> God is all-wise; nothing comes from him which is not good, general and regular: but we cannot see the dispensation and relationship. . . . Whatever happens against custom we say is against Nature, yet there is nothing whatsoever which is not in harmony with her. May Nature's universal reason chase away that deluded ecstatic amazement which novelty brings to us. (808)

This significance of this essay is way out of proportion to its length (ca. 600 words): it may mark the moment in Western culture when the monster, hitherto regarded as a sign from God, is reconceived as a freak *of nature,* for while Montaigne cites God as a kind of benign creator whose creation may exceed human understanding, he also cites a less exalted authority, that of "Nature's universal reason."

Similarly, in his early seventeenth-century essay "Of Deformity," Sir

Francis Bacon argues that deformity is not, contrary to popular conception, a reliable index of bad character: "Therefore, it is good to consider of Deformity, not as a *Signe,* which is more Deceivable; But as a *Cause,* which seldome faileth of the Effect" (134, emphasis added). According to Bacon, people with deformed bodies react to others' patronizing or dismissive responses to them in ways that lead them to be either overachievers or crooks. (That this understanding of deformity was not confined to Bacon is suggested by speeches in which Shakespeare's Richard III glories in deceiving and manipulating others.) The slippage from sign to cause marks a crucial step toward a modern, empirical view of physical anomaly. Indeed, in suggesting that the relation between body and character cannot simply be read off like a code but is mediated by social interaction and human psychology, Bacon's psychosocial approach to disability anticipates the social paradigm; that is, Bacon suggests that any correlation between character and body shape is not divinely ordained but rather a human construction—a response in large part to the scorn of others.

The medical paradigm bids to demystify, de-moralize, and naturalize somatic aberrancy, stripping away any supernatural or moral significance and insisting that human variation is solely a matter of a defect or irregularity in the individual body that medicine may cure, fix, rehabilitate, or prevent. (This is why it is also sometimes referred to as the *individual* paradigm: disability resides in the individual's body alone.) Compared with the symbolic paradigm, the medical paradigm offers much benefit for people with anomalous conditions. People who once might have been persecuted, prosecuted, even executed (as witches) because of conditions like Tourette's syndrome, epilepsy, and schizophrenia might now be regarded as candidates for medical treatment. Exorcism would not be necessary, nor would it be effective. The result for some would be cure, for others institutionalization. Either way, those with disabilities would, in theory, be absolved of responsibility for their conditions.

Yet, as we have seen with the example of obesity, the medical/individual paradigm does not simply replace, but rather supplements, the symbolic paradigm, which survives today. The assignment of responsibility for autism to "refrigerator mothers"—common in the 1950s—is a good additional example; the onus was placed on the parent rather than the impaired individual, much as mothers were often held responsible for deformity in their babies in earlier times. In any case, biomedicine's reach always exceeds its grasp. And in its commendable ambition to explain mysterious medical conditions, it sometimes inadvertently reinscribes prejudicial tropes; rather than abandoning them, it rewrites them in its own language. Typically, this takes the form of the discovery—which is really the invention—of an "X personality." For all his early modern skepticism, Bacon in effect limits people with deformities to two variants of what we might call "deformed personality syndrome." Similarly, as Oliver Sacks has pointed out, for most of the twentieth century migraine was explained (or explained away) as a function of a personality type (*Migraine,* 140). And in his memoir *What's That Pig Outdoors?* Henry Kisor complains of being, as an adolescent, forced

> into the mold of the "deaf personality," a set of traits [thought to be] created by the environment of deafness. Because lack of ready communication at an early age has deprived them of the opportunity to develop emotionally in many ways, the deaf sometimes are psychologically typed as immature, rigid, egocentric, impulsive, and overly trusting. (243)

Thus, when medical (or social) "science" confronts anomalous somatic conditions that elude definitive explanation, it sometimes psychologizes (or neuroticizes) them in a way that betrays the legacy of the metaphorical paradigm (insofar as the "personality syndrome" in effect blames the victim). When biomedicine does not demystify, but remystifies, disability, its narratives or tropes may be more insidious than those of the earlier paradigm in that they claim the authority of science and are often therefore accorded undeserved credence.

This is not to say that the medical paradigm could or should be discarded. Certainly it offers much to people with many impairments; indeed, it makes it possible for people with impairments that once would have killed them not merely to survive but to live productive and gratifying lives. The question here, however, is not whether the medical paradigm has done any good for people with disabilities *in real life,* which is undeniable, but what its implications are as *a mode of repre-*

sentation—a second-order phenomenon, but an important one nonetheless. Although it does not necessarily essentialize conditions, it may represent conditions in ways that are inimical to the best interests of those who have them insofar as it suggests that the problem resides entirely in a defective body. It thus puts the burden on people with disabilities to adapt themselves to their environment; they can function in society only to the extent that their impairments can be normalized.

The third paradigm originated with disability scholars and activists in the United States and the United Kingdom in the last quarter of the twentieth century. It exists in more than one variant, but essential to all of them is the notion that, like race and gender, disability is a social construct that varies both synchronically, from culture to culture, and diachronically, over time. Indeed, the third paradigm is not merely a new paradigm but in effect a meta-paradigm that makes it possible to understand both of the previous paradigms as cultural constructions. A fundamental and crucial distinction is made between *impairment,* which is found in the body, and *disability,* which is located in the social response to, or cultural construction of, impairment. This distinction allows us to recognize, understand, and alleviate disadvantages, like discrimination and exclusion, that seem to be, but are not, inherent in particular impairments.

An often cited illustration is the distinction between being paralyzed (an impairment) and being unable to negotiate one's wheelchair through a built environment that lacks ramps or elevators (a disability). That is, the social paradigm emphasizes the way in which culture (in all its dimensions, not just material) enables and empowers members with particular ("normal") somatic attributes and dis-enables and disempowers members with different ("deviant" or "abnormal") bodies. This paradigm thus places the burden on society to accommodate anomalous bodies. The crucial move made by disability scholars in creating this paradigm, then, was a kind of conceptual figure-ground reversal: whereas the medical paradigm locates the problem in the individual figure, the latter paradigm locates it in the ground. This shift of perspective—foregrounding what had been background—may seem obvious, even facile, in retrospect, but it was innovative in its time, and it has been far-reaching and profound in its implications.

There is debate among disability scholars today over whether the social paradigm—with its insistence that disability is mostly or even only (the strict constructivist version) a cultural construction of physical anomaly—has had the unfortunate, and ironic, effect of denying or effacing the body itself, of stifling testimony about the sometimes painful realities of disability. In particular, Tom Shakespeare has aggressively challenged what he regards as the orthodoxy of the social model, which he sees as limited, indeed gravely flawed, and needing to be replaced. In his most recent book, *Disability Rights and Wrongs,* Shakespeare has criticized the social model for undermining political organization on the basis of particular impairments and for generating unhelpful suspicion of, if not overt hostility to, medical research and development. But the new paradigm has the great advantage for advocacy of diverting attention from what *happened* to disabled people as individuals (what caused their impairments) to what *happens* to them collectively as a result of unnecessary social and cultural restraints. Thus, disability is sometimes *defined* as a harmful social construct. For example, according to Carol Thomas, "disability is a form of social oppression involving the social imposition of restrictions of activity on people with impairments and the socially engendered undermining of their psycho-emotional well-being" (3). Choosing between the conflicting paradigms, however, is not a matter of choosing between true and false; rather, each attends to a different dimension of a knotty issue: how anomalous bodies may function in society. Indeed, choosing between them may not be possible; each has a necessary contribution to make and each may need to be deployed pragmatically in different circumstances to different ends.

The distinction between impairment and disability helps explain why many disabled people were disappointed by Christopher Reeve's disability advocacy after his spinal cord injury: in their view, Reeve was overinvested in a cure for paralysis (impairment) and insufficiently attentive to the many ways in which paralyzed people are disadvantaged by social and cultural restrictions (disability). Successful treatment or cure for spinal cord injury, however desirable, will be slow in coming, difficult and probably expensive to effect, and not applicable to all causes of paralysis; in any case, it will not alleviate discrimination and disadvantage for anyone in the immediate future and never for those who become paralyzed by degenerative illness. It will not make ramps obsolete.

To return to representation, the conflict between the medical and the social paradigms may illuminate the controversy over the Oscar-winning film *Million Dollar Baby* (2004). One critique came from the Christian Right, which attacked the film for its alleged endorsement of assisted suicide. The critique of disability rights advocates was more subtle and more compelling. Their argument was that the movie did little, if anything, to counter—and thus it implicitly endorsed—Maggie's view that her life was not worth living after her injury. The script provided her with a family that was not only not supportive but downright grasping, consigned her to almost complete isolation in a dismal nursing home, subjected her to a preventable complication that cost her a leg, and implied that she had no recourse for relief other than to beg her manager-mentor to kill her. The film's melodramatic conclusion also managed to deflect attention from the protagonist's life-or-death decision to her manager's dilemma as a churchgoing Catholic. All of this is to say that the film presents Maggie as broken, unfixable, and better off dead.

Significantly, no film review that I read noticed a crucial anachronism: although the film is apparently set in the present or very recent past, no one informs Maggie that she can simply request to have her life support discontinued. (Ironically, soon after the Oscar ceremony in 2005, the furor over the Terri Schiavo case educated the general public about their rights in this regard.) The film utterly ignores the possibility that Maggie's despair is in effect a treatable case of depression and, more to the point here, the degree to which her decision may be conditioned by internalized prejudice against people with disabilities. This is all the more likely in someone like Maggie, who achieved upward mobility through sports. Inability to tolerate disability may be especially high among athletes, who come to value physical skill, and mere mobility, very highly. (A sad illustration, in my view, can be found in the 2008 obituary of Barbara Warren, an endurance athlete who, at sixty-five, became a high quadriplegic in a bicycle accident during a triathlon. According to Bruce Weber's *New York Times* obituary, she signaled her wish to have her respirator turned off a mere three days after her accident. Her twin sister is quoted as saying, "No athlete would like to have a life with only their eyes talking" [para. 3].) That is, the film fails to reckon with the extent to which Maggie's condition is not (only) a brute *fact* of *her* life (an impairment) but also to some extent a *social artifact* (a disability).

There is no denying that Maggie's injury is "tragic"—in the vernacular and perhaps even in the literary sense—but the extent to which such injuries are devastating to people's life chances is partly a function of the societies in which they live. Had the film represented her situation with more verisimilitude—acknowledging her right to refuse treatment—it might also have allowed that in order to make a truly autonomous and informed decision she needed time to adjust to her body's new condition and to consult with others who share it.

Thanks to disability rights advocacy, injuries like Maggie's are less "tragic"—that is, unfortunate—today than they once were. As a new professor at Hofstra University in 1982, I remember being taken aback by the sight of paraplegic and quadriplegic students in wheelchairs—a phenomenon I never witnessed during my own undergraduate and postgraduate educations or my first teaching job, at a small liberal arts college in New England. But I have long since become accustomed to it. Indeed, I have come to think of myself as having been mainstreamed when I began to teach at Hofstra at the age of 35; that is, not until that time was I integrated into a truly inclusive educational community. In any case, it is misleading to suggest, as the film does, that her decision is "for the best" and a truly free choice. While presumably no actual paraplegics were harmed *in* the production of the film, it may be fair to say that all paraplegics were harmed *by* it.

Admittedly, this schema of three paradigms is somewhat simplistic as tool for analyzing representation. I do not mean to suggest that reference to it resolves all questions about the impact on vulnerable subjects of their cultural representation. And granted, the first two paradigms are not *necessarily* harmful in cultural representation. Further, the social paradigm is not without its own costs, at least in its extreme ("strict" or radical constructivist) form. Although its intent is to empower people with disabilities, defining their condition as oppression risks characterizing them as victims, rather than agents. As already suggested, claiming that disability is "a construct" risks effacing the body's materiality and denying the pain and suffering caused by impairment. But in "real life" the medical and the social paradigms are not mutually exclusive. Disabled persons can embrace both simultaneously, seeking at once to minimize their impairment and maximize their access and accommodation. After all, many people need wheelchairs because of conditions, like high spinal cord injury, that have physical ramifications other than muscular paralysis, and which therefore require periodic medical monitoring. If they weren't "confined" to their wheelchairs, they would *truly* be confined, excluded from public life, but without medical treatment, they might not survive. (Indeed, Christopher Reeve died of complications from a pressure sore, a bane of people with para- or quadriplegia.) Deployed sensitively and sensibly, the social paradigm enables all of us to distinguish between the suffering inherent in impairment (which medicine may be able to ameliorate) and that caused by social arrangements (which needs to be addressed through rhetorical, political, legal, and other means).

Despite these caveats, I would suggest that, in textual representation, only the third paradigm can be *presumed* to advance the collective interests of people with disabilities—to do them good and not to do them harm. My endorsement of this paradigm should not be mistaken for requiring "positive" images of vulnerable subjects. That is the stock-in-trade of narratives that deploy the individual paradigm, which often feature "supercrips" who "overcome" disability (read: impairment). (Giveaway blurb terms are "inspiring," "uplifting," and "the human spirit.") Rather, it is a matter of encouraging representation that acknowledges that disability is a social and political, rather than merely an individual, concern. Representation that deploys the social paradigm tends to be beneficial because it acknowledges that disability is everybody's business and that disability may be addressed more effectively and universally by accommodation than by rehabilitation. Such representations are also valuable insofar as they tend to challenge the very norms that marginalize and stigmatize disabled people—the norms that make them vulnerable subjects in the first place.

3 ❧ Rhetoric and Self-Representation in Disability Memoir

To members of marginalized groups, autobiography may be the most accessible of literary genres. It requires less in the way of literary expertise and experience than more exalted genres, like fiction or drama; it seems to require only that one have a life—or at least, one considered worth narrating—and sufficient narrative skill to tell one's own story. Most literary scholars would agree that autobiography has served historically as a sort of threshold genre for marginalized populations; within the American literary tradition, witness the importance of autobiography to African Americans, Native Americans, and women, for example. Presumably, it might serve disabled people this way as well. It is not just the apparent accessibility of autobiography—a kind of negative qualification—that recommends it but also something more positive: the notion that autobiography by definition involves self-representation. If marginalization is in part a function of discourse that excludes and/or objectifies, autobiography has considerable potential to counter stigmatizing or patronizing portrayals of disability because it is a medium in which disabled people may have a high degree of control over their own images.

Yet there are serious obstacles in the way of realizing the counter-hegemonic potential of the disability memoir. Difficulty can be found at three distinct junctures: having a life, writing a life, and publishing a life. Like minority racial or ethnic status, disability may disqualify people from living the sorts of lives that have traditionally been considered worthy of autobiography; insofar as people with disabilities have been excluded from educational institutions and thus from economic opportunity, they will be less likely to produce the success story, perhaps the favorite American autobiographical subgenre from Benjamin Franklin onward. That their disqualification lies not in individual incapacity but in social and cultural barriers does not change the fact that people with disabilities are less likely to live the sorts of lives considered narratable and are thus less likely to display their lives in autobiography. (Hence the significance of the emergence of the nobody memoir, which does not require that the author be famous or accomplished.) One aspect of this discrimination, shared with other minorities, is the internalization of prejudices. Those who accept society's devaluation of them are less likely to consider their lives worthy of autobiography; stigma serves to silence the stigmatized.

Writing a life is an aspect of accessibility that may seem secondary, but it is pertinent here because it is peculiar to disability: despite important recent developments in assistive technology (such as voice-recognition software), the process of composition itself may be complicated by some impairments. People who are blind, Deaf, paralyzed, or cognitively impaired are disadvantaged with regard to the conventional technologies of writing, which take for granted visual acuity, literacy in English as a first language, manual dexterity, and unimpaired intellect and memory. For people with many impairments, the process of drafting and revising a long narrative may seem dauntingly arduous. At this juncture, then, people with disabilities may be disadvantaged in ways that do not apply to racial and ethnic minorities and in ways that may not be immediately apparent to those who are not disabled. While these impairments may be worked around with the help of a collaborator, questions then arise as to the agency, authority, voice, and authenticity of the self-representation.

Furthermore, it is not enough to produce a manuscript; *publishing*—as distinct from writing or even printing—a life involves gaining access to readers through intermediaries who may have their own agendas. The rise of self-publishing, through companies like Authorhouse, allows increased access to print (to those who can afford to subsidize their own creations), but self-published texts are rarely reviewed, minimally advertised, and generally reach only minute audiences. A third problem, then, may be located in the genre as defined by the literary marketplace, which may impose hegemonic scripts on a disempowered group. It is here that "rhetoric" and "disability" crucially intersect: in effect, people with disabilities may be granted access to the literary marketplace on the condition that their stories conform to preferred plots and rhetorical schemes. What characterizes these preferred rhetorics is that they rarely challenge stigma and marginalization directly or effectively. Indeed, their appeal to the reading public may vary inversely with the degree to which they threaten the status quo. In this chapter, then, I will distinguish a few of the most common rhetorical patterns of disability memoir with reference to some recent examples, moving from rhetorics that reinforce conventional attitudes—the rhetorics of triumph, horror, spiritual compensation, and nostalgia—to a rhetoric that contests received attitudes about disability—the rhetoric of emancipation.[1]

I use the term *rhetoric* in the neutral sense of persuasive speech or writing, rather than the disparaging sense of meretricious verbiage ("mere" rhetoric). Admittedly, I use the term somewhat loosely to characterize discursive patterns that combine imagery, plot, and theme, but I use it to attend to what I take to be the core of rhetorical analysis. In the case of disability memoir, I analyze discursive patterns to explore how they position a narrator (and his namesake protagonist) with regard to a topic (disability in some form) and in relation to an audience of readers.

The first of the common rhetorics is so obvious as to require little comment. Because disability is typically considered inherently "depressing," it is most palatable as a subject of memoir if the narrative takes the form of a story of triumph over adversity; this positive (and unlikely) outcome is considered inspiring and thus generalizable to the lives of the general reading public. In this formula, a successful individual takes pride in, and invites the reader's admiration for, a recounting of his or her overcoming of the obstacles posed by an impairment (think blind runner, amputee mountain climber, deaf musician, and so on). Needless to say, the lives that fit this paradigm misrepresent the experience of most people with disabilities; this par-

---

1. These different rhetorics are often combined within single memoirs, but in most cases one pattern dominates; my examples are chosen to exemplify particular rhetorical appeals.

adigm holds up the Supercrip, who is by definition atypical, as the model disabled person.

These may be "true stories," but they are not truly representative lives. In any case this approach removes the stigma of disability from the author but leaves it in place for other individuals with the condition in question. In effect, the narrator removes him- or herself from the category of the disabled or, alternatively, denies that his or her impairment need be restrictive. Moreover, this scenario, like the other preferred scenarios, is entirely congruous with the medical paradigm, which locates disability (read: impairment) entirely within a "defective" or "abnormal" body. Disability is presented primarily as a "problem" that individuals must overcome; overcoming it is a matter of individual will and determination, rather than of social and cultural accommodation. The reader is conscripted as an appreciative, admiring witness of this victory but is not encouraged to question the status quo.

Another rhetoric frequently employed in the representation of disability is the rhetoric of horror, gothic rhetoric, which derives of course from the fictional genre that so often features disfigured, deformed, or maimed characters. Here, disability is characterized as a literally dreadful condition, to be shunned or avoided. At worst, gothic rhetoric encourages revulsion from disability; at best, pity for the "afflicted." Such rhetoric might seem unlikely to be used in first-person discourse, such as disability memoir, where it would reflect negatively on the author-narrator. But this deterrent vanishes when impairment is corrected or "transcended." From the standpoint of those who are cured or rehabilitated—or who otherwise destigmatize themselves—it is common to look back upon a period of disability as a gothic horror. In this rhetoric, narrators represent their former condition as grotesque; readers are invited to share narrators' relief at escaping marginalization.

An unfortunate example of this scenario is found in Oliver Sacks's *A Leg to Stand On*, in which the neurologist recounts his experience of temporarily losing the use of one leg after a climbing accident. The following passage may serve as a synecdoche of the book-length narrative.

I had imagined my injury (a severe but uncomplicated wound to the muscles and nerves of one leg) to be straightforward and routine, and I was astonished at the profundity of the effects it had: a sort of paralysis and alienation of the leg, reducing it to an "object" which seemed unrelated to me; an abyss of bizarre, and even terrifying, effects. I had no idea what to make of these effects and entertained fears that I might never recover. I found the abyss a horror, and recovery a wonder; and I have since had a deeper sense of the horror and wonder which lurk behind life and which are concealed, as it were, behind the usual surface of health. (13–14)

Written from the perspective of complete recovery—which he narrates as a mysterious conversion experience—his account redraws, rather than blurs, the line between disability and "health."[2]

Used this way, gothic rhetoric tends, of course, to reinforce common attitudes toward disability—to evoke fear, dread, and revulsion. But such rhetoric is sometimes also used in accounts that do not culminate in the narrator's recovery from the condition in question. When the source of horror is not the condition itself but the *treatment* of the condition, gothic rhetoric has some counterhegemonic potential. Julia Tavalaro's account of the six-year period following her two strokes, during which she was assumed by hospital staff to be completely unaware of her surroundings, is a good example of the latter form of gothic rhetoric—a medical horror story of inattention, indifference, and abuse. In *Look Up for "Yes,"* then, gothic rhetoric serves to indict the medical care of the severely disabled, those who are presumed to be unconscious or beyond rehabilitation.

When Tavalaro is discovered, by a speech therapist, to be cognizant, her treatment improves radically, and what ensues is a narrative of rehabilitation. But even when, as here, gothic rhetoric is used to generate outrage at ill-treatment, rather than revulsion at a disfiguring or disabling condition, it is entirely consonant with the medical or individual model of disability and leaves conventional attitudes in place. It does not challenge the idea that disability resides in the individual body; at most, it calls for more attentive treatment of such individuals.

2. For a more sustained discussion of this book, see my *Recovering Bodies*, 186–89.

The rhetoric of spiritual compensation has also frequently been used to narrate experiences of disability.[3] Ruth Cameron Webb's *Journey into Personhood*, a recent memoir by a woman with cerebral palsy, is a particularly interesting example of this, in part because the rhetoric of conversion was not the only, or even the most obvious, rhetoric available to her. Given the outlines of Webb's life, one might expect her narrative to employ the rhetoric of triumph. For despite delays in her education, Webb got a PhD in clinical psychology and had a successful career counseling people with disabilities. Indeed, because the major obstacle to her eventual success was not her cerebral palsy but blatant discrimination—she was repeatedly expelled from schools and colleges because her disabilities were considered unmanageable—and because she was professionally involved with disabled people, the circumstances of her life might have impelled her toward a more political stance.

Webb does not, however, narrate a secular success story—much less question the medical paradigm—because of a deeply ingrained sense of inferiority associated with her disability. In therapy she traces these feelings to being examined, naked, by physicians at her first boarding school. Her sense of invalidity is so great that it challenges her religious faith: "Often I wonder why God allowed me to be injured at birth. Have I done anything to deserve cerebral palsy? Why can't I walk and talk like everybody else?" (70). This is a classic example of the symbolic paradigm of disability, according to which an impairment is a mark of sin or God's displeasure with an individual. Her double bind is that though her faith contributes to her sense of inferiority, it also condemns her anger, which she finds hard to quell nevertheless. Her religion does hold out some promise of relief, but she has an ambivalent response to faith healing. On the one hand, she feels humiliated and angry when, at a Christian summer retreat, enthusiastic evangelicals form a circle around her and pray for her healing without asking her permission or eliciting her cooperation. On the other, after she volunteers to be healed by Oral Roberts, she sinks into depression when her condition does not improve. (The most that faith seems to be able to accomplish for her is to suppress her recurrent suicidal impulses.)

3. For a discussion of the use of paradigms of spiritual autobiography in disability narratives by Reynolds Price and John Callahan, see my *Recovering Bodies*, 192–98.

There are tantalizing moments when she moves toward a more social and political paradigm of disability. For example, becoming
friends with a biracial couple, she recognizes their kindred marginalization—"Then I'm not the only side show, I think" (79)—and learns
to ignore stares. Later on, through an experience with an African
American colleague, she has another glimmer of minority consciousness: "As a member of a social minority group, she has been discriminated against and excluded. I understand her anger because, after all, I,
too, belong to a minority" (140). Through experiences like these, Webb
approaches the brink of consciousness of disability as a socially constructed condition, a cause (or a form) of oppression. But she always
stops short.

Only late in life does she resolve these issues, through a transfigur-
ing visitation in which a voice tells her to give up her anger and accept
God's love.

> Then, suddenly, these words come into my mind. "Ruth, you have a
> special mission from the Lord, the Great Spirit. Your mission is sim-
> ilar to that of the man born blind about whom John, the gospel
> writer, wrote. You, too, are asked to reflect God's glory in your dis-
> abled body. Without knowing your assignment, you have faithfully
> pursued this mission by helping everyone you met on your journey.
> The time has now come for you to pursue this mission actively. To
> do this, you need to review the battles you have won. Remember,
> with each victory, you have taken another step on our journey into
> personhood." During the next several months, I often awake around
> four o'clock in the morning and watch as a panorama of triumphal
> scenes passes rapidly through my mind. (180)

Webb can regard her life as a success only with the help of faith; indeed, she can only be certain of her personhood—which for her is
somehow compromised by her disability—when it has been conferred
and confirmed by divine authority.

Only through spiritual compensation can she find a comic plot in
her life. Part of the implicit "purpose" of her disability, then, is to make
her a better Christian; she finds solace finally in her sense of value to
God, who has assigned her a special mission on earth. Indeed, the

book might as well have been called *Journey into Sainthood* (in the Protestant meaning of the sainthood of all believers) in that the resolution of her lifelong feeling of inferiority comes from a sense that she has successfully borne her personal cross. In its broad outlines the memoir resembles a conversion narrative. Such rhetoric invites readers to assent to the conditions of Webb's validation as a person. In her view, disability is her problem—a challenge given her by God for his own inscrutable reasons—not a social or political matter. But skeptical or secular readers will see her religious schema as part of the problem, rather than as an ultimate or generalizable solution. The effect of her mystical validation is to remove stigma not from cerebral palsy as a condition but rather from her as an individual. Her resorting to God for validation precludes any attempts to seek a remedy in worldly efforts toward reform, short-circuiting any movement toward the competing political paradigm of disability.

A third pattern, the rhetoric of nostalgia, is illustrated in pure form by a contemporary memoir that was greeted by extensive press coverage and positive reviews: Jean-Dominique Bauby's *The Diving Bell and the Butterfly*. Written by the editor in chief of *Elle* magazine after a massive stroke to his brain stem left him almost completely paralyzed, this memoir was translated and published in the United States in 1997, and in 2007 Julian Schnabel's film adaptation of it (in French) received rave reviews in the United States. Bauby's paralysis was so extensive that it left him deaf in one ear and mute, able to move only his left eye, a condition known as "locked-in syndrome." Nevertheless, he managed to compose a memoir by blinking to select letters, one by one, as an attentive collaborator, Claude Mendibil, recited the alphabet for him.

Partly as a result of this extremely labor-intensive method of composition, the book is very short; it consists of a series of brief vignettes. The text is Bauby's "memoirs" in a particularly literal sense: the chapters range over a number of topics but typically recount isolated memories of his life before the stroke. It is far from a full-life narrative; Bauby makes no attempt to recount his life as a chronological narrative of becoming. The severity of his disability seems to have played a role here; by the time he undertook his narrative, he was past the initial phase of denial, during which he continued to believe he might soon return to work. Aware that he would never recover, though he might improve in certain limited respects, Bauby ceased to orient himself toward the future.[4] Partly, then, because his condition did not allow for his reintegration into the world of the nondisabled, he minimizes narration of rehabilitation, of which very little was possible. If the book has any "narrative arc," it is one of recession.

> I am fading away. Slowly but surely. Like the sailor who watches the home shore gradually disappear, I watch my past recede. My old life still burns within me, but more and more of it is reduced to the ashes of memory. (77)[5]

As a result, there is no consideration of issues of accessibility.

Other contingent circumstances reinforce the rhetoric of nostalgia. Bauby died of a heart attack only two days after the French publication of his book. Thus, by the time the book was available in translation to the American public, readers knew, from the book jacket, that its author was dead. This knowledge confirms Bauby's characterization of himself as already in some sense a dead man. There is a strong undercurrent of morbidity in the book, an implicit equation of severe disability with death. This undercurrent is part of a gothic or grotesque subtext that surfaces—sometimes in the form of black humor—when Bauby looks at himself through others' eyes. Thus, when he sees his image—the face of a "man who seemed to have emerged from a vat of formaldehyde"—reflected in a stained-glass representation of the patroness of the hospital, he experiences a frisson and then a moment of euphoria.

> Not only was I exiled, paralyzed, mute, half deaf, deprived of all pleasures, and reduced to the existence of a jellyfish, but I was also

---

4. It also lacks any confessional dimension. Bauby may have been deterred from a more confessional mode because his stroke occurred at a time of great instability in his life; he had just moved out of the house he shared with his wife and two children. Writing memoir, rather than a more self-exploratory autobiography, he worked around, rather than through, this life crisis.

5. At the same time, his writing of letters to friends and of the book—his letter to the world—is an act of resistance against this seemingly inevitable recession. As his letter to friends seeks to counter the rumor that he is a "vegetable," his book seeks to establish that there is yet intelligent life within his immobilized and silenced body.

horrible to behold. There comes a time when the heaping up of calamities brings on uncontrollable nervous laughter—when, after a final blow from fate, we decide to treat it all as a joke. (25)[6]

An interesting variant of the gothic occurs in a dream in which Bauby visits a wax museum where his orderlies and nurses are on display. Here the tables are turned; it is the staff who are immobilized, exposed, and objectified. A passage like this exemplifies the gothic's potential for political critique, but Bauby draws back, concluding ambivalently, "I realized that I was fond of all these torturers of mine" (111).

Bauby's account of an earlier touristic visit to Lourdes makes clear that his present disablement realizes a deep fear of becoming an invalid. Having become one of "them," however, he does not reevaluate, but rather acquiesces in, the devaluation of disability. Instead of questioning it, he deflects his attention away from his present condition to his "normal" life, which now seems all the more precious and poignant. Thus, although Bauby writes from a position of nearly total paralysis, disability provides not the *subject* of his narrative but only its *motivation* and, of course, its vantage.

For this reason, one could argue that his book is not truly a disability memoir. In some significant respect it is not one, but it demands discussion here because of the way its rare compositional circumstances (its being "eye-typed" and its having been written in a short interval between traumatic injury and death) trigger a response characteristic of much disability memoir. In one blurb, for example, Sherwin B. Nuland, author of *How We Die*, exclaims,

To read this most extraordinary of narratives is to discover the luminosity within a courageous man's mind. His incomparable final

---

6. For a similar moment, see Tavalaro, 150–53; on one of their rare visits, her daughter and her mother "make her over." Even though Tavalaro acquiesces to their desire to beautify her, she finds the resulting image as alien as her previous appearance. Indeed, she describes herself in the third person: "Even all gussied up, I didn't know the person in the mirror. If I had known her, I'd have felt sorry for her. She was skin and bones, a few teeth, some sagging flesh, and fake color. Her hands were like a baby's, always held in a fist. Her head lolled from side to side, and the wig looked awful. I had no idea how much I'd aged in six years. Instead of Judy's mother, I could have been her grandmother" (153).

gift to us is a heartbreaking and yet glorious testament to the wrenching beauty of the human spirit.

Cynthia Ozick's endorsement is even more enthusiastic.

> Jean-Dominique Bauby's extraordinary narrative testifies to the infinitude of the human imagination, to the resilient will that drives boundless courage. The heroic composition of *The Diving Bell and the Butterfly* renders it the most remarkable memoir of our time— perhaps of any time.

Such extravagant responses are encouraged by the purely nostalgic and virtually postmortem perspective of the narration. Since the author did not live long with disability, there is no question of his using his position as a prominent editor to offer personal testimony on behalf of others with disabilities. Rather, he earns praise in part for having undertaken, in forbidding circumstances, to create a book, and for having written a book that is not "depressing," but "uplifting," because, rather than raising disturbing questions about the status of people with disabilities, it offers poignant accounts of pleasures and pastimes no longer available to him.

The diving bell is Bauby's image for his confinement in a kind of hermetic zone removed from the world of "ability"; the butterfly is an image of the compensatory liberation of his mind so that it may float freely over his past, as his eye surveys the souvenirs and snapshots surrounding him in his room (3). The emphasis throughout is much more on the freedom of the butterfly than on the confinement of the diving bell.[7] Indeed, one might say that, despite its occasional gothic passages, the text tends to idealize Bauby's condition as one freeing him from mundane constraints to reminisce, fantasize, and "travel" (103): "There is so much to do. You can wander off in space or in time ... You can visit the woman you love, ... realize your childhood dreams and adult ambitions" (5). In effect, then, Bauby treats his disability not

---

7. The organization of the book around these two opposing images suggests that it, too, participates in the rhetoric of spiritual compensation, even though it is utterly devoid of explicitly religious language.

as an experience *of* the body but as an experience of being "out of the body"; indeed, the memoir has aspects of the near-death narrative insofar as his life passes slowly before his eyes during his months of post-trauma hospitalization. Knowledge of his ensuing death frees readers from the impulse to pity him or to lament his confinement and allows them to enjoy the fantasy of being able to range back over one's life in memory, without having to contemplate the present or the future. (For me, the best aspect of the film was its ability, using subjective camera shots, to simulate the memoirist's point of view, at least optically, and to cut back and forth rapidly between the seen and the imagined.)

The effect is not to challenge or erase, but to mark, a distinction between past and present, function and dysfunction, ability and disability, living and remembering. Although there is little that physicians can do for him other than to stabilize his condition and minimize his discomfort, his narrative in no way challenges the medical paradigm. Compared to the rhetoric of horror, the rhetoric of nostalgia seems benign, and yet it too tends to marginalize disability insofar as it is rooted in an equation between severe disability and the end of life.

In contrast to the preceding memoirs and their rhetorics, my final example realizes some of the counterhegemonic—indeed, postcolonial—potential of disability narrative. *I Raise My Eyes to Say Yes,* by Ruth Sienkiewicz-Mercer and Steven B. Kaplan, is the story of a woman with cerebral palsy so severe that she has never been able to walk, feed herself, speak, or write. After spending some time as a child in rehabilitative facilities, she was sent to a state hospital in Belchertown, Massachusetts, because her father changed jobs and his new insurance did not cover private hospitals. Upon entering this new facility at the age of twelve, Sienkiewicz-Mercer was misdiagnosed as mentally retarded, and she was then warehoused with people who were either cognitively impaired or mentally ill.[8] Eventually, her abilities were recognized and gradually recultivated; in her mid-twenties, she was able to move out of the hospital into an apartment and to marry a fellow former patient. Both she and her partner are thus

---

8. Given her treatment, or mistreatment—her leg was once broken by a careless and clumsy aide and not immediately attended to—Sienkiewicz-Mercer's story, like Tavalaro's, has gothic potential, but the gothic remains a minor element in her account, as in Bauby's.

beneficiaries of the new approach to disability that favored deinstitutionalization.

When she was first institutionalized, she was presumed to be a body without (much of) a mind; though toilet-trained early on, she was diapered, dressed in a hospital gown—all for the convenience of the staff—and supervised, rather than educated or rehabilitated. It was thus not her own severe impairments but the limitations of her physicians that threatened to arrest her development.[9] What saved Sienkiewicz-Mercer from languishing in the institution was her ability, using very limited means, to connect with those around her. Virtually the only moving parts of her body under her control were her eyes and her vocal cords. By making eye contact with other inmates and staff members, she was able to establish vital connections with them; by gesturing with her eyes, and coordinating nonverbal vocalizations with those gestures, she was able to communicate ideas and emotions about life around her in a kind of private language to receptive others. The most receptive were the captive audience of other similarly misdiagnosed patients. It was only through eye contact and private language that she and a few peers could establish that there was intelligent—and intelligible—life within them. In this initial bonding with other inmates we can see the beginnings of political consciousness shared with others in the same predicament, an element that distinguishes her account from those of Bauby and Webb.

The role of her "gaze" in self-construction, then, is crucial. Whereas the disciplinary medical gaze had sized her up (or rather, down) as mentally deficient, through her own inquisitive and aggressive gaze she managed to challenge or defy her misdiagnosis—and, not incidentally, to have a social life. Once her consciousness and intelligence were recognized, she was able to expand on and refine this method of communication, but she could never abandon it. In order for her to com-

---

9. Reading Sienkiewicz-Mercer's and Tavalaro's accounts against Bauby's exposes the role of social class in the ascription of disability. For Bauby, though he never leaves the institution, the hospital is not a site of oppression in the way that it is for her. This is in part because of his socioeconomic status, with all the clout and connections it entails. For him, the major problem is his locked-in condition; for Sienkiewicz-Mercer and Tavalaro, it is the institution's (mis)treatment of their condition, which they have no powerful advocates to question.

municate with the staff and move herself beyond the limits assigned to her, she needed to make them respond to her gaze as well.

The writing of her text is only a more deliberate and extensive application of this means of self-creation; the medium of autobiography is an elaboration of the process of self-possession and self-assertion through manipulation of her gaze. Collaborative self-inscription is the means for releasing herself from the institution; personal narrative is thus crucial to her physical and psychological emancipation. Rather than accepting her dependency as disvaluing, she exploits interdependency as a means of self-assertion. While not achieving independence (or subscribing to the ideology of personal autonomy), Sienkiewicz-Mercer moves herself through reciprocity to a position of greater power, mobility, and personal agency. (The reciprocity of her self-construction is attested to by the way in which her narrative vividly individualizes others also consigned to near-oblivion in the hospital.)

Although, like most personal narratives of illness and/or disability, the narrative has an undeniably comic plot, it is not a story of overcoming disability—at least not in the usual sense. It is not what Arthur Frank calls a "narrative of restitution—a narrative of complete healing in which a physician would play a transformative role" (77). Nor is it primarily a narrative of rehabilitation; though she does learn to use various assistive technologies to communicate, Sienkiewicz-Mercer never manages to walk or talk, nor does she achieve full independence. Her rhetoric is thus not that of triumph. She does not, she cannot, overcome her impairment. Rather, she manages, with a great deal of help, to work around it. The comic resolution is not a function of removing or correcting her impairments, but of getting the world to accommodate them—of removing the physical, social, and cultural obstacles to her integration into the "mainstream." In that sense, her narrative demonstrates what we might call the rhetoric of emancipation.

Indeed, *I Raise My Eyes to Say Yes* has interesting affinities with slave narrative. The narrative is reminiscent of a slave narrative both in the sense that, on the level of plot, it traces a movement from virtual imprisonment to relative freedom, and in the sense that her emancipation is a function of a broader movement to deinstitutionalize disabled people. Like many, if not all, slave narratives, it defies the ascription of mental deficiency to the body of the Other and exposes the confinement of those bodies as a contingent social phenomenon rather than a "natural" or inevitable fate. It has particular affinities, then, with those slave narratives elicited by sympathetic abolitionists, for Sienkiewicz-Mercer's account is in effect promoted and sponsored by individuals seeking to liberate people with disabilities and even to abolish their "institutionalization." In this case, however, neither the disabled subject nor the nondisabled collaborator has made the narrative especially polemical—except, perhaps, in the afterword, where Sienkiewicz-Mercer is quoted as giving a speech that calls for the abolition of institutions like the one in which she was confined.

As with many slave narratives, the collaborative composition of this text raises questions about authorship and authority. In the case of Bauby, who was highly educated and sophisticated about print media, it is probably safe to assume that his collaborator functioned mostly as a scribe—active in prompting him with recited letters, but probably largely passive in the composition of the memoir. With Tavalaro and Sienkiewicz-Mercer, who were far less highly educated, collaborators seem to have played much more active roles in the solicitation and composition of the memoirs. In both cases, the narratives contain texts attributable solely to the women themselves; in both instances, the disparity between the style of those texts and that of the collaborative text suggests that the voice of the memoir is not solely that of its subject and putative narrator—regardless of the *accuracy* of the accounts, which both women were apparently able to ensure.

One of the important aspects of *I Raise My Eyes to Say Yes* is that it represents, by implication, many lives that generally go unrepresented, uninscribed because of disability.[10] In that sense, it suggests not the limitations of people with disabilities but those of autobiography as an accessible medium of self-representation. That is, it suggests that autobiography as traditionally conceived, with its inherent valorization of individualism and autonomy, presents its own barriers to people with disabilities. The book communicates both the limitations of language and the liberation of access to it. Some of the best parts of the book suggest that subjectivity is not entirely a linguistic construct; at least, it

---

10. Of course, new technologies may quite literally write new lives, but in Sienkiewicz-Mercer's case, high-tech methods did not ultimately prove superior to the low-tech word boards.

offers a glimpse of life being lived and communicated in gestures, looks, and sounds—beyond or without the resources of what we usually recognize as language or autobiography.

To associate this disability memoir with slave narrative alone, however, would be perhaps to limit its resonance, at least if slave narrative is thought to have been made obsolete by the Civil War. It might also be considered a form of autoethnography, as Mary Louise Pratt defines the term:

> instances in which colonized subjects undertake to represent themselves in ways that *engage with* the colonizer's own terms. If the ethnographic texts are a means by which Europeans represent to themselves their (usually subjugated) others, autoethnographic texts are those the others construct in response to or in dialogue with those metropolitan representations. (7)

This narrative does display a kind of postcolonial impulse—the impulse to define oneself in resistance to the dehumanizing categories of the medical and health-service institutions (see Frank, 7–11). It's autoethnography, too, in that it's a first-person account of what Erving Goffman calls the "underlife of a public institution," the inmates' view of the asylum—the gossip, the games, the inside dope. Both as individual and institutional history, it supplements, challenges, and indicts official discourse, which assumes that standardized testing can adequately indicate the inner life of the subject in question.

To characterize it as standing in for other unwritten, perhaps unwriteable, accounts is to suggest its affinity with a more current first-person genre: *testimonio.* In an incisive discussion of *testimonio,* John Beverley has distinguished it from "autobiography" as follows.

> *Testimonio* represents an affirmation of the individual subject, even of individual growth and transformation, but in connection with a group or class situation marked by marginalization, oppression, and struggle. If it loses this connection, it ceases to be *testimonio* and becomes autobiography, that is, an account of, and also a means of access to, middle- or upper-class status, a sort of documentary *bildungsroman.* (103)

In this text we have a disability memoir that moves toward, though it may not fully occupy, the position with regard to the disability rights movement that *testimonio* occupies with regard to the movement for the rights of indigenous peoples. *I Raise My Eyes to Say Yes* is *testimonio* to the (considerable) extent to which its narrator speaks not as a unique individual but rather for a class of marginalized individuals, in ways already suggested.

My term *rhetoric of emancipation* should perhaps be qualified here, however, insofar as it overstates the position from which Sienkiewicz-Mercer composes her memoir. To be sure, Sienkiewicz-Mercer is liberated from the confining state hospital, but she narrates her account from within the context of an ongoing personal and collective struggle for recognition of the value and rights of people with disabilities. While the political critique within the text is muted, her story decisively represents disability not as a flaw in her body but as the prejudicial construct of a normative culture. It thus suggests the way in which personal narrative of disability may articulate and advocate the political paradigm of disability and thus align itself with *testimonio* as deployed in other modern liberation movements.

One of the arguments made against *narrating* disability would seem to apply to all forms of narrative, including autobiography: "By narrativizing an impairment, one tends to . . . link it to the bourgeois sensibility of individualism and the drama of an individual story" (L. J. Davis, Introduction, 4). Given the examples I have cited here, there is no question of exempting first-person discourse from this critique. Indeed, most of my examples suggest that the conventional rhetorics for representing disability in autobiography do tend to individualize the condition and, worse, to reinforce its stigma. Thus, although memoir may offer a degree of access that other literary genres do not, and although it may offer a degree of control over representation that other media do not, various cultural constraints limit the counterhegemonic potential of disability memoir. Culture filters and manipulates even seemingly "self-generated" texts in various ways, protecting its interest in marginalizing and ignoring disabled lives.

At the same time, there are signs of promise in some recent texts— narratives from hidden corners, some of which may actually connect with each other in ways that challenge and undermine the limited medical paradigm of disability. Such narratives not only attest to but advance the work of the disability rights movement; in their consciousness of their own condition as culturally constructed and as shared by others, their authors may move beyond the familiar formulas of disability memoir and point the way to broader critiques of the construction of disability in America today.

4 § Double Exposure

Performing Conjoined Twinship

Be two or not be two, that [is] the question.

—HILLEL SCHWARTZ (56)

One of the significant developments in memoir writing in the late twentieth century was an innovation in form: the emergence of the graphic memoir, as heralded by Art Spiegelman's two-volume *Maus* (1986, 1991). Disability has been the subject of a number of graphic memoirs, such as Al Davison's *The Spiral Cage* (2003), an account of living with spina bifida, and David B.'s *Epileptic,* about living with an epileptic brother (2005). Visual representation of visible disability offers new opportunities but also presents new risks and potential pitfalls, because the visual images may overpower verbal cues. But the danger of presenting visible impairment as a voyeuristic freak show is far greater in visual media like photography, especially in video and film.

Documentary films about disabled individuals are hardly new, of course. Indeed, disabled bodies have long been represented in medical documentaries, the very point of which is the visual display of rare "specimens"—for preservation, examination, and analysis. What is new, however, is a turn away from medical perspectives and the medical model. Thus even as disability memoir has taken graphic form, disability life writing is also found in documentary film. Several such films have achieved high visibility and critical esteem; for example, the 1999 Oscar winner, *King Gimp,* is about a young artist with cerebral palsy.

In addition to the single-subject documentary, however, there has

49

also been a rise in documentary group biography or group portrait (visual prosopography). Typically, such films document the lives of a demographically diverse group of individuals who share an anomalous condition. A notable example of this is Lauren Chiten's *Twitch and Shout* (1994), which explores how Tourette's syndrome affects the lives of a photojournalist, a professional basketball player, a waitress and aspiring singer, a visual artist, and a Mennonite farmer. Significantly, the film has no authoritative voice-over and virtually no medical testimony; instead, it is composed of footage of the individuals with Tourette's living, and commenting on, their everyday lives. After introducing the audience to all of these subjects as individuals, the film includes group scenes filmed at a convention of people with Tourette's, at which, being in the majority, they make no effort to stifle their tics, whether physical or verbal. Indeed, as they dance to the tune of "Twist and Shout," many of them seem to revel in their freedom to tic.

As I was at pains to suggest in *Vulnerable Subjects,* visual representation of visible disability runs the risk of objectifying its subjects precisely because of its visual nature: in writing, the appearance of such disabilities may be described in words, then taken for granted; in film, the disability is almost always on display, and the voyeurism inherent in the medium can obstruct attempts to characterize subjects as multidimensional individuals. This chapter, then, explores how and whether nonprejudicial representation is possible when the body in question is conventionally the passive recipient of curious, appraising, or clinical gazes, at best; at worst, a stimulus to pity and revulsion. It does so by analyzing a contemporary nonmedical documentary film concerning two conjoined twins, Reba and Lori Schappell, against the background of the medical documentary. In the age of the some body memoir and the some body documentary, the medical model is likely to be challenged, supplemented, or even replaced by the social model.

There are few bodies as problematic as those (or is it that?) of a pair of conjoined twins. Indeed, one of the fundamental questions raised by conjoinment—with its scientific, philosophical, and moral ramifications—is the issue of number itself: are conjoined twins two connected persons or one divided person? Coming across skeletons of several pairs of conjoined infants in La Galerie d'Anatomie Comparée in Paris led Stephen Jay Gould to ponder this question. Rejecting the commonsense view that the number of individuals is determined by the number of heads, Gould concludes that conjoined twins represent neither one person nor two persons but rather "in part two and in part one," no matter how the body is composed. He argues, then, that such beings represent a very fundamental sort of anomaly; for Gould, conjoined twins, like intersex individuals, defy normative binaries, suggesting that human variation is more a matter of positions along a continuum than a matter of norms and their violation (22).

Conjoined twins are sources of fascination for many people, and revulsion for some, because they violate the seemingly foundational principle of individualism—one body, one person—and thus the notion, idealized in modern Western culture, of the autonomous self. Indeed, they powerfully call into question the application of the term *individual,* whose root meaning is, after all, "indivisible." Furthermore, conjoinment—literally the closest of human relations—conflicts with the modern Western sense of the individual's right to privacy. Conjoined twins seem to have no private space, no private time, no private lives. They seem not to be individuals, then, in the fundamental sense of single, separate, autonomous persons. They present the prospect of being constantly shadowed—or overshadowed—by a sibling from birth to death, for the death of one entails the death of the other (absent emergency surgery to sever the survivor from his or her dead twin). For philosophers in the liberal tradition of John Stuart Mill who associate autonomy with individuality, conjoined twins provide interesting test cases (Ells, 608). Either they are not individuals, autonomy is not a condition of individuality, or conjoinment affords a degree or kind of autonomy after all. For such reasons, many individuals find the idea of being inextricably joined to another person unimaginable or repugnant.

Conjoined twins are commonly viewed at best as curiosities, at worst as monsters. According to Hillel Schwartz, until 1800 or so midwives often smothered conjoined twins at birth (50). In the nineteenth and twentieth centuries, they were typically regarded as freaks. After all, the eponymous "Siamese" twins, Chang and Eng (or Chang-Eng, as they preferred to be called [van Dijck, 540]), became famous when they were exhibited to the public as such—a classic case of the commercial display of anomalous bodies.[1]

Even today the usual assumption about conjoined twins at birth is that their quality of life will be extremely low unless they can be separated. When conjoined twins are born, their conjoinment is usually seen by parents and physicians as abnormal and undesirable—a disorder crying out for surgical correction if at all possible. The conventional medical move is to determine the feasibility of separation, on the assumption that it is desirable to retrofit the twins to the norm of "one body, one person." Indeed, the medical approach tends to prejudge the case, to assume that conjoined twins are "really" two joined individuals rather than one complex and anomalous being. The medical response to conjoined twins, then, is to bestow individuality upon them by dividing them surgically, even at the cost of sacrificing one—treating one as a parasite or a growth (like a tumor, as one physician put it), rather than as a person.[2] One way to think about conjoined twins, then, is as monozygotic (identical) twins whose physical attachment is considered in and of itself a serious, even severe, disability. The dominant medical model, then, favors separation, at the risk of truly disabling or even killing one or both twins.

Two contemporary news stories are pertinent here. In April 2001, Nepalese twins joined at the head were surgically separated in Singapore in a hundred-hour-long operation; in November 2001, they were sent home after a year in the hospital.[3]

However, doctors at a news conference in Singapore cautioned that the 18-month-old girls will not be "like any other children when they grow up."

"We can't really tell for sure what type of disability they will end

---

1. It is worth noting, however, that after having been displayed by others, including P. T. Barnum, they became their own impresarios and, cutting out the middleman, earned sufficient money to retire comfortably.

2. Recently, however, ethicists have begun to challenge this assumption that separation is inherently preferable, especially if it means sacrificing one twin; as counterargument, they cite the testimony of grown twins, who express satisfaction with their lives. See Angier, which cites the Schappell twins prominently.

3. Conjoinment of any sort is quite rare, occurring once in every 100,000 births. Craniopagus conjoinment—joining at the skull—is far rarer, occurring once in every 2,000,000 births ("Outpouring," para. 24).

up with, but there will be some kind of disability," said Prof. Ho Lai Un, a member of the team of doctors who operated on the twins.

Dr. Keith Goh, who coordinated the surgery to separate the girls in April, said the operation had left them with irregularly shaped heads, and they could face social challenges as a result.

"But they do look a lot better than if they remained conjoined," he said. "In that state they could never go out." (Paterson)

This story suggests that even "successful" separation surgery may entail the creation of disability, whether physical or cognitive.

In the summer of 2003 the outcome of a fifty-hour-long attempt at surgical separation was very different in the case of Ladan and Laleh Bijani, adult Iranian twins also joined at the head. (Their heads were joined in such a way that they faced in the same direction, a less awkward configuration than that of Lori and Reba Schappell.) According to CNN news, "Ladan Bijani died when her blood circulation failed after the operation to separate the twins' brains, officials at Singapore's Raffles Hospital say. Her sister Laleh died when her circulation failed one-and-a-half hours later" ("Outpouring," para. 1). Both women had law degrees, but, intent on pursuing different careers, they chose to risk an operation that had never been attempted on adults. This story suggests the powerful appeal of physical autonomy, the desire for which cost both these women their lives.

Not surprisingly, as several scholars have pointed out, the dominant form of representation of conjoined twins in contemporary Western European and North American culture is the medical documentary film that focuses on, and culminates in, (not always successful) surgical separation. According to José van Dijck, in the early twentieth century, within years of the first public movie screenings, a prominent French surgeon, Eugène-Louis Doyen, had himself filmed separating a pair of twelve-year-old conjoined girls, Doodica and Radica Neik.[4] Significantly, although the film was intended for a medical audience, pirated copies were soon shown to lay audiences (544).

---

4. The motive for this belated surgery was to prevent one sister from contracting tuberculosis from the other. Sadly, "although the operation was considered a success, Doodica died a week afterwards, while her sister would live for another year before dying" of tuberculosis (van Dijck, 544).

Indeed, van Dijck argues that the medical documentary has displaced the freak show as the arena for the display of conjoined twins as spectacles. She reminds us that even in nineteenth-century freak shows, exhibits were often presented by "medical" experts. Whereas in the nineteenth century the phenomenon of conjoinment was the focus of attention, today the always risky—and thus dramatic—process of separation is the pretext for display (538): thus, "the medicalization of conjoined twins did not automatically imply their emancipation from popular entertainment" (539).[5] As van Dijck points out, the medical documentary represents the "convergence of media technology and medical technology." Among the features of modern medical technology that give contemporary medical documentary film new dimensions are endoscopes and new scanning technologies; combined, these subject conjoined bodies to unprecedented visual scrutiny (548).

Face to Face: The Schappell Twins, directed by Ellen Weissbrod, is the antithesis of the medical documentary in a number of ways and for a number of reasons. The main factor is that the film calls upon the conventions and resources of the medium to present conjoinment as a familiar, rather than alien, way of being. Lori and Reba Schappell, the subjects of this extraordinary documentary, are conjoined in a particularly awkward configuration: they are joined at their left foreheads in such a way that their faces are offset. Although they are "face to face," they cannot look each other in the eye; indeed, each seems to have only one functioning eye. Their configuration is far more inconvenient and freakish than that of Chang and Eng Bunker. Joined by a band of tissue at the abdomen, Chang and Eng presented mirror images of each other, symmetrical along the vertical axis; in sharp contrast, Lori and Reba are highly asymmetrical as a pair and far from identical in form. Lori is considerably larger and taller than Reba, who can neither stand nor walk because of spina bifida; consequently, Lori carries her or wheels her around on a customized stool. They are bound together quite literally cheek to cheek in an odd and, to most observers, threatening or even repellent intimacy. The challenge to the filmmaker is, of course, to present them visually without placing the viewer in the po-

---

5. For other accounts of the medical documentary, see Clark and Myser, "Being Humaned" (1996), and Myser and Clark, "Fixing Katie and Eilish" (1998).

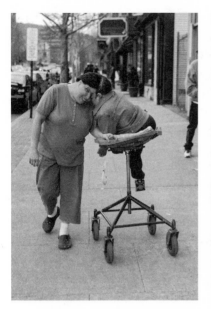

Reba Schappell (seated) and Lori Schappell (standing) on a
shopping trip in their home town, Reading, Pennsylvania.
© Jeffery R. Werner/IncredibleFeatures.com.

sition of the distanced and objectifying viewer—to use the medium to
facilitate empathetic watching, rather than staring.[6]

Although conjoinment is generally considered inherently pathological, even freakish, Lori and Reba Schappell insist that they are content
to be joined; as Reba puts it, "Do not fix what is not broken." They insist that they would not want to be separated until one dies, when it
would be worth the risk of surgery to attempt to save the other's life.
But while they were spared the ordeal of surgical separation after their
birth in 1961, on the grounds that their conjoinment was "God's will,"[7]
they were confined to a state institution for people with mental retardation for the next twenty-four years. As long as their conjoinment
was viewed in terms of the medical, rather than the social, paradigm of

6. For an analysis of staring, see Rosemarie Garland-Thomson, "Ways of Staring."

7. It would likely not have been possible without inflicting serious damage or death on one
or both: a scan done when they were thirty revealed that they share brain tissue in their frontal
lobes.

disability, remedies were limited to separation from each other—which in their case was ruled out on religious grounds—or seclusion, nonsurgical excision from the body politic. They were thus sheltered from the stares of the public—or perhaps the public was thus protected from their threatening presence. Their confinement, rationalized in part on the basis of their lacking autonomy as individuals, effectively deprived them of freedom (and thus autonomy as a pair). As is too often the case, the medical view of people with disabilities as inherently limited was in effect self-fulfilling.

But although conjoinment may seem a terrible fate—a life (and eventually a death) sentence—it may prompt a great deal of creative improvisation on the part of those conjoined. Certainly the Schappell sisters have been performing conjoinment—in different senses, in different venues and media, and before different audiences—all their lives. In their earliest years, they performed it unself-consciously, extemporizing activities most people execute solo, beginning with sitting, crawling, standing, and walking. With the development of self-consciousness, their performance assumed another dimension; even during their years in the institution, they must have been acutely aware of their audience of insiders. (To their credit, some of these insiders, nurses and staffers cited in the film, encouraged the twins to leave the institution and take their performance public—defying the notion of them as lacking autonomy.) Since they began living independently in their twenties—living more public (but also more private) lives—they have been performing in new ways and in new arenas. Lori has attended college and held various jobs. Reba (née Dori) has taken up country-and-western singing (hence the name change, a tribute to Reba McEntire); she has performed in public as well as recording in the studio. They have been featured in photo spreads in glossy magazines, on the *Jerry Springer Show,* and in *Face to Face.* This 1999 documentary thus mediates—shapes and re-presents—what for them is now a long-running act.

Given their history, I find it noteworthy that the film avoids not only the standard medical documentary approach but also the clichéd trope of triumph over adversity—all too common in narratives of disability—which tends to reify the classification of individuals as disabled while congratulating them for succeeding nevertheless. That is, the standard presentation applauds overcoming, rather than removing, obstacles to success. Such a documentary would take the form of a biopic, tracing their lives chronologically from the initial shock of their birth, through the tragedy of their confinement to an institution, to their successful emergence in public; Reba's career as a singer would be the conventional evidence of success. But *Face to Face* is not a conventional biopic; rather, it is a filmed portrait of the twins at a certain stage of their lives. Partly because the film does not recount their lives in chronological order, their crucial move out of the institution—their emancipation—is not made the center of the film; it is relegated to back story. They did face adversity in the form of their institutionalization; they clearly resent this but do not dwell on it. Insofar as they are portrayed as triumphant, they are seen as surmounting adversity in the form of benighted medical and social opinion rather than in the form of their anatomical connection. Thus, they triumph not over their impairment, which they accept, but over their disability—that is, ostracism and confinement. Further, the film proceeds at times by inducing interaction with strangers in order to evoke spontaneous reactions and sample public attitudes about conjoinment; it thus succeeds to some degree in being about "us," rather than—or as well as—about "them." This is the key to its originality and to its value as disability documentary.

In the decade and a half since they moved out of the Hamburg state hospital, the Schappell sisters have made a policy of going out in public as much as possible. Given their conjoinment, which inevitably attracts stares, this takes a certain amount of nerve. Lori, the more outspoken of the two, asserts that any revulsion at the sight of them in public is not their problem but the spectator's. As she puts it, and Reba concurs enthusiastically, if you find the twins interesting, you are welcome to use binoculars (inspect them, but from a distance); if you don't, you should wear blinkers (limit your field of vision rather than intrude into theirs). Thus, they seem to tolerate, even encourage, staring by the curious while denying any responsibility for offending the eyes of the squeamish.

But although they are eager to circulate in public, they are not comfortable with intrusive or objectifying forms of attention. At the heart of the film is footage of the sisters' visit to tourist attractions in New

York City, including the Statue of Liberty and Times Square. In such public sites, meccas for tourists from inside and outside the United States, Lori and Reba themselves become a focus for attention, a sight to write home about or to record on film. When a German tourist snaps their picture, explaining that he is a dentist and that they are "something unusual," both sisters take exception to being described in such objectifying terms. When the man's wife apologizes for his clumsy English, they question the relevance of his being a dentist—the implication being that he regards them as a medical specimen.

In studied contrast to these public scenes, in which they perform their conjoinment, sometimes affably, sometimes combatively, before an audience of other sightseers, the film also contains scenes shot in their apartment. This segment is potentially highly voyeuristic because of the privacy of this zone and because the viewers see without being seen—unlike the German tourist, who can be called to account for his insulting remark. In the event, however, the film manages to minimize or negate the voyeuristic aspect of this sequence. The camera follows the sisters as they arise in the morning. Lori lifts Reba onto the tall, wheeled stool that expedites locomotion, and they proceed into the bathroom, where they brush their teeth.[8] Then on to the kitchen, where they eat breakfast, Lori standing, with her cereal bowl on a high counter, to accommodate Reba's height on her stool.

This footage is at once odd and normalizing (i.e., depathologizing). Rare, strange, and undeniable as their physical attachment is—and it is the most striking thing about their appearance—they are shown carrying out a daily routine, with necessary enabling variations built into it. (The film thus makes the point that radically different modalities may be used to achieve "normal" functioning.) By entering their home to show them in a familiar domestic routine, one that is automatic to many nondisabled "single" people, the film suggests that their unobserved lives are not so different as others might imagine; what may enfreak them is the presence of surprised and fascinated spectators—that is, the implicit assertion of a norm they are presumed to violate. This sequence nicely illustrates that autonomy may be consistent with—in-

---

8. Those who have shared bathrooms with siblings, spouses, partners, parents, or children will recognize that the differences in privacy are matters of degree not of kind.

deed, exercised by means of—apparent violations of privacy. Here the sacrifice of privacy is compatible with autonomy precisely because (unlike that entailed by their institutionalization) it is chosen deliberately and purposefully. Further, by following the Schappells in public and in private, the film dramatizes the permeability of the public/private boundary, which their institutionalization denied.

It is crucial that the medium of this representation is visual, with all its potential for freak-show exploitation. Rather than exhibiting the twins as a spectacle for public perusal, however, the film presents conjoinment in such a way as to expose and unsettle dominant notions of bodily norms. The film is not a show that displays them for the titillation and reassurance of normals but a venue in which they perform their relationship and their lives in ways they manage (for the most part) to control. The sisters are nearly always on camera, and when they are, the fact of their conjoinment is always visible. The medium does not blink their conjoinment, nor can the viewer overlook it. But the director, Ellen Weissbrod, has made clever use of her medium to mitigate its potential for sensationalism. For one thing, the film offers verbal self-representation that is dramatically at odds with the appearance of the sisters. Where viewers may at first see conjoinment and symbiosis, Lori and Reba insist on their individuality and independence (and by all accounts their tastes and personalities are strikingly different—indeed, barely compatible).[9] If at first the viewers appraise them as grotesque or freakish, the sisters proclaim their normality; the film invites viewers, then, to believe the sisters' words rather than their own eyes.

For another thing, putting the sisters in the viewers' face, so to speak, works in the end to normalize their conjoinment, treating it less as a physical impairment than as a condition that constitutes their lives and selves as tightly, permanently, and complexly intertwined. Their constant, prolonged exposure itself has a normalizing effect; over the film's relatively long duration—100 minutes—viewers gradually become accustomed to their (conjoined) faces. Their appearance soon ceases to be shocking, and viewers may focus on one sister at a time,

---

9. According to Nancy L. Segal, who interviewed them, "the twins' behavioral differences are extensive—Lori likes to watch television, Reba does not; Lori loves to shop, Reba does not; Lori craves sweets, Reba does not" (304). And Reba performs as a country singer; Lori does not.

rather than on the *pair* as an anomalous unit; on what one is doing and saying, rather than on the always apparent phenomenon of their conjoinment. Eventually, indeed, viewers may become more shocked by strangers' reactions to them than by their appearance.

The cast of interviewees is also relevant in this regard. They are generally not physicians who see conjoinment primarily as a medical issue, a problem to be solved. This is the most common perspective of documentaries on conjoinment, which typically track twins up to and through surgical separation, with anxious, exhausted parents pacing the corridors.[10] Here, in contrast, the interviewees are mostly women who worked in the hospital, as nurses or volunteers, and who became convinced that the sisters were not retarded and, more important, did not need to be hidden from the public eye. Some advocated their release; one admits she was skeptical about their living independently at first but that they confounded her low expectations again and again. The perspective of these witnesses is experiential, pragmatic, and relational, not medical or rehabilitative. The only academic experts interviewed on camera are Catherine Myser, an ethicist, and Alice D. Dreger, a historian of anatomy: without claiming to speak for Lori and Reba, they minimize their anomalousness. For example, Dreger notes that what upsets most people about conjoinment is its denial of personal privacy. She points out that privacy is a culturally constructed concept and that when "normals" live together they have to redefine the border between the public, the private, and the intimate. Another recognition of the sisters' agency, autonomy, and authority is the film's lack of any voice-over; there is no ever-present host in the form of a loquacious expert like Oliver Sacks, who might dominate the subjects by force of intellect and personal eccentricity. The spoken discourse of the film is overwhelmingly that of the two women, and they defer to no one.

---

10. Indeed, this is true of the BBC documentary *Conjoined Twins*, aired on BBC2 on 19 October 2000. (The transcript is available online.) The film makes a point of offering the testimony of Lori and Reba Schappell and Masha and Dasha Krivoshlyapova as twins content to be conjoined. (In effect, the Russian twins assert their political correctness: "We are a little collective.") But it intercuts this testimony with an ongoing narrative of the separation of Tanzanian twins by South African surgeons. While the consequences of the surgery are far from clear, it is pronounced a success. Despite the documentary's overt attempt to present both sides without drawing conclusions, its effect is to privilege the surgical approach.

Notably absent from the film's cast of characters are other members of their family; the sisters' parents and their siblings appear only in some family photos. It is not clear whether their lack of involvement reflects their wishes or those of the sisters. There is no evidence of hostility on the part of the sisters toward the family that institutionalized them; the absence of other family members from the film may reflect their discomfort with the sisters' public self-presentation, or perhaps it is an expression of the sisters' autonomy and individuality. Whatever its cause, the absence of testimony from family members to some extent works against the normalizing thrust of the film, characterizing them as without "normal" relations. On the other hand, it avoids any risk of the sisters' being characterized as their parents' problem, an embarrassment or a burden to the family. In any case, the absence of any testimony that defines them as freaks or treats them as disabled is evidence either of the sisters' control over who shall speak about them or of the director's respect for their dignity and point of view—or both.

In scenes shot in public, the film often puts the viewers into the privileged position of watching over the sisters' shoulders as others react to them for the first time; the audience is thus aligned with the twins, rather than with the strangers who observe them. For example, in one sequence, passersby are shown the twins' image on a small digital display screen. It takes some of these observers a while to sort out what they are seeing, to make out that what appears as a tangle of limbs and torsos is two joined individuals. When they figure this out, they often blurt out a reaction—usually surprised rather than disgusted, but sometimes pitying or patronizing; one declares, "It's messed up that they gotta live that way." The film also allows those who encounter Lori and Reba to invoke their own normalizing analogies for conjoinment—that it is akin to intense sibling bonding, for instance, or marriage. There's an amusing moment when a middle-aged couple, who have rejected the analogy between conjoinment and marriage on the grounds that marriage is voluntary whereas conjoinment is not, sheepishly realize that each has been finishing the other's sentences. The effect of this is to allow viewers to weigh these outsiders' uninformed responses against what they know of the subjective experience of the sisters, who seem to get along well and to enjoy each other, who do not pity themselves, and who do not regard themselves as freaks or in any way unattractive. One sequence is shot at a beauty parlor, where they get separate hairdos; indeed, their hair is different in color, since Reba dyes hers.

Having entered the world conjoined, Lori and Reba know no other reality. While they cannot but recognize that they are anomalous, they do not define themselves as "abnormal," "freakish," "defective," or even disabled—though they clearly cannot perform some "normal" functions, such as driving a car. They are clearly disabled from a legal perspective, but their mobility is limited less by their anatomy than by the built environment, the accessibility of public transportation, the availability of special transport, and so on. Indeed, paradoxically, Reba is less disabled as a conjoined twin than she would be if separated. As a separate person, she would need to use a wheelchair; as a conjoined twin, she has a sister who either carries her or provides her locomotion when she is seated on her stool. In effect, Lori functions as a human prosthesis, complementing her sister's body.

The film is depathologizing in another subtle respect: its clever use of multiple cameras. This is important because of the sisters' craniopagus conjoinment. The film's title, *Face to Face,* presumably refers primarily to the sisters' configuration, which keeps them perpetually face to face. But it is a little misleading in that the phrase "face to face" usually refers to people situated so that they can look each other in the eye, which these two sisters cannot do. The title's other meaning presumably has to do with the film's bringing the audience "face to face" with the sisters. This is important because the medium provides a visual experience of them that would be impossible in the flesh. People meeting Lori and Reba in person can face only one at a time because the sisters themselves face in opposite directions. This requires significant adaptations in the rituals of greeting; one cannot make eye contact with both at once, and one has to greet one at a time. One can hug both at the same time, but only awkwardly.

In one brief sequence, the sisters self-consciously and humorously disagree over whether they should go "left" or "right," playing on the fact that one's left is perpetually the other's right. In this sense, at least, they are stuck in a posture of constant opposition; they can use some deictics—*here, there, I, you*—in standard fashion, but directional deictics—*forward, backward, left, right*—require reversal (or modification by pronominal deictics: *your* left, etc.). But by using multiple cameras and cutting back and forth from one to the other, the film manages to bring Lori and Reba face to face with the audience almost simultaneously. When they converse, the film presents first one speaking, then the other; as each speaks, the frame contains the speaker's face and the side and back of the other's head. This crosscutting is a simple but ingenious adaption of the conventional way in which films present face to face conversations (as across a table). It takes advantage of the fact that viewers have internalized this convention and are thus not disconcerted by jumping back and forth from one camera angle to a reverse angle.

The film employs the camera in yet another significant way that gives the subjects some control over the viewers' gaze. Of the two, Reba is the more oriented to the pleasures of tourism, and while they are in New York, she carries a digital camera, mainly to record the sights. The normal dynamics of seeing sights together are not possible for the sisters. If one says, "Look!" and points at something, the two must turn nearly 180 degrees to accommodate the other's limited vision. That is, unless her sister has a device such as a digital camera, whose flexible viewfinder allows it to function like a periscope. Reba's camera enables two normalizing strategies. First, this camera's digital display and its small size make it possible for her to look at what Lori is seeing as she is seeing it, by pointing it over her shoulder. The camera functions then as a prosthesis that compensates for their opposing orientation. Second, Reba's camera reverses the voyeuristic gaze. Armed with a camera, like the film crew, Reba—and by extension her twin—is in a position to make others the target of an objectifying gaze—to stare back.

The two sisters differ in their "availability" to the camera. While both seem to tolerate visual inspection (according to their remark about binoculars), at one point on their New York trip Lori tells a somewhat nonplussed observer that it's okay to take Reba's picture without permission, but not hers. The rationale for this is that only Reba is a public figure—in her role as a country-and-western singer; indeed, in New York she wears a satin jacket with the legend "Reba . . . on Tour." In contrast, Lori defines herself as a private citizen. What she acknowledges by deflecting attention, of course, is the perception of the two sisters ensemble as a single freak. By distinguishing her attitude toward picture taking from her twin's, and justifying her sister's attitude in terms of her career, she not only "promotes" her sister but, more importantly, invites the potential picture taker to reconceptualize what she's doing—as "celebrity spotting" rather than "freak spotting"—and to force her to distinguish between the sisters as individuals, to separate and disenfreak them. To treat them ethically, she implies—as the film does—that one must acknowledge their independence and individuality; they have distinct desires, values, and careers. Lori suggests to the voyeur that she has made, or is in the process of making, more than one category mistake.

The film takes advantage of Reba's budding career as a singer by ending as a music video; Reba lip-synchs a song viewers have seen her sing in the studio—significantly entitled "Fear of Living Alone"—while her sister dances beside her and twirls her rolling seat, and others—people interviewed in the film—dance around them in a public park. It is a witty adaptation of the conventions of the music video, whose techniques are devoted here not to glamorous celebrity subjects in some arbitrary "reality" backdrop but rather to subjects portrayed in their home town among friends and acquaintances. This sequence at once mocks the conventions of the music video, alludes to Reba's musical career, and offers a celebratory final image. It takes the twins decisively out of the freak show and into the celebrity culture of their time—in recognition of Reba's genuine, if minor, fame, and in defiance of the distancing emphasis on the grotesque and anomalous.

As a whole, the film flaunts its medium. While the editor never admits the film crew into the frame, keeping them out of view and never allowing the process of filming to be filmed—never letting the story of the story intrude on the story—she uses cameras in a self-conscious way that reminds viewers constantly of the film's mediation. As noted earlier, the sisters are almost always on camera, but they are often filmed in mirrors, or while using cameras, or in images being shown to others. The film fully acknowledges and invites audience members to consider the ways in which point of view and mediation construct reality. Ironically, by offering prolonged exposure and multiple angles of the twins, it tends to deproblematize their conjoinment. In various ways, then, the film challenges preconceptions about identity and in-

dividuality, privacy and publicity, normality and abnormality or disability. It offers an instructive ethical alternative to objectifying displays of vulnerable subjects, and it suggests that those who are geneti-
cally identical and even anatomically attached to one another should
be regarded as autonomous individuals. It further suggests that
scrupulous representation may actively empower them, acknowledging, and even enhancing, their autonomy as well as celebrating their
conjoinment: as represented here, Lori and Reba Schappell are at once
one *and* two.

5 ⸘ Identity, Identicality, and Life Writing
Telling (the Silent) Twins Apart

I was born a twin, and I'll die a twin.

—JUNE GIBBONS (quoted in *The Silent Twin*)

By itself, twinhood does not entail disability; conjoinment of twins, the result of something going awry in utero, is the exception. Still, to be an identical twin, no matter how normal, is still to inhabit an odd, slightly problematic body. And the representation of identical twins presents interesting challenges to conventional life-writing genres precisely because separate but identical (monozygotic) twins challenge Western culture's valorization of the unique individual, which is the basis of both autobiography and biography. In the case of the so-called silent twins, June and Jennifer Gibbons, their extremely strong emotional bond amounted to a kind of involuntary and inescapable conjoinment, psychological rather than physical; more to the point here, coupled with their muteness, it constituted a significant disability, one that made them attractive, but problematic, subjects of biography. Again, the relationship between disability and available modes of representation is a vexed one.

Autobiographies by twins, identical or not, are rare, perhaps because, as theories of child development suggest, being a twin can impede individuation. According to Audrey C. Sandbank,

> clearly identity is a much greater problem for the identical twin. He recognises his twin in the mirror before he recognises himself and is several months behind the non-identical twin in recognising his own mirror image. He takes longer to say "I" and "me" and more often answers to his twin's name. (169)

As children, twins may collapse the distinction between them in various ways; they may use their names joined with a hyphen to refer to themselves or, more dramatically, use "me" instead of "us" in referring to themselves (as in, "sit between me" [Segal, 61]). And while mothers can facilitate their infants' separation from *them*, it may be harder to enable infant twins to separate from each *other* (Ainslee, 77). In adolescence, too, "twins may not be ready for the thrust towards separation until much later than their physical maturity would suggest" (Sandbank, 179). This may be less a function of genetic identicality, however, than of being raised with an exact age peer: "It is probable that 'look-alike' nonidentical twins have the same problem" (Sandbank, 169).

Ainslee concurs.

> The presence of two infants, faced with the same developmental needs and tasks, profoundly alters a child's usual environment. . . . Although zygosity may play a role in shaping parental perceptions, as some research suggests, it is not in and of itself the preeminent force in shaping twin development. (x–xi)

So the lack of twin autobiography may not be a sign that twins are less fully individuated than nontwins; it may rather reflect the fact that twins—identical or not—have an intimate lifelong mirror in which to reflect—and to whom to express—their sense of individuality.

Biographies of identical twins—that is, life narratives of *both* twins—are also quite rare, perhaps because few pairs have achieved the requisite eminence. Marjorie Wallace's *The Silent Twins*, a biography of identical twins whose lives were intertwined to an extreme, even pathological, degree, is an exception that demonstrates, even as it surmounts, the difficulty of representing identical twins. The "silence" of June and Jennifer Gibbons—their elective mutism—was a deafening one in that it was a manifestation of a serious pathology, a psychological bond that at once sustained and stifled them, cutting them off from vital relations with anyone else; for most of their lives they were deaf to voices other than their own, cut off from the discourse of the family and the larger community surrounding them.[1]

---

1. I use the past tense because Jennifer Gibbons died suddenly in 1993 of heart disease (acute myocarditis).

The Gibbons twins at school age. Photo reprinted from *The Silent Twins*, by Marjorie Wallace (Random House, 1986). Courtesy of Marjorie Wallace, founder and chief executive of the mental health charity SANE.

Of Barbadian descent, June and Jennifer Gibbons were born in 1963 and grew up in Yorkshire and Devon, England, and in Wales, near Royal Air Force bases where their father worked as a technician (Als, 74). The third and fourth children of Aubrey and Gloria Gibbons, they were followed by a younger sister, Rosie. Slow to learn to talk, the twins developed what seemed a private language. (A speech therapist, however, determined that, rather than a "secret" language— or as one "expert" supposed, an African "click" language—they used a sort of patois combining Barbadian slang and English, spoken very quickly [Als, 75].) They were quite literally inseparable as small children, even in school. Major factors contributing to their mutual dependence and apparent mutism were their isolation in white communities, where they were bullied and subjected to racial taunts, and a speech impediment, which made their speech difficult for others to understand.[2] They grew up not only identical in appearance and similar in manner, then, as is often the case with monozygotic twins raised together (MZTs, in clinical parlance), but very much absorbed in each other, moving in synchrony, quickly establishing a shared fantasy life that excluded other people and other aspects of life.[3] By the time they had been marked out for special education, the intense bond between them and their refusal or reluctance to speak to anyone else cut them off from most other people. They spoke rarely even to family members, except for their younger sister; instead, they communicated largely through notes.

By the time teachers and school administrators recognized the intensity of their relationship, they were already eight and a half years old. At that time, the degree of their psychological bonding was viewed as so threatening to their individual integrity that school authorities not only proposed forcibly separating them, but framed the suggestion in the very terms used to justify the surgical separation of conjoined twins: "They are dying in each other's arms and we must save one of them, even if it is at the price of the other" (quoted in Wallace, 31). In an odd instance of inappropriate medicalization, the twins' tongues were operated on despite uncertainty among medical consultants as to whether lingual mobility was an issue in their mutism.

No doubt separation seemed appropriate—and both twins expressed a desire for it—but when it was attempted, neither could tolerate it. In any case, the administrators' language suggests the extent to which this sort of relationship violates some implicit standard of individuality, such that it was considered ethical to "sacrifice" one twin, as if one was physiologically parasitic on the other. (It implies that, like conjoined twins, identical twins violate the tacit rule of personhood: one person, one body. Conjoined twins seem to be two persons in one body; identical twins seem to be the same person in two bodies.) It also suggests why the twins may have resisted so mightily, responding perhaps to ruthless methods rather than to a presumably beneficent goal.

---

2. This residual impediment is audible in *The Silent Twin—Without My Shadow,* which relies heavily on interviews with June Gibbons.

3. Oddly and surprisingly—given their appearance and their excessively close bond—their mother regarded them as nonidentical twins until blood tests revealed their identicality when they were about twenty.

When they left school for good, at sixteen, they became reclusive, keeping to themselves in a room from which they barred their parents. There they compensated for their lack of social life with a rich fantasy life, played out first with dolls, then with books.[4] After taking a writing course—necessarily by correspondence—they wrote prolifically: fiction, poetry, and especially diaries. As adolescents, they ventured forth and acted out, experimenting with sex, drugs, alcohol, and crime—first shoplifting, then vandalism and arson. Their forays out of the house coincided with the onset of puberty, a juncture at which they might have been expected to grow apart; ordinarily, socializing and dating would introduce a little latitude into sisters' relationship at that age. But it was not to prove so for them. Indeed, some of the most dramatic evidence of their inability to exist—or even conceive of themselves—as completely independent and separate beings has to do with the inauguration of their sex lives. After having for a time strongly resisted the physical changes of puberty, they reversed course and aggressively sought sex and love. Or rather, perhaps uncomfortable relating intimately to others—especially boys their age—they treated sex as a substitute for love. (Their impersonal sexual encounters provided material for incongruously romantic fantasies in their diaries.)

Their sexual initiation also had a voyeuristic and narcissistic dimension. Both twins were deflowered in successive weeks by the same unappreciative young man; moreover, each twin witnessed the other's initiation. A rite of passage that might have helped differentiate them by giving each a healthy intimacy with someone other than her twin proved just another shared experience—shared but intensely competitive, as each vied to be first to lose her virginity and to be foremost in the young man's affections. After they set fire to a public building in 1982, they were arrested (together), tried (together), and sentenced (together) to be detained indefinitely in Broadmoor Special Hospital in England—a notorious high-security facility for the criminally insane—where, by far the youngest inmates, they were at times forcibly separated for therapeutic purposes. Ironically, then, it was only when

---

4. An interesting detail of their elaborate world of interrelated families of dolls is that the twins in that world were always nonidentical, indeed of different sexes (40).

they were literally imprisoned together that they were finally (but not successfully) isolated from one another. The death of Jennifer while in custody—on the day of the twins' transfer to a minimum-security facility—suggests that the proposal to sacrifice one to save the other was carried out, indirectly and inadvertently, in the end.

While the nature of their relationship gave the Gibbons twins a degree of notoriety and thus qualified them for biographical treatment, it also seemed to defy standard life-writing genres. Certainly, the twins' pathology was inconsistent with autobiography or memoir. Although they were given to minutely detailed and copious journal writing—the essential raw material and primary source of the biography—the twins were disinclined to (and possibly incapable of) the sort of sustained *reflection* that autobiography or memoir would require. And their exclusive relation with each other made it impossible for anyone else, inside or outside the family, to write about them in any sustained or authoritative way. Even as their unusual relationship cried out for clinical or therapeutic intervention, it seemed to defy life writing of any sort (except, of course, their journals).

The challenges for Marjorie Wallace were at once logistical, methodological, and ethical: how to interview twins who were virtually mute, how to ensure that they spoke for themselves; most of all, how to represent twins so tightly bound together without collapsing the distance between them—how to represent their inseparability without denying their separateness. The very qualities that made them biographical subjects—their oddness, their muteness, their inseparability—also rendered them liable to objectification and stigmatization—indeed, enfreakment. They are thus a striking, if atypical, example of subjects particularly vulnerable to misrepresentation.

Identical twins present a special *narrative* challenge for the biographer, in any case. In the case of identical twins raised together, it might seem that the narrative could treat at least their early lives simultaneously, rather than alternately, using the third-person plural, rather than singular, pronoun. But scrupulous biography needs to acknowledge the existence of differences, to acknowledge that identicality does not mean duplication of identity and experience. While *collective* twin biography may seem appropriate, even unavoidable, it minimizes au-

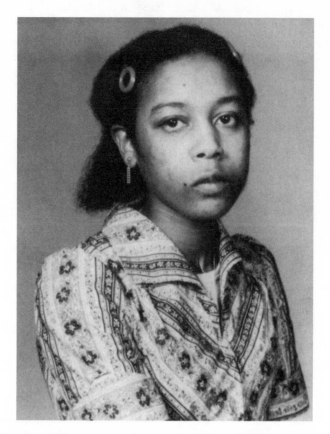

Jennifer Gibbons at Broadmoor Hospital, 1982. Photo reprinted from *The Silent Twins,* by Marjorie Wallace (Random House, 1986). Courtesy of Marjorie Wallace, founder and chief executive of the mental health charity SANE.

tonomy and individuality. These challenges are heightened with *insep-arable* twins, such as June and Jennifer. Although it is a limit case, their example can illuminate the dynamics and ethics of writing the lives of closely related individuals and of writing the lives of individuals who may be indisposed to, or incapable of, representing themselves.

The pathology of the twins' bond also bears on the issue of their agency in their representation. If biography involves getting inside the subjects' position in some way, the mute, reclusive Gibbons sisters would seem highly unlikely subjects for, much less collaborators in,

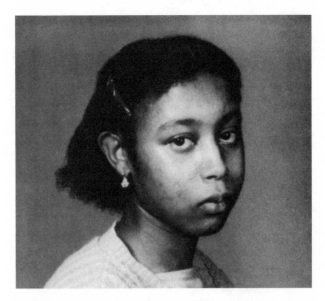

June Gibbons at Broadmoor Hospital, 1982. Photo reprinted from *The Silent Twins,* by Marjorie Wallace (Random House, 1986). Courtesy of Marjorie Wallace, founder and chief executive of the mental health charity SANE.

their biographical representation. Locked in a tight orbit around each other, Jennifer and June were barely able to acknowledge or interact with outsiders. A biographer who depended primarily on their oral testimony would get nowhere; one who depended exclusively on others' testimony about them would fail to render their lives with any depth or insight. Granted, their case generated a considerable amount of documentation in the form of therapeutic, medical, and legal dossiers, but their mutism severely limited *personal* testimony; even— perhaps especially—within the family they were not well known or understood.[5] Their relationship presented special problems for a biographer, including the ethical issue of authorization and the extent to

5. Indeed, some of their pathology seems linked to a distanced, laissez-faire style of parenting that left them pretty much to interact with each other. There is no way of knowing whether different parenting might have resulted in their relating to others differently; what seems clear is that the nature of their relationship would have alarmed some parents more than it alarmed theirs.

which they could collaborate in the biographical process, in view of questions about their competence.

One of the manifestations of, or compensations for, their mutism, however, was their prolific writing, much of which was self-life-writing. Both kept detailed journals, and both wrote fiction and poetry, especially after they co-enrolled in a writing course as a single student. (Both wrote novels as well as short stories, and June published a novel, *The Pepsi-Cola Addict,* with money they pooled from their unemployment benefits.) The upshot was that their biographer had abundant written testimony from their points of view. And as we shall see, Wallace managed to represent June and Jennifer in ways that register their separate identities and respect their individuality.

Their criminal career first brought the Gibbons twins to public attention, and Wallace's interest in them began when she reported their trial for the *Sunday Times* of London. In the course of investigating their story, she met their parents, who gave her access to their pretrial writings. She first met June and Jennifer at their father's invitation, while they were in custody awaiting transfer to Broadmoor. After an awkward introduction, she broke the ice by asking them about their writing (Shapiro and Wagonner). After her newspaper coverage appeared, Wallace was summoned to the hospital by Dr. Boyce Le Couteur, a consultant psychiatrist, who hoped that she might be able to stimulate the sisters to resume their writing and that that might lead them to interact more with others.

Her privileged access to them made her, in a sense, their authorized biographer. As such, she was in an extremely delicate position; like many biographers, especially those writing about living or recently deceased subjects, in order to research and write her book she needed the cooperation of parties—June and Jennifer, their parents, and the staff at the hospital—whose interests did not necessarily coincide with hers or with each other's. Indeed, the various parties' interests were not merely different but arguably opposed to each other. She faced other methodological problems, as well: negotiating with and interviewing apparently willing, but virtually mute, subjects; doing justice to the complex bond between them; trying to distinguish between them without advancing either one's interests at the expense of the other's (even as the hospital staff was trying to wedge them apart); and sorting out and sorting through the immense volume of their writing (over a million words of diaries alone). What she produced is not only a nearly unique thing, a biography of identical twins; it is also a case study in a very tricky problem in the ethics of life writing, for her double subject presents particular, perhaps irresolvable, problems.

Generically, the book defies definitive classification. Despite the fact that the subjects were accessible to her, it is not what we usually mean by a memoir: although Wallace sat through the entire trial, her contact with the twins while writing the book over three years was necessarily limited and intermittent. Her relation to them was more professional than personal and more through correspondence than face-to-face; she could see them only on prearranged prison visits. In any case, their continuing mutism made a personal relationship difficult to sustain, much less to develop beyond the minimal trust required to make biography possible. Although the book begins with a chapter recounting her first contact with them in the hospital, it is focused on them, rather than on Wallace's relationship with them; for the most part, it is a third-person, not a first-person, narrative. For the same reasons, the book could not be a collaborative (i.e., "as-told-to") dual autobiography; the twins were not inclined to *tell* their lives to anyone though they had documented them to an extraordinary degree in their journals.

As a life-writing project, then, Wallace's book raises a number of important issues. Two questions loom above the rest. The first is whether it is essentially a *patho*graphy, which emphasizes the subjects' pathology and represents them as *patients,* or a *bio*graphy, which portrays them as *persons* (with an admittedly pathological relationship). A related issue is whether the book is a *dual* or a *collective* biography— that is, whether it treats its subjects as linked but separate individuals (June and Jennifer Gibbons) or as an anonymous unit (the "silent twins").[6] This is perhaps the crux of Wallace's ethical predicament, for if she collapses the already dangerously small distance between them, then she has reified their pathology and validated their marginalization. To put it differently, she will have enfreaked subjects who are all too vulnerable to objectification.

---

6. There is a good deal of misinformation about them in print, which extends to their names. June is sometimes called "Jane" or "Jean."

Before I explore these issues, I need to note an additional complication of her delicate position as an authorized biographer. The only way to write an extended narrative of the twins' lives was with their permission, since, as I have suggested, they lived so reclusively that even those within the same household could not have offered much in the way of informed or detailed testimony. However, unlike most authorized biographers, Wallace would not get much cooperation from her subjects, as that would require a kind of interaction of which they seemed incapable. Thus, cooperation meant not "collaboration" in the sense of give-and-take, much less extended interviews. Rather, it meant being granted access to their copious writings, the one indispensable source for the book. Wallace first gained access to some of their writing not only apparently without the twins' permission, but before she even met them; their parents gave Wallace permission to read the materials when she approached them after sentence was pronounced. These had just been returned to them by the police, who had seized them as part of the criminal investigation. (To the utter surprise of their parents, investigators who entered the sanctuary of their room found not only stolen loot but journals in which they admitted to—indeed, boasted of—their arson.)

Their limited ability to cooperate raises an important ethical issue: whether their participation in the project, however limited, can be said to involve truly informed consent. If, as the court determined and their psychiatrist maintained, they were psychopaths, there must be some real doubt as to their competence to consent, and thus of the ethics of accepting access to private and potentially embarrassing journals.[7] In court, the diaries were used to represent them not only as guilty but as unrepentant; thus, their diaries served quite literally to indict and convict them. Their life writing constituted "life sentences" with a vengeance: based on its evidence, a judge sentenced them to life, if necessary, in seclusion (though not necessarily in *prison*)—thanks to their guilty plea and psychiatric testimony. Thus, their own life writing was used to justify consigning them to an institution until they could be considered cured—that is, sane.

---

7. Their initial forensic diagnosis was psychopathic borderline disorder, and they were diagnosed as schizophrenic at Broadmoor, but some of those familiar with them are skeptical of these diagnoses (Als, 80); Wallace's account gives little evidence of schizophrenic symptoms.

I am in no position to assess the twins' sanity and thus their competence, of course, and it is hard to tell whether two individuals so turned in upon each other could have fully understood the implications of Wallace's project. But some considerations seem to justify her apparent belief in their competence and to validate their consent to the writing of their biography. First, both had sought fame and celebrity as writers of poetry and fiction—although their only publications were self-financed. In addition, the twins had been accorded considerable publicity—as delinquents and to some extent as psychological freaks—during the course of their trial; they were no longer merely private citizens. More to the point, perhaps, their "private" journals had already been seized, read, and used against them in their trial. It seems likely that they granted Wallace access to the copious diaries they kept in prison in hopes of moderating or offsetting the uses to which their pretrial journals had been put. Perhaps they sacrificed further privacy in hopes of more favorable publicity. (Their legal representation was successful only to the extent that they were placed in a medical, rather than a penal, institution; it did not contest their pathology, nor did it represent them separately.) Of course, without independent access to them—and even perhaps with it—this question cannot be definitively answered. If they had been deemed legally incompetent, however, authority would devolve upon their parents, who were clearly inclined to help Wallace. Thus, it would appear that Wallace was legally, if not ethically, in the right.[8]

It is difficult to tell to what extent June and Jennifer—or any of the other permission-granting parties—had any control over Wallace's text. The acknowledgments do not indicate this, other than to say that a social worker "checked" the chapter on Broadmoor. There is no record of the twins' being shown the work in progress, for example, as might be the case with a truly authorized biography or a collaborative autobiography. One would welcome, then, more of what Paul John Eakin calls, in rather different circumstances, "the story of the story," or what I call transactional visibility (*Vulnerable Subjects*, 25). The more an author offers in the way of an account of access to the parties

---

8. It may be worth noting, too, that June Gibbons apparently cooperated fully and willingly in the documentary *The Silent Twin—Without My Shadow.*

and materials used in producing a life of a cooperating subject, the more a reader can be satisfied that the procedure was ethical. It would be naive to assume that an author's story of how she got the story—in this case, how Wallace interacted with the twins and their parents—would necessarily be trustworthy, but we don't have to assume that the author's account is reliable to welcome an account of the transaction. At the very least, a public accounting enhances credibility because it invites challenge and can be proven false.

Perhaps as important as whether the twins fully understood what they were consenting to is how the resulting life narrative represents them—whether it wrongs them or harms them. If it violates their privacy, it would *wrong* them, but it would not necessarily *harm* them, that is, adversely affect their interests. It appears to me that it does not harm them. My sense of the book is that Wallace made responsible use of their consent, whether or not it was truly free and fully informed. As we shall see, Wallace made sensitive use of the journals, leaning toward sympathy for and advocacy for the twins, rather than merely echoing the authorities who institutionalized them.

Wallace also needed the cooperation of the parents, however. They initially granted physical access to the early diaries (which were at home, not in the hospital) as well as access to themselves. Apparently, they were very cooperative, and Wallace acknowledges their "courage" and "strength" "first and foremost." (Oddly, Wallace does not formally acknowledge the twins' permission or help; rather, the acknowledgments are devoted entirely to those who had responsibility for them at various stages in their lives: parents, teachers, and psychologists.) The delicacy of her relation with the parents is that a candid account of the twins' development might represent their parents as distracted and permissive to the point of negligence. (If anything might have saved the twins from bonding to one another in such a powerful and damaging way, it would have been early and aggressive parental intervention.) As it happens, Wallace treats the parents gently, perhaps too generously.

Wallace's having been invited by the twins' psychiatrist to meet them added a further degree of complexity to her situation as biographer, for it involved her in their therapeutic regimen. The biographer-to-be was summoned as a kind of adjunct therapist, the hope being that with her stimulus the twins would resume writing and that that would facilitate their recovery—an indirect form of scriptotherapy. (The twins' particular pathology made them poor candidates for the "talking cure.") Insofar as such writing would be a sign of their recovery, which was a condition of their eventual release, this positioned her on the twins' side. Wallace's sympathies were clearly with them, as against those who incarcerated them. She makes it plain that she considers their sentence extreme and undeserved: she calls the chapter on their trial "Blind Judgment" and presents the trial as ignoring the complexity of their predicament.

In the hospital, the twins' therapy took the form of an elaborate program of forced separation and behavior modification designed to reshape them into normal, or at least functional, young women. Both legal and medical scripts, then—forms of institutional life-writing—were working against the twins' desires and possibly against their best interests. While Wallace acknowledges the twins' need for therapy and is grateful for their assignment to a medical, rather than penal, institution, she does not approve of their separation, which they resented and schemed to defeat. Thus, she is in an awkward position with regard to their keepers. She is suspicious of their "therapeutic" methods, but she depends on them for access to her subjects.

Wallace especially thanks Dr. Le Couteur for his encouragement, but the evidence of the narrative proper is that she finds his "treatment" of the twins ill-advised. She does so partly on the basis of her privileged knowledge of them. (Apparently, the hospital staff had neither the time nor the inclination to investigate the twins' earlier journals, and Wallace points out that Le Couteur had not even read the journals they wrote in the hospital, to which he apparently had access.)[9] Indeed, with her access to *all* of their writings, Wallace ironically has a much fuller picture of their psyches and their complex relationship with one another than any other observer, including their most intimate relatives and those responsible for their therapy. Whether consciously or not, the twins' cooperation with Wallace made her an ally, at least potentially, in their resistance to the institutional regime.

---

9. The ethics of a physician's reading his patient's "private" journals is always debatable, but in this case the journals would seem to provide valuable, pertinent, and otherwise unobtainable insight into their psyches.

At the very least, it makes her a uniquely privileged confidante—apparently the only one who read very much of their diaries. Indeed—and this reveals how very privileged her position was—it gave her access to each twin that the *other* twin didn't have. (Though they read each other's writing in other genres repeatedly, they appear not to have shared their private diaries with each other.) Thus, it gives each twin a potential ally against the other. The unusual extent and intensiveness of their journal writing gave her the sort of godlike perspective on her subjects that most biographers only aspire, or pretend, to have.

On the whole, Wallace manages her complex role quite admirably—responsibly and fairly. There are moments, especially early on in the book, when she seems to succumb to prejudicial folkloric responses to them, passing on the view of Jennifer as a kind of "evil" twin who dominated and controlled June (5). But for the most part she avoids such sensationalism; at her best, she works to demystify and thus disenfreak the twins. When describing their relationship, Wallace mostly avoids using moralizing or melodramatic metaphors, stigmatizing them, or demonizing one of them.[10] As indicated earlier, perhaps the most important issue is whether she manages to "tell them apart"—to represent them in a way that acknowledges their individuality despite their obviously stifling bond.

The challenge of keeping them separate goes well beyond the difficulty many people have experienced in everyday life of distinguishing between physically identical twins. The biographer's problem here is a special case of representing monozygotic twins raised together. In most cases of identical twins raised together—even when they are treated identically (dress and naming are key indexes of this)—the lives of the twins eventually diverge. And with the conventional foreshortening of life spans in biography, such that childhood is covered relatively quickly, a biographer might get away with treating the twins as a unit in childhood, then increasingly differentiating between them as they matured and their lives diverged. The problem af-

---

10. Compare the book's review in the *Times Literary Supplement* by Anthony Clare, who describes the twins much more prejudicially—he speaks of Jennifer's "peculiar blend of charm, the sinister practice of West Indian magic and downright physical violence"—and who explicitly criticizes Wallace for underestimating "the formidable and largely destructive impact the two girls exert on those who struggle to help and understand them" (212).

ter that is whether to present their lives as parallel or divergent and how to solve the narrative problems that derive from their no longer being in the same place at the same time.

Wallace's problem is the opposite of that; it is the problem of distinguishing between twins in narrative when in "real life" they are almost never apart, never *not* in the same place at the same time. (Indeed, until they were forcibly separated, they were together almost as constantly as conjoined twins—and far more difficult to distinguish from one another than the Schappell twins.) The easy way to tell the story of identical twins who are virtually always together doing the same things is to adopt the third-person *plural* pronoun as the typical pronomial sign for them. To do that, however, is to erase any meaningful distinction between them, to deny their individuality and separability; it mimics the discourse of many of their teachers, which risks reifying their pathology.

> "One day I was in with the school secretary, whose window looks out on the playground," says Cyril Davis, their headmaster, "and there were the twins doing a kind of goose-step, walking ten yards one behind the other, very slowly as though in some strange stately procession. 'Do they always walk like that?' I asked the secretary. 'Yes,' she said. I couldn't believe it and jumped in my car to see how long they would keep it up. I followed them through the town, still doing their dead march, one following the other." (15)

For the most part, Wallace alternates between advancing the story by employing the convenient third-person plural pronoun and distinguishing between them by introducing the third-person singular pronoun.

> June and Jennifer set about learning the craft of writing in a professional way. They really did try hard. . . . They drafted dozens of stories, rewrote and rewrote them to refine the characters or improve the plot.
>
> Jennifer's life centred round the course in creative writing; she studied the lessons, wrote the exercises, waited impatiently for the anonymous tutor to return them covered in his spidery red scrawl. June was less diligent in doing the exercises, but both girls learned

about key characters and plots. . . . They taught themselves grammar and punctuation. (56–57)

Without their participation, this would be difficult, if not impossible. After all, the two twins not only do the same things at the same time; they experience many of the same emotions, though not necessarily simultaneously. (Some of their keepers in prison claimed that they acted in synchrony even when separate [Wallace, 138].) Thus, one could claim that not only an "outward" but an "inward" biography could be plausibly written of them in the third-person plural.

For Wallace to distinguish between them she required access to their separate consciousnesses; given their mutism, only the journals could provide this. It is perhaps no surprise, then, that some of the most incisive passages in this biography are provided by the subjects' own life writing. (While these are attributed to one or the other, they are not dated or otherwise documented.) The best evidence of differentiation is their own testimony, then. Indeed, she uses their prison diaries—when they are in an environment that at times reinforced their confinement to each other's orbit—to suggest that there are undeniable, if subtle, distinctions between them.

> Juxtaposing June and Jennifer's descriptions of the same day is an extraordinary experience. They were like two cameras, each focused on the other and recording her every movement of gesture. From time to time, one or the other would swing away and look at the prison world around them, but inevitably they would return to their strategic positions. . . . June and Jennifer describe the same events and emotions in extraordinary detail, yet the two diaries never quite fit. All the distortions of each twin's vision of the other make the double perspective as disconcerting as a surrealist painting. Reality lies somewhere, exhausted, between their furious perceptions. (138)

What's odd and revealing here is that Wallace seems to expect their descriptions to coincide exactly rather than to differ like stereoscopic images. One could argue that some difference between identical twins in virtually the same environment is inevitable—the difference that separate consciousnesses and memories would supply. But the difference here is necessary in a different sense as well; even as each sister obsessively observes the other, she is distinguishing herself from her sister. They may seem to mirror each other in gazing upon each other, but the gaze of each is one-way. Here elective mutism has given way (or given rise) to mutual surveillance; the two points of view are proof of a degree of individuation and distancing, even when the sisters are closest—literally imprisoned with one another. Indeed, such journal entries constitute not just the *evidence* but perhaps the *enactment* of their existence as individuals; each inscribed *herself* by observing and inscribing her alter ego. Here Wallace describes their situation in the mandatory intimacy of their cell, then offers June's view of it.

One twin could not stir, breathe or swallow without irritating the other. In that brittle atmosphere their childhood rituals became, as June described, a form of mutual torture.

> This morning in bed I lay there. I didn't move. I didn't breathe. For I knew it was the beginning of a game. . . . I wondered to myself, should I call her? She was up there snoring, breathing heavily. But was she really? She lay there like a person awaiting execution. Paralysed. . . . She did not think of moving. One move would be the biggest mistake she made. Fatal. So she lay unmoveable, I lay likewise, as though paralysed by her stillness, her refusal to move. For I knew it was a refusal; it was not an inability. She had not lost her power to move. . . . I read her mind, I knew all about her mood, in that split second I awoke from my unconsciousness to the sound of her perception; her perception which made mine ten times as sharp. My mood. Her mood. Clash. Like spilled blood. . . .
> And where will it all end? In death? In separation? I cannot help it. She cannot help it. It comes over us like a vague mist.
> (163)

As Wallace puts it elsewhere, from outside they may appear as one,

but their unison was only an artefact of the years they had spent playing games against the world. They had practised the skill of appearing to be identical. Even the twins themselves believed they could read each other's thoughts, but as they probed more deeply into their inner selves, it became clear their minds did not match.

Despite the identical front they presented, there was almost as great a divide between the twins as between them and the rest of the world. They were always watching, but usually misinterpreting the movements of the other. They each developed exaggerated scenarios of what the other was thinking and planning. (149–50)

Their behavior here goes a step beyond their mutism, which at least involved talking to each other. They seem not to have read each other's diaries but rather used their private diaries as retreats from each other, though each was the other's obsessive object of contemplation. The paradox is that had they read each other's journals they might have gained more confidence in the difference between them, which each was at pains to assert and to enact by keeping a *private* diary. This is perhaps the opposite of what Susanna Egan calls *mirror talk,* in that it is not collaborative or responsive, not shared or responded to. Each stimulates the other, but there's no dialogue—rather, there are two competing monologues. Only Wallace and the readers of her biography are in a position to overhear both voices in this "conversation."

This is not to say that she adopts their point(s) of view; rather, she allows them to "speak" through quoted journals, in a way that directly and effectively counters the *confessional* use to which those journals are put by the court and the hospital. Thus, much of Wallace's project is in effect rehabilitative, not in the sense that, as Dr. Le Couteur seems to hope, she can precipitate some therapeutic change in them, but rather in the sense that her representation of them will communicate their separate points of view and thus recuperate their individuality; rather than speaking *for* them, she lets them speak *through* her. To do that, it is not enough to quote them. (Indeed, one can imagine a book built much more around their testimony, annotated and contextualized, rather than subordinated to a third-person voice-over.) Wallace needs, like the editor of a slave narrative but for very different reasons, to vouch for the authority of the speakers she introduces—not just for the discrete times when she quotes them (when their authority or lack of it can more readily be judged by the readers) but also for her pervasive reliance on their testimony for the color and detail in her book. Thus, her fly-on-the-wall details are, according to Wallace, not a function of prose license, but rather of minutely detailed and accurate records kept by the twins.

There's an interesting degree of mutuality here. She vouches for the authority of her "psychopathic" subjects, but by establishing the authority of their testimony from the position of an independent "fact-checking" journalist, she also shores up the credibility of her own account.

> Each day the twins analysed their feelings towards each other and their imprisonment in their diaries, more perspicacious than any psychiatric reports. The memoirs they kept during April and May of 1982 are masterpieces. (152)

She presents their testimony as both indispensable and questionable— neither buying into it nor discrediting it. A good example occurs when they report their sentencing as glamorous. She quotes June.

> A dangerous, evil, ruthless criminal! Me! At last my torment, my self-consciousness, my violence is known. I am labelled! Ah! Now I know my fate! June Alison Gibbons, just aged 19, going down in history as psychopath. (187)

Then Wallace comments:

> Inwardly they were elated by the glamour of their sentence. Their years of suffering had been vindicated and they felt the relief that sick people sometimes feel when a long unrecognized illness is given a name and therefore a status. (187)

At the same time, Wallace is sensitive to the issue of responsibility to the historical record because, like many biographical subjects, these twins are not always reliable reporters. An obvious way in which their diaries proved unreliable was that what they reported as a "good talk" with someone was neither "good" by most standards—or even real "talk"—but rather mostly mime and passing of notes, and here, by definition, their testimony could be checked. Further evidence of their unreliability is found in their accounts of sexual encounters, which they invest with romantic feeling that was apparently not mutual. So she does at times openly function as a reality check on their testimony.

> The twins, who had no experience of tenderness or even concern in human relationships, thought nothing odd about . . . the way they were made to wait and were punched and kicked. This, they believe, must be love. . . . Like addicts the twins returned the next day, Jennifer holding a hand over her face where Carl's blows had caused an unsightly bruise. Jennifer wrote:
>
> > My mind is now undoubtedly at peace. My boy Carl, he doesn't know how good he's been to me. His arms caressing mine. His lips brushing my lips. I could feel the intense hotness of his eyes slowly studying my body. At that moment I felt like a very beautiful girl. I knew he was infatuated with me, my looks and my mysterious style. (98–99)

But mostly Wallace uses their testimony in a way that counters how it was used to put them away. In this regard, she edges toward advocacy, and the twins' testimony serves at different times both as institutional and as anti-institutional confession. Indeed, Wallace's representation of the twins had an indirect but noteworthy impact on its subjects; her newspaper coverage led to a BBC docudrama *The Silent Twins*—with a screenplay by Wallace—that made the twins realize how hard their relationship had been on their parents; this moved June to write to them to apologize (Goleman).[11]

Twin autobiography, though rare, is likely to register the identity and experience of twinhood strongly—on some level and in some way.

---

11. The docudrama is sometimes engaging, but although it uses the twins' diaries in voice-over, it offers a rather external view of them; compared to the biographical book of the same title, it is a one-dimensional portrait of them. It does, however, feature some skillful impersonation by two pairs of identical twins who portray the Gibbons twins at different ages, accurately mimicking their synchronized movements, which had been filmed by educators and therapists. The BBC film *The Silent Twin—Without My Shadow* (1994), a straight documentary, includes some archival footage of the young twins. Made after Jennifer's death, it culminates in June's release to the custody of her parents. June and Jennifer have also entered popular culture as the inspiration for "Tsunami," a song by Nicky Wire of the Welsh band Manic Street Preachers.

With biography, twinhood may be even more prominent; it is more likely to be the motive and occasion for biography than for autobiography (for, as I have suggested, the experience of being a twin may impede or suppress the autobiographical impulse). The questions raised by the representation of living twins have to do with balance—between June and Jennifer and between self-consciousness as *twins* and as *individuals*. The case examined here complicates the questions built into twin biography because of the inseparability of the twins. The difficulties here are not just methodological but ethical.

This case raises the stakes because the pathological nature of the bond is the occasion of the life writing. The twins become the subjects of life writing not so much because they are twins as because they are the sort of twins they are. The biographical challenge is to refrain from exploiting this by enfreaking them. In my view, Wallace met the challenge quite successfully. Granted, the book does not give its readers much insight into the process of its production nor any sense of the division of the proceeds. And the twins had little say in its preparation; that is, they seem to have interacted only prospectively and minimally with Wallace. Of necessity, she relied heavily on their diaries to document their lives, and to a large extent she uses their written testimony—none of which was *elicited* by the biographical process—to differentiate between them in ways that most who knew them and had direct personal contact with them could not or did not do. Thus the readers' experience of the Gibbons twins is more intimate than that of family members. So while Jennifer and June Gibbons had almost nothing to say about how their biography is written, their voices do inform it; they are heard in the text in ways that they were not in the "real world" of family, school, court, and hospital—where in many ways, they were *silenced* twins.

While June and Jennifer exhibit striking pathology, Wallace represents them as individuals who became unwilling patients, rather than patients who exist to illustrate or personify a particular pathology, such as folie à deux.[12] *The Silent Twins* manages to present its subjects as persons who asserted their individuality—not always successfully—in a relationship of extraordinary closeness and constraint. Though

---

12. They are cited by Sandbank as an instance of this pathology (181).

the text can provide only vicarious experience of its subjects, it affords a kind of nonexploitative access to them that would be impossible in everyday life. It brings us into virtual contact with twins who devised individual subjectivities while perpetually face to face with each other. One measure of its success may be that it offers what seems a fair—and surprisingly positive—estimation of the quality of their lives. The life writer's estimation of the worth of their lives is far different from that implied by the institutions that housed—but did not adequately *care* for—them at different points in their lives. And not incidentally, it establishes that the quality of their lives was not determined by their genetic anomaly—their "identicality."

6 § Autoethnography and Developmental Disability

Riding the Bus with My Sister

Traditionally, ethnographic life histories were written by profession-ally trained Western academics about subjects from non-Western cul-tures. In the last several decades, however, the nature and authority of ethnography have been called into question (Clifford). To a large ex-tent, this is a function of concern among professional anthropologists about the complicity of ethnography in Western imperialism. There is a new concern among ethnographers, then, with what we might call macroethics, the ethics of the enterprise as a whole, and contemporary ethnographers have become particularly wary of exploiting or patron-izing their human subjects.

One ethical crux of contemporary ethnography is this: by conven-tion, if not by definition, ethnography is the study of the Other (one of the meanings of the word's Greek root, after all, is "foreign"), but as a rational empirical enterprise, ethnography seeks to avoid reinforcing the pejorative implications of that term. That is, the subjects of ethnography should be represented as different but not alien; they are of necessity Other, but they should not be *othered*. To this end, ethno-graphers have experimented with ways of deploying their methodol-ogy more sensitively and responsibly, of minimizing or subverting their own authority, of giving voice to the "native."[1] The politics and ethics of ethnography have thus been reexamined in the aftermath of classic Western colonialism.

---

1. On the "crisis" in ethnography, see Clifford (1988) and Clifford and Marcus (1986).

The status and representation of disabled people have not been much attended to in this reconsideration of ethnography, but disabled people warrant ethnographic attention for a number of reasons. First, some groups of disabled people—most obviously Deaf people, who consider sign language their native "tongue"—constitute culturally distinct populations. Second, contemporary disability studies has embraced the paradigm of disability as a cultural construct; the work of scholars in the humanities, which focuses on ways in which disability has been represented in various media and historical periods, needs to be complemented by participatory interactive research on how disabled people may differ from mainstream populations. At the very least, disability communities are repositories of lore that elude notice by most nondisabled people; understanding how the lifeways of disabled people are shaped by their impairments can helpfully illuminate majority as well as minority culture.

Disabled people have largely been ignored by ethnographers, arguably to the detriment of both disabled people and the discipline of anthropology. But although disability communities are ripe for ethnographic investigation, disabled people, long subjected both to marginalization and objectifying examination, may resent and resist such attention. Indeed, like indigenous people, disabled people have sometimes been treated as colonial populations, and disability ethnography faces some of the same ethical challenges as ethnography involving populations subjected to classic Western imperialism.

The notion of disabled people as colonial subjects may be counter-intuitive, since colonialism is typically imposed on populations that are ethnically or racially different from their colonizers and geographically distant from the metropolitan center of empire. Yet disabled people have at times been literally and overtly colonized: consider the leper colony. And there are troubling similarities between the exploitation of non-Western and disabled populations. Disabled people have been subjected to the same genocidal practices—sterilization and execution—as the ethnically and racially different, and the institutionalization of people who are mentally retarded or mentally ill amounts to a kind of internal colonization. In *The Mask of Benevolence* (1992), Harlan Lane, a hearing psychologist, has argued that Deaf people have been subjugated by an "audist" establishment. More broadly, many

disabled groups consider themselves subject to well-meaning but patronizing domination by medical experts and charitable organizations
that control the terms of their integration into society as a whole. According to Lennard J. Davis, "people with disabilities have been isolated, incarcerated, observed, written about, operated on, instructed,
implanted, regulated, treated, institutionalized, and controlled to a degree probably unequal to that experienced by any other minority
group" (*Reader*, 1).

Whether one accepts or rejects the notion of the disabled as a colonial population, one needs to reckon with postcolonial attitudes
among them. A classic statement of this stance is James I. Charlton's
Nothing About Us Without Us: Disability Oppression and Empowerment
(1998), whose title sums up its argument. The ethnographic representation of disabled people, then, is at least as problematic as that of non-
Western "natives." It involves the same issues of the imbalance of
power between those who write and those who are written about. Further, disabled people pose particular methodological challenges to
ethnography. When they are concentrated in institutions, they are virtually invisible to anthropology (though not to sociology; see Goffman, *Asylums*); when not institutionalized, they are often geographically dispersed in a way that also makes them difficult to study
collectively. In any case, since disabled people do not share a single
condition, they cannot be—nor should they be—represented as a
monolithic community. Their representation requires alertness to the
internal politics of a divided community that sometimes displays subtle forms of ableism.

One phenomenon that has emerged from the recent crisis of ethnographic authority has been the writing of ethnography by "natives"
who were once its subjects. Indeed, I would claim that this gesture—
which puts the *auto* in *autoethnography*—is the distinctive sign of the
postcolonial turn. As argued in chapter 1, this gesture has also been
characteristic of disability life writing contemporary with the disability rights movement. Yet neither the practice nor the theory of representing disabled populations has been given the critical attention lav-
ished on the ethnography of non-Western subjects. In what follows, I
hope to begin to redress that imbalance. To that end, I address several
distinct but connected topics: disability as a distinctive form of human

diversity that poses special challenges for ethnography; the various meanings of the term *autoethnography,* which can denote various forms of discourse characteristic of postmodernism; and finally Rachel Simon's *Riding the Bus with My Sister* (2003) as a contemporary life narrative that exemplifies both the promise and the problems of disability autoethnography. While not ethnography by a strict definition, Simon's account of sharing the life of her mildly retarded sister, who spends most of her waking hours riding the buses in her Pennsylvania hometown, is an example of disability memoir that approaches ethnography in its method and that suggests what disability and ethnography have to offer each other.

Disability is a fundamental aspect of human diversity first in the sense that, worldwide, an enormous number of people are disabled. In 2005, the Web site of the United Nations Population Fund (UNFPA) characterized about 10 percent of the world's population (or 600,000,000 people) as disabled. Other estimates range considerably higher, from 15 to 20 percent of populations, with the higher numbers typical of rural areas of developing countries, the lower ones typical of developed countries like the United States. At the same time, this minority is at least as heterogeneous as groups based on race and ethnicity, gender, and sexual orientation. Disabilities may affect one's senses or one's mobility; they may be static or progressive, congenital or acquired, formal or functional, visible or invisible. All these differences create potential fault lines within the group as whole; far from monolithic, then, the category of disabled people is inflected with differences that profoundly affect identity politics. For example, people with congenital disabilities are likely to identify as disabled and to express pride in their anomalous bodies and distinctive lives; in contrast, individuals with acquired disabilities are likely, at least initially, to resist or even reject identification as disabled and to invest, financially and emotionally, in the quest for cure or rehabilitation.

In any case, the border between the disabled and the nondisabled may be less distinct and more permeable than those between races and genders. On the one hand, with the help of biomedicine or rehabilitation, individuals may pass from the status of disabled to that of nondisabled; on the other hand, anyone can become disabled at any time, and, barring sudden or accidental death, most people will eventually become disabled to a significant degree. So as a form of diversity, disability is distinct in its extent, its variability, and its contingency. Thus, if a disability community may be said to exist, it is not a monolithic entity; rather, it tends to split along one of various fault lines—for example, that between physical and cognitive disabilities. So the pertinent community whose interests should be taken into account may be more limited in scope: those with a particular condition.

As a constellation of stigmatized differences, disability creates groups vulnerable to subjugation and control. But the very diversity and dispersion of the disabled population have also kept it below the radar of traditional ethnography; in contrast with race and ethnicity, disability is generally not concentrated in families (with the obvious exception of hereditary conditions) or in neighborhoods (with the exception of its association with poverty or old age). Disabled populations have thus not been as visible, accessible, or attractive to ethnographers as ethnically distinct and geographically distant populations.

The situation has begun to change, however; disability has begun to garner ethnographic—and, in a postcolonial age, autoethnographic—representation. *Autoethnography* is a slippery, ambiguous, but useful—indeed indispensable—term. Interestingly, it seems to have been coined separately in different disciplines (literary studies and anthropology) to refer to distinct new forms of discourse. Over time, however, the forms of writing that the term was coined to name have converged. The result is that today the term can be applied to several genres or subgenres that overlap somewhat. So the term's ambiguity is a function of its broad interdisciplinary utility. As defined by Françoise Lionnet in the field of life writing (where I first came across it), *autoethnography* refers to "the defining of one's subjective ethnicity as mediated through language, history, and ethnographical analysis; in short, . . . a kind of 'figural anthropology' of the self" (99). In this sense, it was first applied to memoirs by members of ethnic minorities, for example, Zora Neale Hurston's *Dust Tracks on a Road* (1942) or Maxine Hong Kingston's *The Woman Warrior: Memoirs of a Girlhood among Ghosts* (1976). Here it designates a more or less self-consciously ethnic or ethnographic autobiography. (As my examples suggest, however, autoethnography in this sense is not necessarily written by professional ethnographers: Hurston was a professionally trained anthropologist, but Kingston is not.)

As used within anthropological discourse, the term may refer to autobiographical (i.e., confessional) ethnography—texts in which trained observers explicitly address and analyze their personal relations with the natives they are writing about. These two senses of the term seem quite distinct and are fairly easy to distinguish: the former is a subgenre of autobiography, the latter of ethnography. But, as Deborah Reed-Danahay has pointed out, the term also has at least one additional meaning. In the introduction to *Auto/Ethnography: Rewriting the Self and the Social*, Reed-Danahay traces the provenance of the term (primarily in anthropology) and offers the following overview.

> Autoethnography stands at the intersection of three genres of writing which are increasingly visible: (1) "native anthropology," in which people who were formerly the subjects of ethnography become the authors of studies of their own group [also known as auto-anthropology]; (2) "ethnic autobiography," personal narratives written by members of ethnic minority groups; (3) "autobiographical ethnography," in which anthropologists interject personal experience into ethnographic writing. (2)

According to Reed-Danahay, these three distinct genres have converged because

> anthropologists are increasingly explicit in their exploration of links between their own autobiographies and their ethnographic practices. . . . At the same time, "natives" are increasingly telling their own stories and have become ethnographers of their own cultures. [And] practitioners of ethnography have become increasingly aware of the politics of representation and of the power relations inherent in traditional ethnographic accounts. (2)

The multiple meanings of the term—in Reed-Danahay's words, native anthropology, ethnic autobiography, and autobiographical ethnography—may result in some confusion, but the convergence of the three types of discourse is a function of the collapsing of conventional binaries and hierarchies in a postcolonial age.

The literary scholar Mary Louise Pratt has used the term to refer to any writing "in which colonized subjects undertake to represent themselves in ways that *engage with* the colonizer's own terms" (7), a sense more or less equivalent to Reed-Danahay's "native anthropology." As Pratt defines it, then, autoethnography is decidedly post- or anticolonial in its thrust. Although, like most ethnographers, Pratt thinks of colonialism in terms of cultural and geographical differences, I have suggested here that it is equally pertinent to the condition of some disabled populations, who have been required to conform to arbitrary norms, subjected to control and domination by medical experts or others claiming authority over them, and even confined in institutions or isolated settlements, such as leper colonies. Like other postcolonial subjects, disabled people are beginning to produce texts that are autoethnography in the senses of ethnographic autobiography and native anthropology—texts that explore the creation of identity within particular subcultures and texts that contest the way the author's community is characterized from outside.

Yet most of this writing focuses on individuals, rather than exploring the boundaries and values of distinct communities; it is more ethnographic autobiography than native ethnography. Thus, while the advent of the social paradigm of disability—which locates disability not in anomalies of individual bodies but in exclusionary features or practices of the social and cultural environments—has fostered autobiographical rejoinders to the prejudicial constructions of disability, it has not yet generated a substantial body of genuinely ethnographical treatments of disability. Symptomatic of this irony is the fact that perhaps the best-known practitioner of disability ethnography is not an anthropologist at all but rather a neurologist, Oliver Sacks. Granted, he does not literally claim the title of disability ethnographer, but his self-identification as a "neuroanthropologist" in *An Anthropologist on Mars* (1995) implies that his extraclinical work with neurologically impaired subjects combines the insights of medicine with those of ethnography. As I have argued in *Vulnerable Subjects* (74–122), his best work does suggest what genuine disability ethnography might look like, but more often his work betrays the fact that it is grounded in medicine and not in anthropology; indeed, it suggests that he is not well versed in contemporary ethnography, much less in disability studies.[2] In any case, his work is not autoethnography in *any* sense; Sacks is not himself disabled and thus he is not a "native," and there is little personal or professional self-reflexivity in his writing.[3]

The prototypes of disability autoethnography have been more serendipitous than systematic, more informal than academic. For example, in *The Body Silent* (1987) Robert Murphy reflected professionally as well as personally on the impact on his identity and life trajectory of his progressive (and finally fatal) paralysis. *The Body Silent* is therefore an early example of disability autoethnography.[4] Since he was a denizen of the world of physical disability as well as a professional anthropologist, his book has a claim to being native anthropology and autobiographical ethnography, yet because it focuses mainly on his own experience, it corresponds most closely to ethnographic autobiography. A related work is Irving Zola's *Missing Pieces* (1982), which records Zola's sojourn in a Dutch community for people with disabilities. Although Zola's conduct there involves a degree of simulation—a polio survivor, he adopted the use of a wheelchair that he did not require in everyday life—his account is ethnographic in that (1) he was a professional social scientist (though not an anthropologist), (2) he lived for a significant period of time in a distinct and segregated community, and (3) he was attentive to how the distinctive lifeways of that community were shaped by the disabilities of its inhabitants. (Its confessional dimension, having to do with his rediscovery and affirmation of his identity as a disabled person, makes it autoethnography also in the sense of autobiographical ethnography.)[5] Finally, *Venus on Wheels* (2000), Gelya Frank's recent book about Diane De-Vries, who was born without arms or legs, qualifies as a genuine ethnographic life history, replete with the self-reflexivity and self-exposure

---

2. In Sacks's oeuvre, his volume on Deafness, *Seeing Voices* (1989), is more ethnographic than his individual case studies in that it addresses a community of people—significantly, those who claim Deaf identity, a matter not so much of the degree of hearing impairment as of the use of sign language, cultural allegiance, and identity politics. And yet even there, Sacks remains more the neurologist than the anthropologist, addressing himself to questions that are nonissues for his subjects, such as whether prelingual deafness entails mental retardation.

3. An exception is *A Leg to Stand On* (1984), which concerns an injury to his leg that temporarily deprived him of sensation in that limb (discussed in chapter 3).

4. I discuss Murphy's book at some length in *Recovering Bodies* (205–11).

5. For further discussion of Zola, see Couser, *Recovering Bodies* (211–14).

of postcolonial anthropology; in addition, insofar as Frank acknowledges having invisible disabilities, the book has an autoethnographic dimension.

Aside from these signal texts, disability ethnography and autoethnography are still quite rare; there is not yet a very substantial body of autoethnographic discourse concerning disability. Disability life narrative more generally, however, is increasingly common and prominent; to some extent, it has begun to fill the gap. As noted in the introduction, whereas twenty-five years ago, there were few published accounts of living with most disabling conditions, today one can find narratives of a large variety of disorders—intellectual, emotional, and physical.

Although ethnographic autobiography written by amateurs may lack the rigor and theoretical underpinning of academic work, its freedom from some of the drawbacks of academic ethnography—extensive theorizing or excessive abstraction, for example—may compensate somewhat. Little of it is explicitly ethnographic in its goals or its methods, but insofar as it is infused with the paradigm of disability as culturally constructed rather than naturally produced, disability life writing has tended to assume an ethnographic dimension or to have ethnographic significance. Certainly most narratives challenge the prevailing cultural scripts of the conditions in question and offer a degree of intimacy and access that is not found in academic ethnography.

More closely approximating ethnography are memoirs produced by former inmates of institutions for those with mental illness and mental retardation. A good example of the former is Susanna Kaysen's *Girl, Interrupted* (1993), an account of her sojourn in the late 1960s in McLean Hospital, a mental hospital near Boston known for its privileged clientele. Rather than narrating her experience in linear chronological form, Kaysen produced a book comprising chapters of various kinds. Some are vignettes of other patients; others (e.g., "Velocity vs. Viscosity," "Stigmatography") satirically suggest the inadequacy of medical terminology; still others incorporate and interrogate the actual documents that effected her diagnosis, supervision, and discharge. Her book approaches ethnography in its inclusion of other patients, in its analysis of the customs and conventions of life in the institution, and in its suggestion that the discourse of psychiatric medicine functioned for her generation of rebellious women in part as a mechanism of social control.

An example of a memoir by a former inhabitant of an institution for mentally retarded people is *I Raise My Eyes to Say Yes* (1989), which was discussed in chapter 3. Its collaborative composition, made necessary by the nature of Ruth Sienkiewicz-Mercer's impairments, means that, like many life narratives produced with native informants, it is not completely self-written. But it is ethnographic to the extent that it details the workings of the asylum, a kind of self-contained world. Furthermore, it is a postcolonial narrative in an unusually literal way, for the author's emancipation from the institution coincided with the disability rights movement and benefitted from new policies favoring self-determination and deinstitutionalization. It is certainly autoethnographic in Pratt's sense of the word. These examples point the way for an emerging autoethnographic critique of disabled lives in what Lennard Davis has referred to as the "United States of Ability" ("Rule").

In *Riding the Bus with My Sister: A True Life Journey* (2003), Rachel Simon has produced an unusual piece of life writing that realizes some of the potential of such a critique. The sister in question is Simon's slightly younger sister Beth, a woman in her late thirties with mild mental retardation. Beth lives by herself on Supplemental Security Income (SSI) and occupies herself six days a week by riding the buses in and around her hometown in Pennsylvania. Unlike her fellow riders, she rides the buses for the sake of the stimulation and companionship she finds on them: what is for others a means (of transportation) is for her an end in itself. (Beth's knowledge of bus routes and timetables is such that management sometimes informally relies on her to orient new drivers.)

Beth dresses eccentrically, even outlandishly, in bright, clashing colors, and she is very strong-willed. Her habit of talking loudly and incessantly causes a good deal of friction with some passengers and repulses some drivers, even those who are initially sympathetic. She arouses strong feelings, then, both positive and negative. Even when other riders engage in hostility and harassment, however, Beth is undaunted. The book's most powerful message is that—whatever her social workers, her family, or the readers think of it—Beth *has* a life that is her own idiosyncratic creation and that she will pursue it in defiance of convention and criticism.

By a process of trial and error—not without painful rejection—Beth has discovered which drivers welcome, or at least tolerate, her presence riding shotgun. And she has developed ongoing relationships with a number of these drivers. Some of these relationships take the form of crushes on handsome male drivers, but her driver-friends include some women. In any case, they go beyond casual comradeship and idle flirtation; she sometimes socializes with drivers and their families on Sundays, and when she had to check into a hospital for minor surgery, one of them accompanied her and several visited her. This may be anomalous, but it is not entirely serendipitous; Rachel learns that it is part of a new approach to mental retardation in the community.

> I learn, on the phone with Olivia [a case worker], that this is how it's supposed to work. The system that supports independent living relies on it: the cultivation of friends in the community, who will, out of kindness and generosity, help out. (214)

A writer, journalist, and teacher, Rachel Simon had grown somewhat distant from her sister as they reached adulthood. But when she was in need of a topic for a newspaper feature article, her editor suggested that she ride with Beth for a day and write up the experience. The result was a *Philadelphia Inquirer* article that got national distribution; it was well-received by readers and, not incidentally, by its subject (11). Not long afterward, for a mixture of personal and professional reasons, Rachel agreed to ride the bus with Beth several days a month for an entire year. The book does not make entirely clear what the terms of the arrangement were or how they were arrived at, but apparently Beth made riding the bus a condition of Rachel's visiting her; in effect, then, the year-long experiment was initiated by Beth. But Beth did not commission a book about herself: writing the book was Rachel's idea, a way of taking professional advantage of the time spent. The significance of that for our purposes is that the enterprise morphed from human interest journalism to memoir; it was not conceived of as ethnography, and the text is silent on issues of process and method in ways that would not pass muster in professional ethnography.

The book consists of thirteen units, one for each month from January of one year to January of the next, followed by a brief coda. The foreground narrative, in roman type, consists mainly of detailed accounts of particular days on the bus; it reproduces—or more properly simulates—incidents and conversations with Beth's favored drivers, whom she monopolizes by taking the seat closest to theirs. (Nearly every chapter features a different driver, which suggests a high rate of turnover, or burnout, among her favorites.) Interspersed, in italics, throughout the foreground narrative of riding the bus are chronologically arranged episodes from the girls' childhood and adolescence. The family's early history was quite tumultuous: the girls' father moved out of the house and their parents divorced; after taking up with an abusive man, their mother forced her children out of the house. Although this backstory is highly dramatic, it remains in the background until that narrative line catches up to, and converges with, the foreground narrative near the end.

Riding the Bus does not correspond exactly to any of the three distinct senses of autoethnography distinguished earlier: native anthropology (because the author is not herself developmentally disabled), ethnographic autobiography (because the author is not the main subject), or autobiographical ethnography (because the author is not an anthropologist). Yet I would locate the book at the nexus of ethnography, disability, and life writing; in any case, it illustrates both how disability can challenge and enrich ethnography and how ethnography can illuminate the otherwise obscure lives of some "ordinary" disabled citizens.

Like most powerful life narratives, *Riding the Bus* is a hybrid of genres. Most obviously, it is an example of "relational life writing," that is, a personal narrative that concerns a subject with whom the writer has a preexisting close relationship. Rather than being ethnographic *autobiography*, then, we might consider it an ethnographic *memoir* of growing up and entering adulthood with a sibling whose disability sets her apart and that shapes the family history in significant ways. However, to the extent that its foreground focus is on Beth's odd lifestyle, which Rachel samples over the course of a year, it approaches ethnography proper. While Simon is not an anthropologist, she refers to herself at one point as having been a top student in anthropology in college (238), and *Riding the Bus* has a claim to being disability auto-ethnography because, in researching the book, Simon functions as a kind of participant-observer. Thus, unlike most relational life writing, this book did not grow out of everyday contact and the preexisting familiarity between subject and writer; it was not the organic by-product of an ongoing relation but rather the result of a deliberate decision on the part of the writer to devote a good deal of her time and energy to sharing, investigating, and documenting an aspect of her sister's life that would otherwise have remained opaque to her.

Beth's habitual, even compulsive, bus riding was not just a mystery to the rest of the family; it was an "issue." Her three siblings and her parents all felt that she should be doing more with her life. Thus, the book was the part of a project and a process that brought the two sisters back together physically (and emotionally) not in either one's home but rather in the unusual public zone in which Beth chooses to spend most of her waking hours. At the same time, of course, it differs from professional ethnography in that its genesis is primarily personal, and it falls short of ethnographic rigor in its lack of an explicit and fully forthcoming account of the arrangement between subject and writer.

The extent to which the book is a function of Beth's eccentric lifestyle is unusual if not unique, and it makes the book particularly interesting as ethnography. For in her daily life Beth becomes a virtual inhabitant of a world in constant motion aboard vehicles that function for most people as interstices between the sites at which they do their "real" living. Whereas the others ride *in order to* get to work or to get home, Beth rides *instead of* working or staying at home. (As is her prerogative under the social programs that apply to her, she consistently declines to get a job.) Beth's world is foreign to Rachel, then, for reasons related to Beth's particular disability. For one thing, no "normal" person would take up such a pastime with such single-mindedness. For another, a woman like Rachel, for whom the bus is a means of transportation rather than a site of habitation, would not become as involved as Beth does with the drivers. For most passengers, the drivers are pure functionaries; their personalities and the details of their lives are not of interest except insofar as they affect how they perform their jobs. But clearly, anomalously, Beth is most at home when she is on the bus, not in her own apartment, where she sleeps or passes the time until the buses start running again. Although Beth had been trained to ride buses, the life she develops as a rider (much more than her writer-sister's work-oriented life) is very much her own unorthodox invention, a product of her ingenuity—a trait not

> generally ascribed to people who live on the periphery of society's vision. Like indigent seniors, people with untreated mental illness, and the homeless, Beth is someone many people in the mainstream don't think much about, or even see. (3)

If Beth's disability renders her an interesting ethnographic subject, it also presents formidable methodological challenges. In particular, the anomalousness of her life presents a dilemma concerning the ethics of such enterprise. The most obvious danger in life writing involving siblings is violation of privacy. And while Rachel Simon is rightly concerned about this, it is not really possible for her to represent her sister anonymously: she could hardly publish a nonfiction book about her sister under her own name and at the same time conceal her sister's identity. On the other hand, since Beth spends most of her waking hours in public by choice, one might ask how much privacy she has to protect.

Even if we were to let Rachel Simon off the ethical hook when it comes to the representation of Beth as a bus rider, however, such exemption would not apply to the disclosure of her private life, and there is a good deal of that both in the background narrative of their childhoods and in the frank discussion of Beth's present sex life. All of this is made more sensitive by Beth's disability, which renders her a more vulnerable subject than she would otherwise be. In the event, Rachel Simon recognizes that the publication of her book could render Beth prey to voyeurism of a very direct and intrusive kind: people might travel to her hometown to marvel at "the retarded lady who rides the buses all day." Simon's solution to this is to disguise the details of the location, and she also changes the names of all other persons who appear in the narrative.

Another aspect of the project is reassuring on a second ethical issue. Although Simon does not say that she has allowed Beth to vet the manuscript before it was published, she does report that Beth was "tickled" by the publication of the newspaper piece. If we can trust this report, then in effect Beth previewed and approved a sample of the longer manuscript. This is rarely the case with relational life writing and even with formal ethnography. In any case, Rachel Simon seems to have done what she could to get Beth's informed consent to the project. The fact that Beth is only mildly retarded is important here. Severe retardation would make it impossible to get truly informed consent.

Despite the publisher's telling, marketing-driven label, "Memoir/ Inspiration," *Riding the Bus* is ethnography to the extent that it involves the writer's entering into a life other than, and very different from, her own with the goal of understanding it on its own terms and as part of a larger social and cultural whole. Simon sees that while Beth is not living in a distinct disabled community—she dislikes and thus avoids living in a group home—she cannot be represented in a social and cultural vacuum. As any good ethnographer (professional or amateur) would be, Rachel Simon is attentive to the way in which Beth's life is both enabled and constrained by the institutions with which she interacts and the attitudes of the general public.

Granted, *Riding the Bus* is not, and could not have been, autoethnography in the sense of native anthropology because Rachel is not retarded and because Beth is not its author. Though able to read and write, Beth is neither interested in nor apparently capable of documenting her life at length or in a systematic way. She does, however, produce copious amounts of correspondence in the form of notes and cards, much of it to Rachel, apparently her closest sibling, and some of this correspondence finds its way into the book. It is clear that Beth expresses her sense of identity in part through written correspondence, a way of sustaining relationality that supplements regular phone calls. As reproduced in the book, her writing is more or less correct in grammar and spelling but highly idiosyncratic in capitalization. It is primarily concerned with expressing love and regret, which she seems to have difficulty doing face to face. In any case, if her life is to be written, it must be by someone else; hers is a disability that does impede certain forms of self-representation. Fortunately, however, Rachel has a privileged relation with her and steps into the breach.

Riding the Bus is autoethnography, then, in two distinct senses.

First, like the authors of *Girl, Interrupted* and *I Raise My Eyes to Say Yes*, Simon is improvising a quasi-ethnographic account of an episode in the life of a person with a distinct disability. Her book is a memoir whose ethnographic dimension is made necessary by her sister's disability; despite having grown up with Beth, Rachel is not, at the outset, well versed in the culture and politics of the life of an adult person with mental retardation. As a newcomer in Beth's world, she has to watch closely to intuit and articulate the implicit codes, rules, and values of that subculture. (Significantly, Simon resists quantifying Beth's intelligence or mental age, preferring to explore how, and how well, she functions in a world not designed for her.) Second, it is autoethnography in the sense of confessional ethnography; as Beth's sister, she cannot approach her dispassionately and objectively. Rachel finds her own sense of identity, her own emotions, and, most of all, her own sense of family history at stake as she shares and recounts Beth's life. Appreciating Beth's life on its own terms is a difficult challenge; at first, Rachel finds herself desiring something more for Beth. Only very gradually does she surrender her own expectations and come to understand why Beth does what she does and why she enjoys it so much.

The book functions as disability ethnography most obviously in documenting Beth's life as a response to the constraints placed on her not so much by her particular intellectual limitations (her impairment) as by the society in which she lives (her disability). Simon makes no claim that Beth is typical of a cohort of women with mental retardation; on the contrary, she is presented as sui generis. But Simon notes how many people like Beth there are in the United States (in 1990, approximately 7 million people, or about 3 percent of the total population). Insofar as she gives a very full account of the daily life of an independent person with mental retardation, she portrays Beth's life as shaped, but not wholly determined, by laws, institutions, and an economy that allow her very limited options. For one thing, it is only when Beth invites Rachel to her annual Plan of Care meeting that Rachel learns the basic economic facts of life for Beth; what her SSI covers, how it discourages working (since financial benefits are cut back in proportion to wages earned), and, for that matter, what SSI stands for. Here Beth is the competent—though not always engaged—insider, while her older sister is the neophyte in need of orientation.

In her periodic meetings with her social workers, Beth is quite impatient with their concerns about her unhealthy diet (mainly snacks and soft drinks consumed on the bus), her health problems (which she tends to minimize or ignore), and her lack of ambition. The sorts of jobs for which Beth is deemed qualified—such as light manual labor in sheltered workshops, bagging groceries, or filing in her father's office—bore her, and at some point she always rebels, manifesting her dissatisfaction through absenteeism, sabotage, or other subversive gestures. Since she can afford to live on her SSI checks, she chooses not to work. This is an issue less for the social workers who monitor her on a monthly basis than for her family, who think that Beth should aspire to a more productive pastime than riding the bus. It is also an issue with fellow passengers, many of whom, one suspects, have jobs that bore them and think it unfair that Beth lives off their taxes.

In her meetings with her consultants, Beth reiterates that she likes the life she lives and that she desires to make no changes. Which is to say that, given the limited options her impairment and her society allow, she has devised a way of life that she finds gratifying. Though not drawn to other people with her condition, she has a boyfriend, Jesse, who also has mental retardation. (He spends much of his time riding a bicycle and competes in endurance events.) They chat on the phone regularly and occasionally meet to socialize and have sex. (Beth agreed to be sterilized after her family learned that she had become sexually active.) Jesse is African American, and in Beth's conservative hometown, interracial couples are highly conspicuous and not widely accepted. As a couple, then, Beth and Jesse are vulnerable to discrimination—and sometimes surprisingly overt hostility—on dual grounds: their disability and their transgression of a local taboo. So Beth's daily life involves negotiating a social and cultural minefield. Undaunted, she challenges racism whenever she encounters it; she is in fact quite outspoken on the subject. Interestingly, then, the book suggests that as a victim of one kind of prejudice, Beth is sensitized and resistant to others; and her retardation may disinhibit her from voicing objection to prejudice on the part of "normals."

Perhaps the most important way in which Rachel Simon puts her sister's life in "ethnographic" perspective is by illuminating the rules and principles governing her government assistance and "care." For example, the notion of Beth's autonomy is new to her, and as an older sister used to being protective of her, Rachel Simon is not always comfortable with the idea of self-determination. But Rachel comes to realize that her sister's life is not just happening but being shaped by a disability rights movement that endorses autonomy even for those with mental retardation: "She is, in many ways, an embodiment of self-determination" (166).

Rachel comes to three related revelations, as well. One is that, given the constraints on her, Beth has used her own ingenuity to forge a life of her own.

> Beth has sought out mentors in places where others might not look, and moreover, taken the time, and endured the pain, to weed out those drivers who are decent and kind and reflective [perhaps one-sixth of the total] from those who are indifferent or hostile. (166–67)

A second is that Beth is far less vulnerable, far more capable of independent living, than she had thought.

> She's got her own streetwise code of behavior, I see, as she finally stops at a corner. It's a code born of circumstances she has not shared with me, and that have taught her a level of discernment I do not possess. Indeed, throughout this break from the bus, I've felt far more naive than the street urchin chugging along in front of me. (64)

The third is that "the invitation that I join her in her travels didn't 'just happen,' either. I realize . . . that Beth might well have wanted me to meet her drivers because I needed them, too" (167). This is at once a touching and a fraught moment. It is affecting that her sister may have sensed an emotional void in Rachel's life, the equivalent to the void that Beth has filled in her life with her new relationships. But Rachel's appreciation of this is complicated by her awareness that it alters the dynamics of their relationship. As an older "normal" sister in a broken home, Rachel has, she realizes, "matronized" her disabled sister. It takes her nearly a year of periodic immersion in her sister's life to discover that their reaching out is reciprocal and that she, Rachel, may have as much to gain from it as Beth does.

Somewhat surprisingly, the conclusion of the book involves a wedding. This is a standard resolution for a comic plot, but it is not the protagonist who gets married; Beth and Jesse seem quite content to remain single and live apart most of the time. Rather, in the epilogue, "A Year and a Half Later," it is Rachel who, after dating one of the drivers at her sister's urging, resumes her relationship with her old boyfriend and marries him. She explicitly credits Beth with this development.

> The biggest change has been my own, and . . . I know that it would never have happened had I not spent my year with Beth. It was she whose very presence caused the ice around my heart to thaw and who nudged me tenaciously to find the courage to go out with a man again. (292–93)

At this point, the book is in danger of reproducing an unfortunate convention of fiction and film, in which disabled characters are used to facilitate the romantic pairing off of the nondisabled characters. (As Lennard Davis has noted, all too often in literary representation, "the [disabled] character is placed in the narrative 'for' the non-disabled characters—to help them develop sympathy [or] empathy" ["Crips," 45].)

But Simon's scenario does not in fact conform to this convention. For one thing, Beth is emphatically not desexualized or made pathetic; she has an ongoing sex life with Jesse—about which she is quite uninhibited—and an active social life aboard her buses. Nor is she being introduced into a fictional narrative for the purpose of bringing about an anagnorisis in a protagonist; rather, her role seems to emerge organically from the sisters' midlife reunion. Rachel Simon's immersion in Beth's life seems to divert her from her own self-absorption and to make her aware of the deficits in her own life. It is Rachel's awakening to the surprising fullness of Beth's life that makes her resolve to do something about the emotional emptiness of her own. Only through Beth does Rachel discover that the drivers too have lives, and only because Beth has formed relationships with some of these otherwise anonymous public servants is Rachel able to see some of them as multidimensional and interesting people. The exposition of their lives also makes the book more ethnographic than if it had focused narrowly on Beth.

But there is a larger resolution as well. Rachel's time with Beth eases an underlying worry that nags at all the members of the family: what will become of Beth in the long run? Rachel's fears are eased by her sense that there is a network of institutions and friendships exclusive of the family in which Beth matters and also that Beth is surprisingly resilient and resourceful. She may have difficulty anticipating, planning for, or averting future problems, but as they arise, she manages to cope. Also working against sentimentality is that, just after Rachel attends her second annual Plan of Care meeting, Beth announces suddenly that the year's experiment is over. Rachel is not only surprised but hurt by this. More important than her wounding is her underlying realization that in this matter it is up to Beth to call the shots. This is a climactic, salutary but painful, reminder of Beth's self-determination.

As noted earlier, *Riding the Bus* is not, by any strict definition, ethnography. But it does occupy the intersection of the various streams of discourse that Reed-Danahay designates with the elastic term *autoethnography*. My purpose has been not so much to laud the book, although I do find it a praiseworthy piece of life writing, as to suggest how disability and ethnography can benefit each other. I hope I have established that disabled people have largely been overlooked by ethnographers, why they now deserve the attention of ethnography, and what special challenges disability ethnography involves. Addressing those challenges can only enrich the sophistication and repertoire of ethnography, and it promises to address a major gap in our understanding of cultures and subcultures.

While disability ethnography is (as indicated previously) fraught with danger, it has the potential to corroborate and substantiate the cultural paradigm of disability, showing how culture constructs disability and, conversely, how disability produces its own culture. Ethnography can do this by recognizing and documenting the lives of disabled individuals and communities. *Riding the Bus* points the way by mapping (almost literally) a life that would otherwise be hidden in plain sight.[6]

---

6. The book's success was such that it was quickly (2005) adapted as a made-for-television movie directed by Anjelica Huston and starring Rosie O'Donnell as Beth and Andie MacDowell as Rachel. Of course, that the film is a biopic (rather than a documentary) raises questions about a fraught form of disability representation: the impersonation of people with disabilities by nondisabled actors.

That is, Beth's life is lived almost entirely in view of a public that is largely indifferent to and uncomprehending of it. That Beth lives her life the way she does is a function of a new and relatively enlightened approach to her condition. But it is not enough that she be allowed or even encouraged to live such a public existence. In order to live as she likes, Beth has had to develop a tough skin. Fortunately, she seems to have been predisposed, or brought up, to assert her rights and her sense of her own worth; whatever their failings, her parents had always insisted on her value and had steadfastly refused to hide her away from others' eyes. Rachel's very valuable contribution to Beth's life is to write it and thus render it visible to a public beyond Beth's fellow travelers.

Writing such an idiosyncratic and otherwise obscure life in a quasi-ethnographic fashion provides a desirable complement to the usual meaning of access. If people like Beth are to live independent and fulfilling lives, it is not enough to give them nominal access to public areas in the form of, say, bus passes and training in how to use them; the public also benefits from being given controlled access to their lives. Such mediated access enables the population at large to understand what the Beth Simons among them may be like, why they should be regarded as possessing dignity, why they should be welcomed into the public realm. In writing the bus, then, Rachel Simon has performed a public service very much in the spirit of the disability rights movement. In this way, I think her book suggests ways in which more overtly ethnographic treatment may further the understanding of disability. But equally, I think, disabled people offer ethnographers long overlooked subjects; addressing their lives sensitively is a new challenge for ethnography. Taking up that challenge promises to help ethnography fulfill its mission of illuminating the relation between the body, the self, and culture.

7 ❧ Disability as Metaphor

What's Wrong with *Lying*

A mere two years after the publication of her popular and critically acclaimed memoir *Prozac Diary* (1998), Lauren Slater published another, *Lying: A Metaphorical Memoir* (2000). Like its predecessor, *Lying* belongs to the subgenre of disability or illness narrative (autosomatography); this one, however, concerns not depression and Prozac but epilepsy and surgery (corpus callosotomy, or separation of the right and left hemispheres of the brain). Readers familiar with Slater's earlier narrative may have been taken aback at what seems a radical revision of her medical history in *Lying*. *All* readers of *Lying* may have been disconcerted by Slater's undermining of her own credibility (beginning with her title). Predictably and understandably, then, the first wave of response to *Lying* has focused on the book's truthfulness as self-representation—particularly the question of whether Slater really has epilepsy. For the most part, reviewers and critics have concentrated on the way in which she challenges, plays with, or violates the "autobiographical pact"—the genre's implicit contract between writer and reader.

The terms of the autobiographical pact, as defined by Philippe Lejeune, are somewhat limited, and it is well to remember that it is a critical conceit, or a convention of reading, rather than a legal or ethical requirement of the form. According to Lejeune, "What defines autobiography for the one who is reading is above all a contract of identity that is sealed by the proper name. And this is true also for the one who is writing the text" (19). According to Sidonie Smith and Julia Watson, for Lejeune, two things indisputably distinguish autobiography and, by implication, a wide range of life narratives, from the novel: the "vital statistics" of the author, such as date and place of birth and education, are identical to those of the narrator; and an implied contract or "pact" exists between author and publisher attesting to the truth of the signature. (8)

This may amount to little more than saying that autobiography is read as nonfiction, that is, that it is the story of a real human being, namely, the person listed as its author. (Whether it is *written* by that person, at least without assistance, is a different matter.) But it is generally taken to extend to an obligation on the part of the memoirist to present a factually true story, unless readers are alerted to the contrary, either by explicit disclaimer or by postmodernist gestures like those made by Slater. It is this more legalistic sense of a pact that caused a media furor when James Frey was exposed as having exaggerated key details in his memoir of recovery from addiction, *A Million Little Pieces* (2003). Frey's downfall was all the more dramatic because his memoir had been first promoted, then defended, by Oprah Winfrey; in response to a groundswell of dismay from readers and book club fans, Winfrey reversed herself and then flayed Frey in front of a live audience on her television show. Similarly, his publisher, which initially stood behind the book, eventually offered disgruntled buyers a refund and agreed to add a disclaimer to future editions. Such scrutiny of factuality is rarely and inconsistently applied to memoir; Frey's liability to it seems to have been a function of the great acclaim for his book and the fact that he claimed to have recovered from addiction by sheer willpower and resolve, rejecting the 12-step approach. This was a story that appealed to millions of readers, and their outrage at having been deceived was proportional to their initial desire to swallow it whole.

Far more egregious have been numerous violations of the pact by recent memoirs that are based on entirely false claims to identities and pasts that happen to have high market value. For example, a Swiss adoptee, Benjamin Wilkomirski, falsely claimed, in *Fragments: Memories of a Wartime Childhood* (1996), to have been a Polish survivor of the Holocaust, and a privileged white suburbanite, Margaret Seltzer, writing as Margaret B. Jones, falsely asserted in *Love and Consequences* that she was half Native American and grew up involved in gang life in South Los Angeles. These memoirs are out-and-out hoaxes that blatantly violate the pact's implication of the validity of the author's "vital statistics."

On the one hand, *Lying* is not an outright hoax or a fraud; on the other, the issue is not one of misrepresenting minor details of Slater's life. Rather, if there is an ethical problem, it lies in the matter of vital statistics, which are crucial to the pact, loosely constructed. In addition to one's age, gender, race, and ethnicity, vital statistics would presumably include major elements of one's medical history, such as whether one has a disability or not. One way to put Slater's narrative and rhetorical strategy in perspective is to imagine the response if a prominent memoirist made claims regarding her ethnicity or race analogous to those that Slater makes with regard to disability—that is, if she claimed a racial, gender, or ethnic identity she did not in fact have. As we'll see, Slater shrewdly and playfully stops short of making that claim; or rather, she makes it only to take it back, thus avoiding any liability for fraud. The problem, I shall argue, is that even as she undermines her claim to being epileptic, she characterizes that condition in outdated and prejudicial terms. And that has implications for others who *do* have it.

Slater's complex self-representation in this volume is certainly interesting, if only because it does for the memoir what postmodernism has done for the novel (touched upon later). What concerns and interests me more than her *self*-representation, however, is something that seems to have escaped notice by most critics: her implicit representation of *others*, namely, those who have epilepsy. I am less concerned with whether Slater herself has epilepsy—a claim she qualifies and hedges, in any case—or with her right to write a hyperbolic, metaphorical, or even deceitful memoir, than with the possibility that her choice of a disability as a metaphor for her experience involves her in a misrepresentation of those who have that condition. For me, then, the ethical crux of *Lying* is not that Slater may be lying about having epilepsy, but that in exercising prose license she commits herself to an essentializing and mystifying characterization of a still stigmatic disability. The book's relation to the recent proliferation of personal accounts of disability and illness is thus troubling. On the one hand, with its humor and literary self-reflexiveness (which I enjoy), it expands and enriches the repertoire of that literature; on the other, its glibness about Slater's own health status threatens to discredit the genre. Above all, it may cause unnecessary harm to vulnerable others.

Born in 1963, Slater was the author of four autobiographical volumes by the age of forty, and *Lying* is best understood in the context of the other three volumes. The first, *Welcome to My Country* (1996), is a collection of case studies of her patients (Slater is a psychologist); the second, *Prozac Diary* (1998), is an account of being one of the first patients to go on Prozac; the third is *Lying* (2000); and the fourth, *Love Works Like This* (2002), is an account of her first pregnancy and the first "trimester" of motherhood. As different as they are in their concerns, they share one characteristic: all approach her experience somewhat obliquely or indirectly, rather than candidly and confessionally. Insofar as *Welcome* is mainly about her patients, it would seem to be *patho*graphy rather than autobiography, somatography rather than autosomatography. But nearly all of the case studies swerve toward autobiography as her patients' conditions echo some aspect of Slater's own psyche.

One might expect that *Prozac Diary* would be more directly autobiographical, a narrative dedicated to her suffering from, and being treated for, depression. But as its title suggests, it focuses not on the experience of depression but rather on her drug regimen. For the most part, readers have to gauge the depth of Slater's depression from her description of what it felt like to emerge from it: "an experience of the surreal, . . . a disorientation so deep and sweet you spin" (24). Thus, it is far less self-revealing than one would expect. This is often the case, of course, with narratives of mental illnesses. Communicating what it is like to be acutely depressed is notoriously difficult since the condition tends to impede the very act of composition; once the mood has lifted, it may be difficult to recreate or describe.

Finally, *Love*, her volume about becoming a mother, is written from the vantage of a long-term Prozac user who faces a difficult choice: whether to go off Prozac and risk relapse in order to spare her fetus possible harmful side effects or whether to stay on it in order to get through her pregnancy in good mental health. After all, as Slater notes, "being a mother and being a mental patient are really mutually exclusive, at least according to the law, and according to private opinion as well" (13). The element that one might expect to dominate the book—Slater's being haunted by her failed relationship with her own mother—is dealt with only intermittently and obliquely.

In fairness to Slater, it should be noted that her life writing has generally been ethically sensitive and responsible. Indeed, ironically, what I see as her ethical lapse in *Lying* may be a function not so much of disregard for others as of a concern for the privacy of those close to her. In the front matter of *Welcome,* Slater demonstrates that she has a keen sense both of the constraints on her as a therapist who moonlights as a life writer and of what is at risk for others in self-life-writing.

> The tales related in this book are based on my true experience with real patients whom I have treated. However, in every case the patient's name, physical characteristics, and specific geographical details have been altered so as to protect and respect the confidentiality of all involved. All involved have approved their disguises. In a few cases, the individuals represented are complete composite portraits, made up of many different images and from the many different stories I have heard in my practice as a psychologist. My aim has been to remain true to the subjective experience of mental illness as I have perceived it, while at the same time honoring the ethic of privacy inherent in any doctor/patient relationship.
>
> In all cases where the story is based on an individual patient, however loosely (as opposed to a complete composite portrait), I have obtained written consent from the individual involved. In all cases, patients were eager to have aspects of their suffering, however disguised the form, shared with the wider world in the hopes that others might come to a better understanding of their plight. (v)

If what she says here is true—and I have no reason to doubt it—Slater goes beyond minimal professional standards, which require only that she either conceal her patients' identities *or* obtain their permission to represent them sans disguise. (The redundancy of the privacy protection in her cases moots the issue of whether one can get meaningful informed consent from a psychiatric patient.) As I noted in *Vulnerable Subjects* (chapter 2), standard restrictions on professional life writing protect patients only against recognition by others, not against the potential harm that could be caused by *self*-recognition. Slater's protective measures do not utterly prevent this, but they minimize her responsibility for it.

In addition to her deontological (principle-based) justification of her practice, she offers a utilitarian (consequence-oriented) one: that her representation of her clients has a social benefit—furthering the understanding of "their plight," mental illness.[1] This effect is characterized not only as desired by her patients but also as beneficial to them (as well as to the general public). This is the standard rationale for case studies addressed to lay readers, and while it is appealing, it is not always clear exactly how this benefit is effected, what it means, and whether in fact a particular case study does further the claimed goal. That is, it should not necessarily be taken at face value, in part because such goals can be achieved through different means, not only by case studies, which carry the risk of harm to their subjects.

At the outset she wisely acknowledges the autobiographical dimension of her case studies (in sharp contrast, I would note, to her neurological counterpart, Oliver Sacks). In her preface, she cites Alfred Adler's suggestion that self-analysis begin with one's earliest memory; from her own earliest memory, she concludes that her fundamental psychic need is for repairing rifts in intimate relationships (xi).

> And I have learned that the only way to enter another's life is to find the vector points where my self and another self meet. . . . Similarly there is no way, I believe, to do the work of therapy, which is, when all is said and done, the work of relationship, without finding yourself in the patient and the patient's self in you. In this way, rifts within and between might be sealed, and the languages of our separate lives might come to share syllables, sentences, whole themes that bind us together.
>
> These, then, are not just stories of my patients; they are stories as well of myself, of interactions and conflicts, of the way one psychologist watches her past meet her present, coming to see herself in the complicated lattice of her patients' lives. These are stories of reflec-

---

1. For a useful discussion of the differences between deontological and utilitarian ethics, see Beauchamp and Childress, 340–50.

tions and routes, including the route I have traveled to cope with my own psychiatric difficulties. (xii–xiii)

She suggests, then, that self-exploration is built into the work of therapy and that autobiography is implicit in pathography.

Two things are worth noting here. First, in comparison to the neurologically compromised individuals Sacks represents, Slater's patients are mostly treatable, if not curable; she can hope to ameliorate their conditions more than Sacks can the conditions of most of his subjects. Second, the indispensable mode of her interaction with them is dialogical. While Slater's patients, like Slater herself, may be on psychoactive medication, she is not a medical doctor; her therapy consists exclusively of talk. As a result, in contrast to Sacks, who often gets a good deal of mileage out of merely observing and describing his subjects, Slater is dependent on dialogue with hers; as a writer, then, she is thus much more "in the frame" with them. This sort of interaction may be more conducive to sensitive representation of vulnerable subjects.

Slater makes, or at least claims, a personal connection with nearly every one of her psychiatric charges. From her work with a group of six male schizophrenics ("Welcome to My Country"), she offers an interpretation of schizophrenia as a radical form of a common human condition (one she has identified as central to her own life): loneliness. By acknowledging past episodes of bulimia, she finds unlikely common ground with a patient who has antisocial personality disorder and a nasty misogynist streak ("Striptease").

> Hadn't I once striven for his same goals, to control the random, fleshy facets of female life, to eradicate the weak part of the self who hurts and bleeds and feeds? In a sense we were both murderers and we were both crying out from our crimes. (44)

She makes the provocative claim that "the recovering anorexic is . . . ironically, in a particularly good position, via therapy, to treat the misogynist male" (50). She finds an obvious link with the chronically depressed "Marie" ("Holes") and acknowledges that she, the purported therapist, may be the primary beneficiary of their sessions.

> She . . . went with me into marrow. Or perhaps I should say I went
> with her, for I was the one now learning about pain. . . . I began to
> notice small things as therapy continued, and sometimes my sight
> felt so clear objects were transformed. (141)

With a schizophrenic/catatonic ("A Great Wind"), she wonders
whether catatonia is an overreaction to extreme sensitivity (like her
own).

It is only in "Three Spheres," however, that she offers details of her
own distress. When she meets a new patient at the site of her own hos-
pitalizations, she finds herself in the very conference room in which
her mother announced that she was giving Slater up to foster care
when she was fourteen. Obviously, Slater's wound has yet to heal.
Moreover, this patient shares the same vague but devastating diagnosis, borderline personality disorder, that Slater discovered was hers
when she read her own chart upon her final discharge—the same diagnosis received by Susanna Kaysen at McLean Hospital and contested
by her in *Girl, Interrupted*. Slater's sense of identification with her patient serves to trigger fuller disclosure of Slater's personal difficulties.

She acknowledges feeling that contemporary North American culture is awash with often distasteful and unproductive confessions and
questions what she is about to do.

> For what purpose will I show myself? Does it satisfy some narcissis-
> tic need in me—at least I can have some of the spotlight? Perhaps a
> bit, yes? But I think I set aspects of my own life down not so much
> to revel in their gothic qualities, but to tell you this: that with many
> of my patients I feel intimacy, I feel love. To say I believe time is
> fluid, and so are the boundaries between human beings, the border
> separating helper from the one who hurts always blurry. Wounds, I
> think, are never confined to a single skin but reach out to rasp us all.
> (179)

In the final scene in this chapter (which is the final chapter in the
book), Slater gives her new patient the key to the conference room in
which they are to conduct their first session. The gesture is one of sym-

pathy and empowerment but also perhaps of *self*-empowerment. The implication is that Slater is empowered as a therapist and as a person by surrendering her professional authority and privilege and by her confession of mental illness. Indeed, it is at this point that Slater *becomes* an autobiographer.

This final chapter may provide a key to Slater's own life writing in two complementary ways. First, as is perhaps now obvious, it reveals how her work as a therapist stimulates her practice as a memoirist; that is, it may illuminate *why* she becomes a memoirist. Second, and less obviously, it may help to explain Slater's tentativeness and restraint as a memoirist, her avoidance of overt confession; that is, it may illuminate the *way* she is a memoirist. The key is in the "gothic" detail, which hints that her mother molested her, or seemed to, when she was about ten years old: "She murmurs a Hebrew prayer and I imagine her hands exploring me, and a darkness sprouts inside my stomach" (182). This veiled accusation suggests that for Slater to explore her own past too explicitly might entail a kind of character assassination from which she shies away.

This would help to explain her entire oeuvre as a life writer, at least on one level. It would explain her focus in *Prozac* on her recovery from depression rather than on its genesis and course. And it would help to explain why the book, for all of its ambivalence about Prozac, in effect endorses the doctrine of contemporary psychopharmacology, which one would think would be anathema to a therapist without a license to prescribe: that "the patient's past, the story of self, is no longer relevant" (108). It might also account for the way *Lying* retreats from painful literal truth behind a prism of metaphor. Finally, it may illuminate the subtext of her fraught pregnancy in *Love*. Behind the foreground concern with the effect of her medication on her fetus lies the larger issue of Slater's becoming a mother, a role Slater expresses a great deal of ambivalence about—not surprisingly, considering her history with her own emotionally troubled mother.

Significantly, Slater and her mother seem to embark on a process of rapprochement at the very end of her pregnancy. On the first night of Passover, Slater had called her mother, long divorced from Slater's father and remarried, only to hang up, terminating what proved an unsatisfactory conversation (79). Months later, Slater's mother called her in the hospital after being informed by Slater's sister that Slater was in labor (126). The acknowledgments to *Love* suggest that the contact restored at this moment may have brought mother and daughter closer after a long estrangement.

> I also wish to thank my mother, who reentered my life after a very long hiatus literally as I labored to bring my own child into the world. Her ability to tolerate my written explorations of our relationship is exemplary. She has modeled for me flexibility and forgiveness; I will try to emulate these qualities as I navigate the motherhood that is now mine. (n.p.)

Slater must be referring here to her oblique accounts of her childhood and adolescence in *Welcome, Prozac,* and *Lying.* Her expression of gratitude to her mother reveals that she did not have her mother's permission, much less her blessing, for these earlier "explorations." Rather, her mother seems to have accepted them after the fact. Thus, it is quite possible that Slater's reticence, her holding back from detailed accusations she apparently might have made, kept the door open for a resumption of mother-daughter relations, which would be all the more precious to Slater when she has a newborn daughter of her own.

Textual evidence supports this hypothesis. The real crux of *Love* is not whether motherhood and mental illness, pregnancy and Prozac, are compatible, but whether a woman so wounded by her own mother can become an adequate mother herself. And while the first trimester of maternity proves nothing either way, Slater provides closure to her narrative by affirming that she does finally "feel" like a mother; by some mysterious process, motherhood finally "takes" with her. In light of the fact that she anticipates her daughter Eva's eventual perusal of her book, the language in which Slater expresses this may seem oddly impersonal and much closer to an essentialist or mythic conception of motherhood than someone of Slater's feminist persuasion might be expected to use: it suggests that the genesis of love has little, if anything, to do with any endearing characteristics of her daughter. Rather, the development of mother-love is a function of gestation itself: "Love grows like the embryo grows, without any effort from your fine mind. Love grows despite you, in the interstices of each entry, in the white space, without a word" (169). On the one hand, Slater doesn't find mother-love as all-consuming or as overwhelming as she expected; on the other, its development seems quite automatic and instinctual. Slater's expression of what she yearns for in motherhood can be read as an invitation to her own mother to help her repair the rift in their relationship.

> Intimacy, I am coming to understand, is corporeal. It has to do with the distance between bodies. I wish for more. I wish for a passion that transcends space. When I am with Eva, she is my heart. When I am gone from her, at work, or with a friend, she ceases to exist. (169)

Slater's oeuvre suggests that as a life writer she has recognized, tacitly, at least, the fundamental relationality of identity, and that she has grasped the ethical implications of the fact that all biography is autobiography and vice versa. I have discussed her other books to suggest not only *that* Slater has enacted ethical precepts in her life writing but *how* she has done it. As suggested earlier, however, I think that her impulse to protect the privacy and reputations of those closest to her may have backfired in *Lying,* which fails to respect the porous boundaries between individuals—in this case, between her and the community of people with epilepsy.

One of the case studies in *Welcome* may shed further light on Slater's seemingly compulsive yet generally nonconfessional life writing. "Some Kind of Cleansing" has to do with "Joseph," a schizophrenic with hypergraphia (compulsive nonsensical writing). After he enrolls in a college course in creative writing, Slater begins to edit his writing. At first, she limits herself to paring away random words to expose hidden sense, but she soon takes greater license with his prose—so much so that she comes to question its authorship. Acknowledging that her editing of one of his stories drew upon her own experience with her mother, she wonders,

> Does that, then, not make me the author, possessing both the theme and the poetry of the piece? . . . But this is the story I heard Joseph tell me; this is the story we shaped together. And no, I think he is not any less the author because his efforts merged with mine. All stories,

as Elliot Mishler, an ethnographer, claims, are "joint constructions of meaning." No author, in other words, writes a story without the pressure of an internalized culture pruning the sentences, shaping the tale. (109)

She then addresses a complementary question, whether she can be regarded as the sole author of this case study.

I can't say that the pages you have before you here come from only me, for at every point the words—which pass from *my* axons to *my* dendrites and finally emerge in blessed sentences—are tangled in Joseph's rhythms and history, as well as in my own. Perhaps narratives are the one realm that cannot ever—despite the consumerism and capitalism in the publishing industry—be confidently claimed by any individual. I am not sure. (110, emphasis in original)

In any event, she asserts that she and Joseph made some kind of therapeutic connection through collaborative writing.

It is all well and good for writers of case studies such as this to acknowledge that their texts are not the sole product or property of those who write them; it is appropriate (and all too rare) to acknowledge that authority is shared. But it is all too easy for Slater to declare common ownership of a text whose royalties accrue to her alone, and it may be facile of her to rationalize her editing of Joseph's prose by resorting to such general propositions. While it is desirable for therapists and writers of case studies to acknowledge the permeability of the borders between therapist and patient, writer and subject, the acknowledgment of the porosity of the border between apparent collaborators or partners should not embolden those in possession of diplomas or professional credentials to take liberties at the expense of those who lack those qualifications; rather, it should be a warning to tread warily. The danger of transgression is latent in all such life writing, and authorial self-examination is welcome but not sufficient. Thus, even as *Welcome* begins by demonstrating that Slater has exceeded the minimum protection of her subjects, it ends by revealing, implicitly, that such disclaimers may not necessarily protect subjects against all forms of misrepresentation or appropriation of their lives and life writing.

Lying is a significant departure from her other work, for at least three reasons, all related to its ethical crux. First, here Slater claims to have epilepsy, a condition never mentioned in her other three volumes of life writing; this claim thus raises questions of truth and authenticity. Second, Slater explicitly, frequently, and aggressively undermines her own credibility. The self-created doubt about her truthfulness extends of course to her claim that she has epilepsy; she alternately hedges, waffles, and backs away from this claim only to reaffirm it in her epilogue. Third, unlike either of her previous volumes, *Lying* divulges considerable detail about her childhood and adolescence; it approaches full-life narrative and confession far more closely than any of the books that precede or follow it.

It is worth noting that this book departs from a trajectory apparent in its predecessors. If in *Welcome,* she "came out" climactically as a former mental patient (directly, as a writer to her readers, but also indirectly, as a therapist to colleagues past, present, and future), and if in *Prozac* she acknowledged a painful history of mental illness, by recounting its remission under treatment, it would seem that in her next autobiographical volume she might fully and candidly explore her troubled past. This is not quite what happens, however. Rather than delving into the "gothic qualities" of her past, she distances herself, and her readers, from the literal truth of her life through the displacement of metaphor. This way, as I have suggested, she can explore her past without violating the privacy of other family members.

And yet her laudable impulse to protect, preserve, and perhaps salvage relations within her nuclear family may come at the cost of vulnerable subjects beyond the boundary of that family. She provides no particulars of her foster parents, for whom she has only praise and gratitude and whom she credits in large part with her quite remarkable recovery from mental illness so severe that she was hospitalized five times between the ages of fourteen and twenty-four. Thus, her life writing may illuminate the limitation of the bioethical principle of "respect for the person" when it comes at the cost of respect for a community at risk, in this case epileptics.

Whether Slater has epilepsy is an interesting but finally undecidable issue. The evidence of her extensive oeuvre is ambiguous, if not self-contradictory. On the one hand, if epilepsy—not depression, bulimia, or borderline personality disorder, all of which she claims to have had—is the condition that she chooses to define her in her most fully confessional volume, one might ask why it is not even mentioned in her other three memoirs. If it looms so large in her life as to provide the central metaphor of one memoir, one might expect that it would at least be mentioned in the others. On the other hand, among the drugs Slater mentions renouncing and then resuming during her pregnancy is Klonopin (clonazepam), an anticonvulsant prescribed to prevent petit mal seizures. If this inventory of her medications in *Love* can be trusted, it confirms her claim in the epilogue of *Lying* that she takes anticonvulsant drugs daily. My own guess is that Slater does have a history of mild seizures but that epilepsy is far less important to her identity than her mental illness; thus, it functions, as she suggests, more as a metaphor for other conditions than as a literal condition in and of itself.

But the question of whether Slater has, or ever had, epilepsy may finally be beside the ethical point. Slater is under no ethical obligation to tell us definitively one way or the other whether she has epilepsy. Nor, if she has epilepsy, would her account of her history as an epileptic have to be factually true. I fully endorse her right to write in the metaphorical mode, to stretch the autobiographical pact to the breaking point, to take great liberty in representing herself, to go far afield for a trope that might capture the complexities and contradictions of what it is like to be Lauren Slater.

And yet I think her choice of epilepsy as that metaphor—*even if she has it herself*—is unwise and her deployment of it unethical. She makes two distinctive uses of epilepsy as a trope for her life. The first is to model the four major units of her narrative after the stages of a classic grand mal attack: onset, the rigid stage, the convulsive stage, and recovery. The effect of this strategy is to liken the course of her life as a whole to that of a single massive seizure from which she eventually recovered. This could be an apt metaphor for the way the course of any, or all, of the other conditions that she says she had shaped her being and her life narrative. But the fact that her description of this phenomenon is drawn from a medical text over a century old, *The Text*

Book of Grand and Petite [sic] *Mal Seizures in Childhood* [1854], suggests how little concerned she is with contemporary developments in
understanding and treating this condition.

The other use has to do not with the structure of her life but with its
subjective quality; she uses the condition of epilepsy as a metaphor for
the existential or phenomenological reality of her life—what it feels
like to be her, to live in or as her body. This trope brings us closer to the
literal. That is, while this too could be a trope for other conditions, this
deployment of the metaphor claims some sort of equivalence between
them; it asserts that living her life was somehow not only analogous to,
but actually felt like, having epilepsy. (And of course it would help to
make this trope convincing if she had some experience, rather than
mere textbook knowledge, of epilepsy.) This trope comes into play
when the autobiographical subject begins to manifest the classic
symptoms of epilepsy, auras and seizures. One of the most interesting
aspects of her masterly working out of her central metaphor is the way
in which the account of her very first seizure suggests a kind of co-
dependent relationship in which the daughter's epilepsy, whether real
or not, served her *mother's* emotional needs as well.

> She touched my head gently now, . . . like it was whatever she was
> not, a wild and totally true world in there, a place she had forsaken
> for artifice, etiquette, marriage, mediocre love, and which I had re-
> turned to her; here, Mom; have my head. (23)

> When a seizure rolled through me, it didn't feel like mine; it felt like
> hers—her ramrod body sweetening into spasm. She gave it all to me,
> and I returned it all to her, this wild, rollicking, hopeful life. . . .
> Rest with me when it's over.
> This the gift I gave you.
> How we held each other. (24)

All of which is to acknowledge that the metaphor of epilepsy is apparently well suited to communicating certain home truths about Slater's
life and self (which is of course her rationale for it).

The trouble with this narrative strategy is that it involves what is
known as a familiarizing metaphor. Unlike the defamiliarizing
metaphors prized in, say, metaphysical and modernist poetry, which

enable, or require, readers to perceive common things freshly, familiarizing metaphors domesticate alien or abstract entities by likening them to something already known or understood. What George Lakoff and Mark Johnson refer to as the "metaphors we live by"—those pervasive, unavoidable metaphors we use to negotiate daily life—are such. (Thus, we say we "grasp" an idea, rendering a complex mental process in terms of a manual action. Or we characterize an inchoate emotional state by saying we are "down.") What Slater seeks to do in *Lying* is to communicate her otherwise ineffable sense of self by reference to a somewhat exotic but relatively accessible entity, epilepsy.

Presumably much of the appeal of epilepsy for Slater was that it is a mysterious and unpredictable condition involving uncontrolled and uncontrollable behavior. Epilepsy serves her well because, as a somewhat unstable signifier, it provides a good correlative for her unstable personality and chaotic emotional life. But it may *disserve* epileptics (even if they are "fellow" epileptics—that is, even if she has the condition herself) because of what her metaphor implies is "known" about epilepsy. The ethical lapse in her book has little, if anything, to do with whether she has epilepsy herself, either as a matter of authenticity or as a matter of identity politics. The problem is that in order to employ epilepsy as the basis of a familiarizing metaphor, she has to attribute specific characteristics to it that will stand for aspects of her life. That is, in order to appropriate epilepsy as a trope for her individual existence and state of mind, she has to assign to it a stable and particular essence. Among the problematic attributes Slater ascribes to epilepsy is a tendency toward mythomania.

> Epilepsy is a fascinating disease because some epileptics are liars, exaggerators, makers of myths and high-flying stories. Doctors don't know why this is, something to do, maybe, with the way a scar on the brain dents memory or mutates reality. (6)

As historians of epilepsy are at pains to point out, epilepsy has been a particularly and peculiarly stigmatic condition throughout history.[2]

---

2. As Joseph W. Schneider and Peter Conrad point out, epilepsy is perhaps best thought of not as a disease but as a symptom of a brain disorder that could have many different causes (29). Similarly, it may be regarded as an episodic rather than a chronic disability (30).

Indeed, it has proved an especially tricky historical subject; Oliver Wendell Holmes once said, "If I wished to show a student the difficulties of getting at truth from medical experience, I would give him the history of epilepsy to read" (quoted in Temkin, ix). This is in part because epilepsy has been susceptible to so many mystifying constructions over the centuries since it was first identified in Mesopotamian civilization (if not earlier). "Showing both physical and psychic symptoms, epilepsy more than any other disease was open to interpretation both as a physiological process and as the effect of spiritual influences" (Temkin, 3). Indeed, epilepsy is usually thought to be the affliction suffered by the son brought by his father to Jesus, who drives out his "unclean spirit" in Mark 9:14–29 (Schneider and Conrad, 25).

As early as in ancient Greece, the battle over its status was joined in the book *On the Sacred Disease,* a collection of Hippocratic writings that argued against the proposition that it was supernatural in origin (Temkin, 4). Nevertheless, even in the contemporary era, as Schneider and Conrad point out, it has been susceptible to three detrimental myths: that it is hereditary (a belief that made it the subject of eugenic marriage prohibitions); that it is, or can lead to, a form of psychopathology; and that it may cause aggression and crime (31–43). "These ideas are sometimes reinforced by various professional people," and "they have served to perpetuate and even legitimate epilepsy as a stigmatized disorder" (Schneider and Conrad, 30). Mervyn J. Eadie and Peter F. Bladin concur in the view that epilepsy is best seen as distinct from a psychiatric or personality disorder: "At the present time very few, if any, would take seriously the possibility that psychological factors play any major role in the cause or mechanism of epileptic seizures" (156).

Of these three myths, Slater's book certainly reinforces the second. For example, she wonders, "Is epilepsy mental or is it physical?" and passes on (without endorsing) one therapist's theory that her seizures were a function of repression (81). More insidious, Slater trades heavily in the notion of an epileptic personality. This idea was given medical authority in the early twentieth century, but as Schneider and Conrad observe,

Whether epilepsy causes increased psychopathology remains an open question. To the extent that there is a higher incidence of mental and emotional problems among people with epilepsy, it is equally likely to be a product of the social reaction to epilepsy [and thus a kind of self-fulfilling allegation]. (38)

Thus, although Slater's strategy and intention may be to compare the turmoil inside her psyche to powerful electrical impulses within her brain—rendering the intangible relatively tangible, and making the obscure accessible—the traffic on the metaphorical bridge runs both ways, and the implication of her trope is that epilepsy is, leads to, or is tantamount to mental illness, or at least a personality disorder. This is the symbolic paradigm with a vengeance.

I have omitted from this discussion so far an important aspect of the book, the evident pleasure Slater takes in her self-reflexive play with what she realizes is a fashionable genre. Perhaps the best evidence of this is the episode in which she finds succor and support among members of Alcoholics Anonymous, despite the fact that she is not an alcoholic. (She implies that it is her mother who should be a member.) This episode ends in a hilarious, but also serious, send-up of the 12-step recovery program. When Slater, who has always held back from narrating her own story, finally undertakes her "fifth step," coming clean, she confesses that she is not an alcoholic and has thus been misrepresenting herself. Predictably, the other members deflect this confession as denial, evidence that she is not yet ready to confront her drinking problem.

Her defense of misrepresenting herself to the AA members as a fellow alcoholic in the text may double as her defense to her readers for having (possibly) misrepresented herself to them as an epileptic.

> They wanted my story, I would tell them my story. I was not an alcoholic, I suffered from a different disease. I had told them I was an alcoholic because in some deep sense it seemed true. Alcoholism can stand in for epilepsy, the same way epilepsy can stand in for depression, for disintegration, for self-hatred, for the unspeakable dirt between a mother and a daughter; sometimes you just don't know how to say the pain directly. (203–4)

As such, it may be her attempt to defuse the charge that her book is in effect "false testimony" of the sort that has been exposed in various online support groups. In those cases, a real wrong seems to have been perpetrated because individuals have gained emotional and sometimes financial support on patently false premises. Because of all of her postmodernist self-undermining gestures, however, Slater cannot be accused of this as a writer (which is not to say that her book may not be disingenuously self-aggrandizing).

She has not betrayed her readers, to whom she readily reveals her artifice, the way she betrayed those present at AA by pretending to be one of them and sharing their dysfunctional and stigmatic condition. On the other hand, she has not falsely represented alcoholism in the way that she has epilepsy; in claiming to be an alcoholic, she did not reinforce or exacerbate its stigma. In claiming to have epilepsy and an epileptic personality, however, she may not only have misrepresented herself, she has perpetuated a harmful notion of epilepsy as entailing a character defect. Thus, she can be faulted for ignoring the rights and interests of people with epilepsy, who suffer from her remystification of a condition still in the process of being demystified. Her disregard for the larger community of people with such conditions is all the more remarkable, and culpable, in someone who is a professional therapist—one who, I repeat, was careful not to harm those she represented in her memoir.

The same is true, I think, for the way she dismisses the growing body of more literal and admittedly often literal-minded accounts of illnesses and disabilities.

> Therefore, despite the huge proliferation of authoritative illness memoirs in recent years, memoirs that talk about people's personal experiences with Tourette's and postpartum depression and manic depression, memoirs that are often rooted in the latest scientific "evidence," something is amiss. For me, the authority is illusory, the etiologies constructed. When all is said and done, there is only one kind of illness memoir I can see to write, and that's a slippery, playful, impish, exasperating text, shaped, if it could be, like a question mark. (219–21)

What is particularly problematic about her claim to have epilepsy is that it promotes discredited assumptions about the condition. Although she is not a physician, her depiction of epilepsy gains authority from her position as a psychologist and therapist. Her autobiographical conceit deploys a particularly crude version of the metaphorical (symbolic) paradigm of disability, which a generation of disability advocates has energetically criticized as oppressive. While she deploys epilepsy as a metaphor in highly creative and inventive ways, underlying the various meanings she ascribes to it is the idea that it is more than a merely physiological or neurological condition. This strategy imposes a script and a judgment on those who have it; it is simply a milder form of the sort of thinking that regarded epileptics as possessed by demons in earlier centuries. In writing her own life in the way she sees fit, a prerogative to which she is entitled, she unfortunately chooses a trope that involves inadvertently, but prejudicially, scripting others' lives as well.[3]

---

3. Autobiographical accounts by people with epilepsy are not numerous. One such account, Jill Robinson's *Past Forgetting,* is autobiographical almost by accident. Robinson's memoir is primarily concerned with her loss and recovery of her memory after a stroke in midlife. Only in the aftermath of that stroke did she remember that, although she was never told she "had" epilepsy, she had been given anticonvulsants as a child. Her family's response to her episodes was a function of its stigma: "All of these instance of passing out were rationalized, excused and no connection among them was ever made. This was only natural in the time I grew up [during World War II], when epilepsy was seen as an unmanageable and unmentionable disease, like alcoholism" (150).

8 § Lucy Grealy and the
Some Body Obituary

When most of us—including, perhaps especially, academics in the field—think of life writing, obituary is hardly the first genre to come to mind. But I will argue here that the obituary is in fact a very interesting and important (and widely consumed) genre, and thus one worthy of close scrutiny. Available to newspaper readers on a daily basis, it has remained hidden in plain sight, so to speak. I will argue also that, because it is prompted by and published on the occasion of the subject's death, it may, in the case of disabled subjects, give undue prominence to their impairment (and not enough to their disability). Finally, I will argue that the obituary is a particularly fraught genre when the subject is herself a life writer, because it may overwrite her own life writing and thus taint her legacy.

On 21 December 2002, the *New York Times*, often described as the "newspaper of record," published an obituary under the headline: "Lucy Grealy, 39, who wrote a memoir on her disfigurement." Needless to say, those of us who had read and liked—and in my case, taught—that memoir, *Autobiography of a Face*, were shocked and saddened to hear of its author's early death. Grealy was a minor literary celebrity, and the unanticipated death of any celebrity arouses curiosity about its circumstances and cause. On this matter, the obituary's author, Christopher Lehmann-Haupt, was at once circumspect and coy. While declining to specify a cause of death, the obituary presented its circumstances in a sequence of sentences that implied one.

Lucy Grealy, the poet and essayist who wrote a noted 1994 memoir, *Autobiography of a Face*, about her experience growing up with extreme facial disfigurement and repeated surgery to repair it, died at a friend's house in Manhattan . . . . No cause of death was announced. Friends said she had been despondent over operations she underwent two years ago.

I think that many, if not most, readers of this short passage would infer that Grealy committed suicide and did so because of continued, or increasing, unhappiness about her appearance. (My conjecture about this has been reinforced in the years following her death when people I have met have casually referred to Grealy as having killed herself.) To put it crudely, many would conclude that she killed herself because she thought she was ugly.

According to Alden Whitman, chief obituary writer for the *New York Times* in the 1960s and 1970s, "a good obit should not be a partisan document. . . . [rather] it ought to be as dispassionate and as many-sided as possible" (9). Historian Janice Hume characterizes the obituary in different but related terms, suggesting that it needs to balance two functions: chronicling and commemorating (14). By either set of standards, the Grealy obituary is deficient. While it is not "partisan," it is hardly multidimensional, and it chronicles at the expense of memorializing. Its main offense is to insinuate what it seems unwilling to state (that Grealy killed herself) and, further, to imply what could not be known (even had Grealy left a suicide note): namely, the reason or motive for the (implied) suicide. If Grealy actually died, as her sister Suellen Grealy has said, of a drug overdose, without leaving a suicide note, the obituary seems all the more irresponsible because of the inherently ambiguous nature of such a death.[1] Although the writer's intention may have been to protect Grealy's reputation from the scandal of dying from a self-administered drug overdose, the obituary errs by inscribing its own very questionable interpretation of her death. It at

---

1. Suellen Grealy, "Hijacked by Grief," para. 4. On the matter of causes of death, generally Janice Hume notes that "when medical science took hold in the United States in the mid- to late nineteenth century, obituaries began listing more specific causes of death." Some causes were effectively taboo—notably murder and suicide—but the reluctance to mention suicide as a cause of death has weakened significantly (2000, 143–44). The *New York Times* does report suicide as a cause of death under some circumstances. See, for example, the obituary of the artist Fred Sandback: "Mr Sandback, who suffered from depression, committed suicide, said his wife, Amy Baker Sandback" (Johnson, para. 2).

once withholds and interprets facts about her death, replacing the stigma of illegal drug use with that of suicide. It is thus not only bad journalism, to the extent that it does not confine itself to the known facts; it is also bad life writing. Indeed, in my view this obituary is particularly insidious because it is the obituary of a memoirist. I shall argue that, by overwriting her memoir, it patronizes her even as it purports to memorialize her.

An accomplished writer who published poems and a book of essays, Grealy was known primarily for her memoir; it is doubtful that she would have been considered worthy of a *New York Times* obituary had she not published *Autobiography of a Face,* which gained her a large audience. (The obituary's identifying clause, "Who wrote a memoir on her disfigurement," acknowledges as much.) Grealy's disfigurement was undeniably central to her identity and her life course—as her memoir's striking title declared—but the thrust of her book, as I read it, was that she had begun to understand that her real life would not, as she had long believed, commence when her face was "fixed" but rather that her fate was to live with a face that surgery could alter but never normalize. Lehmann-Haupt's obituary overwrites her literally painstaking self-representation in two distinct but related ways; its brief narrative of her life reconstructs it in terms of the tritest script of disability—that of triumph over adversity—and then characterizes its ending as a tragic reversal of her presumed victory. It suggests, then, that her reconciliation with her face was in the end transitory, if not illusory.

Debra Taylor observes that "despite the fact that the obituary is such a vital component of the modern newspaper, it is not a highly valued form of journalism" (668).[2] Precisely because it is seen as mere journalism—at least in the United States—it is infrequently regarded as a significant form of biography. But the obituary is undoubtedly the

---

2. In a piece called "News of a Lifetime," Max Frankel, a *New York Times* editor and columnist, acknowledged this, even as he exempted his own paper: "In most newsrooms, obituary writing is thought to be work for neophytes or burned-out veterans. . . . On many days, the *New York Times* is a glorious exception. . . . The *Times* assigns obits to good writers, often those with direct knowledge of the person's achievements, and to sensitive editors who aim to balance candor and respect." He also acknowledges that the British model is different: "As a handful of British newspapers have repeatedly shown, obits should be written by articulate history buffs and affectionate biographers" (28).

most widely disseminated life-writing genre and thus the one most
widely consumed by the general public: according to Alden Whitman,
"the obit page is the most widely read in most newspapers" (8). I con-
fess that, although I check the *New York Times* obituaries daily, I gave
very little thought to the obituary as a form of life writing until recently. Such a popular genre is surely worthy of sustained critical attention. (It does get an entry, by Taylor, in the *Encyclopedia of Life Writing,* but the article's bibliography is rather short, suggesting that the
obituary has not received its due from scholars and critics [668].) Indeed, insofar as it is presumably universal among print cultures, it
would seem ripe with potential for cross-cultural analysis. In any case,
its implications are thrown into high relief when an obituary both
depends on, and departs from, the self-written life of its subject, as
Grealy's does.

I would not argue that autobiographers should be privileged subjects of obituaries. Indeed, I would not claim that obituaries should
defer to their subjects' desires, no matter who those subjects are. In the
United States a sharp distinction is made between the obituary
"proper" (sometimes known as the "news obituary") and the "death
notice." Death notices generally concern individuals who do not merit
obituaries; they are generally quite short. While they may be edited by
the media in which they appear, they are written by and paid for by
friends or relatives of their subjects; they are thus not journalism but a
form of eulogy—and also, as their name implies, public announce-
ments of the deaths of local people. In contrast, obituaries, which concern public figures of note, are news stories, the first draft of history;
they are written by professional journalists employed by newspapers
or news agencies.

Interestingly, this distinction is not observed in Britain; according
to the American critic Elaine Showalter,

American obituary writing . . . remains primarily a news item rather
than an aspect of belles lettres. Lapses of days or even weeks between
a death and an obituary are routine in the U.K., while in the U.S.,
timeliness is all-important (para. 4); while American newspapers
treat obituaries of public figures as occasions to record historical
facts, British newspapers in the past 15 years have increasingly used

the obituary as an interpretation of the life and career of the deceased, often written in the first person by someone who knew him or her. (para. 2)

The British obituary is often informal, chatty, anecdotal, informal, affectionate, making no pretense of objectivity or comprehensiveness. Indeed, some British newspapers publish letters that supplement obituaries with additional stories in the obituary section. This practice, which moves the obituary even closer to eulogy, is unknown in American journalism.

In both countries, of course, obituaries are devoted to persons whose lives have a public dimension and therefore a claim on the public's attention. In the United States, however, the public is considered to have a "right to know" things about "public figures"; in the United States, then, celebrities have diminished rights to privacy and protection against defamation, whether written (libel) or oral (slander). According to Joseph Gibaldi:

> Most states . . . recognize the right of privacy in four respects:
> 1. Unreasonable intrusion on the seclusion of others
> 2. Appropriation of another's name or likeness without permission for advertising or purposes of trade
> 3. Unreasonable publicity of another's private life
> 4. Publicity placing another in a false light. (58)

But such strictures do not apply to individuals who are of "public concern." Similarly, whereas "in law, defamation is a published false statement of fact about a living person that exposes the person to public hatred, ridicule, contempt, or disgrace, induces an evil opinion of the person in the minds of others, or deprives the person of friendly relations in society" (53), to be found guilty of defamation of a public figure one must not only make a false statement, one must also know it to be false and make it with malicious intent or reckless disregard for whether it is true (55–56). This diminished protection is considered the price of fame.

It would seem odd and unreasonable to grant autobiographers greater protection than other public figures from verbal harm. After all, autobiographers have made themselves public figures in a particularly deliberate and distinctive way—by publishing their own lives. As we have seen, one of the distinctive features of the so-called memoir boom of the 1990s—in the United States, at least—was the phenomenon of the nobody memoir: the autobiographical volume by a hitherto unknown person, often quite young, often female, and often with a medical or psychiatric condition (e.g., Susanna Kaysen, Lauren Slater). Such subjects seem to have sacrificed, if not violated, their own privacy by the self-conscious public-ation of their private lives. Even if one could defame a dead person, memoirists would have no claim to special protection when it comes to obituary writing. And yet where legal issues are mooted (e.g., by death), perhaps we are justified in looking past merely legal considerations. In any case, the predicament of those who become public figures by way of their self-representation highlights both the power and the weakness of the obituary as a form of life writing. Before I address how autobiographers, particularly those with disabilities, may be especially vulnerable—though not necessarily privileged—subjects of obituaries, however, I would like to address a more fundamental issue: whether (and how) obituaries can harm their subjects.

The broader question of whether it is possible to harm the dead at all may seem to have a self-evident answer. To me, the answer seems obvious: of course the dead can be harmed. But in discussing this issue with friends and colleagues, I have found that responses vary considerably. At a colloquium on ethics and life writing at Indiana University in the fall of 2002, this issue aroused heated discussion, much to my surprise. Not only did I discover that others think quite differently from me; I also discovered that they consider their position—of course the dead *cannot* be harmed—to be self-evident. (This discovery confirms what poststructuralism claims: that "common sense" is often neither common nor sense.)

Indeed, one member of the colloquium, the late Diane Wood Middlebrook, author of a controversial biography of Anne Sexton, boldly declared, "The dead belong to us." It may be convenient, even necessary, for biographers to believe that. But the first-person plural is a particularly tricky deictic; in this biographer's pronouncement, its use may be an example not of the royal but of the imperial *we*. Since, as

John Maynard Keynes remarked, we are all dead in the long run, perhaps we (the living) should not distinguish ourselves too hastily and
too sharply from the dead. In any event, I do not consider myself to be
part of this biographer's "us." I do not consider the dead to belong to
me; to pick up an earlier thread, I think that at most only some of the
dead—namely, public figures—"belong" to the living, to be disposed
of as we see fit.

A provocative and, to me, compelling, account of the issue of harm
to the dead can be found in Joel Feinberg's *Harm to Others* (vol. 1 of
The Moral Limits of Criminal Law). The position that the dead cannot
be harmed, which is implied in the legal limitation of defamation to
the living, appears to have the strength of tautology. According to Feinberg, "in order to be harmed, common sense reminds us, a person
must be in existence at the time, but death . . . is the cessation of one's
existence, the first moment of a state of nonbeing, which is beyond
harm or gain" (79). In this view, it is impossible to harm the dead, since
the dead are no longer persons—and "*there cannot be harm without a
subject to be harmed*" (80). The drawback of this position becomes evident, however, when we realize that by its logic *killing* a person does
not entail *harming* that person, since death obliterates the very subject
whose existence is a precondition of harm. (It may be difficult, but it is
not impossible, to kill someone without causing pain to that person in
the process; and in this view, painless killing does not constitute harm
to the subject.) This is a counterintuitive and ethically problematic position, to say the least. (So much for arguments against the death
penalty—not to mention euthanasia.)

Feinberg's way out of this ethical dead end is through the definition
of harm as "setback interest, [which], given the universal interest in
not dying, implies that death is a harm" (81). That is, to kill us *is* to
harm us insofar as it entails a setback to our interests, which we can no
longer advance when we are dead. Feinberg suggests that much of our
dread of death stems from the realization that, once dead, "we have no
chance whatever of achieving those goals that are the ground of our
ultimate interest," most of which "require not simply that some result
be brought about, but rather that it be brought about *by* us, or if not by
us, then *for* us" (81).

Feinberg's argument that death harms the subject leads him to the conclusion that posthumous harm is also possible. For "if the prior interests set back by death justify our characterization of death as a harm (even without a subject), then equally some of them [i.e., prior interests] warrant our speaking of certain later events as posthumous harms" (82). He thus arrives at the conclusion that undergirds my argument concerning Grealy's obituary.

> We can think of some of a person's interests as surviving [her] death, just as some of the debts and claims of [her] estate do, and ... in virtue of the defeat of these interests, either by death itself or by subsequent events, we can think of the person who was, as harmed. ... [She] is of course at this moment dead, but that does not prevent us from referring now, in the present tense, to [her] interests, if they are still capable of being blocked or fulfilled, just as we refer to [her] outstanding debts or claims, if they are still capable of being paid. (83; I have taken the liberty of transgendering Feinberg's pronouns)

This argument provides a philosophical foundation—if one is needed—for the custom, in all cultures with which I am familiar, of treating most corpses with respect and for the legal institution of last wills and testaments, which enable one to enact one's desires after one's demise. In summary, while in some sense the dead are invulnerable to harm, their interests survive them, and a posthumous setback to those interests may be regarded as posthumous harm to them.

Feinberg's account of posthumous harm is pertinent to the obituary of Lucy Grealy in two respects. First, it helps to account for

> why we grieve for a young vigorous "victim of death" [her]self, and not only for those who loved [her] and depended on [her]. We grieve for [her] in virtue of [her] unfulfilled interests ... The moment of death is the terminating boundary of one's biological life, but it is itself an important event within the life of one's future-oriented interests. When death thwarts an interest, the harm can be ascribed to the person who is no more, charged as it were to [her] "moral estate." (85–86, transgendering mine)

More important for my purposes, Feinberg nominates "the interest every person has in [her] own reputation" as the best example of interests "from the purely self-regarding category" (87). He argues that, just as a setback to one's reputation of which one is unaware while alive constitutes harm, posthumous damage to one's reputation also involves harm (87). If one accepts Feinberg's argument—as I do—then the obituary is a particularly potent and fraught genre of life writing insofar as it is the genre that first represents the dead—who are not only, according to Feinberg, still subject to harm but intrinsically incapable of defending themselves against it. Lucy Grealy's obituary is a particularly ironic example of death writing inflicting posthumous harm on its subject. But before turning to her case, I would like to expand on what I see as the special status of the obituary among life-writing genres.

Life writing can be fundamentally divided into first-person and third-person forms, forms of autobiography and forms of (hetero)biography. Less obviously, but perhaps equally significantly, life writing can also be arranged along a time line; on this continuum the operative distinction is not between first- and third-person points of view but between first and last (i.e., earlier and later) words. In this schema, the death of the subject is decisive because it puts an end to life writing by, but not about, a particular subject. Indeed, biography may not only continue after the subject's death but may be stimulated and authorized by an event that may unseal lips and written records.

At this critical juncture on the time line are found those genres we might refer to as "death writing." Among these, in the United States the death notice may be (but usually is not) first-person in point of view, as it is written by someone who knew the subject; the obituary proper is always third-person in point of view. The obituary occupies an especially, perhaps uniquely, important place among life-writing genres not only for the obvious reason that it announces and marks the passing of the subject but also because it may, at least temporarily, fix the subject's image in the public mind. Obituaries are not always the last words on their subjects, but they are such for the vast majority who never receive subsequent biographical treatment. At the very least, then, the obituary is the first *posthumous* word on its subject; as such, an obituary in a major newspaper like the *New York Times* in the United States or the *Times* of London in the United Kingdom may determine the image of its subject for a substantial postmortem period—until and unless it is supplemented or supplanted by more extensive biographical consideration.

One irony of its status as the first last word is that the obituary is typically *antemortem* in composition, though never in publication. The very famous—those guaranteed obituaries—are thus subject to having their lives inscribed in the past tense well in advance of their deaths; their obituaries thus precede rather than follow their deaths, which simply confirm them: So-and-so is now actually dead. (Only satirical media may spell this out, as *The Onion* did to mark the passing in 2003, at the age of 100, of a man who served as South Carolina's U.S. senator for some fifty years: "Strom Thurmond finally, finally dies.") Such canned obituaries, waiting to be precipitated into print, are akin to tombstones with the date of birth already engraved and followed by a hyphen; I like to think of them, then, as pre-posthumous. (One ironic consequence of such obituaries' being written well before the death of their subjects is that they are sometimes published after the deaths of their authors, as was the case with the *New York Times* obituary of Bob Hope. Like Thurmond, Hope was 100 when he died; his obituary was written by Vincent Canby, who predeceased him by three years.) According to Alden Whitman, a complex calculus determines when a celebrity's obituary is assigned. That calculus takes into account prominence and power (so in the United States, presidents have top priority), age, health, the availability of materials, and "complexity." In addition, as Whitman delicately puts it, priority goes to those "whose careers and lifeworks are substantially behind them and on whom, therefore, little updating is required at the moment of death" (9).

Along with newspaper clippings found in the appropriately named "morgues," prospective obituary subjects sometimes serve as sources for their own death writing. Whitman denies that such interviews are "ghoulish" or that he ever felt like an "undertaker," let alone the Reaper himself: "elderly people have reconciled themselves to mortality and are thus often willing to look back over their lives with a mixture of pride, candor, detachment, and even amusement" (10). Indeed, he says, "from these conversations—all the more frank and open because the person knows that what he says is not for immediate quotation—emerges some of the best material" (12). Still, such luminaries may be justified in feeling a bit apprehensive when they are approached by obit writers ready to put the finishing touches on their stories. And in the case of someone like Lucy Grealy, whose death is sudden and unexpected, the subject has no opportunity to contribute to, and thus shape, his or her own obituary.

Another inherent characteristic of the obituary calls for mention with respect to the obituary of Lucy Grealy: its brevity. Though length and placement within an issue are calibrated to their subjects' purported significance, obituaries are of necessity among the briefest forms of life writing. (It is their brevity, of course, that enables us to consume so many of them.) Life is long, the obituary short. Therein lies the challenge: the obituary must be condensed and highly selective, but it should not be reductive or formulaic, as I think Grealy's is. Given her youth and the unexpectedness of her death, we can be sure that Grealy's obituary was composed posthumously and hurriedly, and we should take that into consideration in our judgment of it. Aside from interviews with friends, Lehmann-Haupt apparently gleaned much of the substance of his obituary from the *Times*'s review of her memoir by Margo Jefferson. One senses that Lehmann-Haupt's account of Grealy's life is based not on his reading of her memoir but on his reading of a review of it. In any case, her life is gravely diminished by its simplistic representation.

The obituary credits Grealy with having survived the medical ordeal of dozens of operations from childhood well into her thirties and the emotional ordeal of being stared at and ridiculed. But this account of her life renders it in the familiar and mildly oppressive formula of triumph over adversity, giving little sense of the maturity with which she came to view her own predicament. The problem with the script of overcoming adversity is that it represents disability entirely as a personal tragedy rather than as a social and cultural construct, removing stigma from the overcomer but not from the condition in question. In Grealy's case, rather than attending to the forces that shaped her, it attends only to the shape those forces threatened to impose on her. Such a script is patronizing: she's "brave Lucy" as long as she struggles, "poor Lucy" when she becomes "despondent." Such an account of her life denies social and cultural complicity in her predicament. Indeed, it tends to characterize her as a monomaniac, if not a narcissist—concerned only with her appearance (even as the obituary acknowledges that her book gives a very different impression of her).

Perhaps the obituary's most telling passage is this: "'When my face gets fixed, then I'll start living,' she said she told herself" (para. 12). This is one of only two quotations from her book; presented uncontextualized and unqualified, as it is in the obituary, where it is given a paragraph of its own, it is somewhat misleading. Had Grealy believed that her life would begin only when her face was fixed, then she would not have had a life, and she could not have produced any "life writing," much less the book she wrote. The story of such a life would have had to begin with her surgical normalization, but the book she wrote is about living with an unfixed, and unfixable, face. Indeed, if there is a false note in *Face*, it is the closure Grealy provides, quite suddenly and somewhat facilely, in its final pages, where she suggests that she had passed a turning point: "And then I experienced a moment of the freedom I'd been practicing for behind my Halloween mask all those years ago. As a child I had expected my liberation to come from getting a new face to put on, but now I saw it came from shedding something, shedding my image" (222).

As her obituary indicates, however, she continued to undergo operations on her face, confirming that the narrative's closure was somewhat forced, supplied perhaps in response to the presumed requirement of the form. In any case, the obituary's account of her death cancels out its own narrative of triumph and is at odds with her twin sister's testimony that, with the publication of her book, she "saw her life in a different way. She felt [that] she had gotten her message out, that she had found herself, that her face had become acceptable" (para. 14). The implication that she committed suicide out of despondency about her appearance suggests that the pride and determination the obituary ascribes to her were not enough in the end.

We should remember that Christopher Lehmann-Haupt had to produce his obituary under the pressure of a deadline and by means of interviewing grieving colleagues, friends, and relatives. What I perceive as the shortcomings of his obituary are in part literally that, characteristics related to the brevity of the form rather than to his execution of it. Let me explain by reference to another bit of death writing about Lucy Grealy, a reminiscence published in *New York* magazine in March

2003, within months of her death, by a close friend, the writer Ann Patchett. Beneath its title appears the following text, as a teaser.

> In her dazzling *Autobiography of a Face,* Lucy Grealy detailed her quest to reclaim her jaw, disfigured by cancer. Suddenly, she was the toast of literary New York, beloved for her quick wit and wild streak, saluted for her grit. But her endless surgeries left her so weak, impoverished, and dependent on drugs that even her dearest friends couldn't save her. (30)

Here again, a compact narrative inscribes her life as a complex tragic plot—a rise in fortune followed by a fatal decline; moreover, this summary suggests that this friend's memoir will corroborate, rather than challenge, the obituary's representation of her as a pathetic and possibly suicidal victim—of cancer, rather than of depression, or oppression.

In fact, Patchett's reminiscence does imply that Grealy's self-destructive behavior, which involved heroin addiction, was suicidal in effect, if not in intent; to that extent it corroborates her obituary. (This is perhaps not surprising: Patchett may have been one of the friends interviewed for the obituary.) Yet her reminiscence is less disturbing to me than the obituary. Why? For one thing, it is evidently written by someone who knew Grealy well and cared deeply about her. For another, it does not attribute her emotional trouble solely to her disfigurement. (The title, "The Face of Pain," suggests that her emotional pain did not stem solely from her disfigurement, and also perhaps that she suffered a good deal of physical pain, which contributed to her substance abuse.) Further, Patchett's story is long enough to contextualize Grealy's persistent pursuit of outer beauty and to suggest what was behind it. It begins, then, to supply what her obituary tends to elide or erase; it thus highlights the partiality and peculiarity of the obituary as a form of life writing. Reading Patchett's account made me realize how obituaries, despite their seemingly obligatory lists of known survivors, are conventionally, if not inherently, non- or even antirelational in their approach. Among life writing genres, it isolates and individualizes its subject to an extreme degree.

So while Patchett's magazine memoir (which she later expanded into a book, *Truth and Beauty*) to some extent confirms the obituary's implications about Grealy's death—by detailing her loneliness, depression, and self-destructive habits, including addiction to prescribed painkillers and illegal drugs—it does so with greater authority and transparency than the obituary: at least it gives some biographical evidence for its interpretation. Also, and not incidentally, it suggests that Grealy's most significant disability was not her disfigurement but clinical depression, which may have manifested itself in terms of feelings of ugliness but which must have been a function also of physiological factors—brain chemistry—and cultural factors—the cult of female beauty.

At the same time, I am somewhat troubled by Patchett's piece for some of the same reasons that I am troubled by the obituary. Both tend to reinforce a view of disability that is misleading and marginalizing. Portraying Grealy as triumphing over adversity or as succumbing to it by suicide are in the end not such radically different representations of her: they are two sides of the same coin, the comic and tragic versions of the same agon experienced by an atomistic individual. Both ignore the larger context of Grealy's disfigurement and the way in which it represents institutional and cultural oppression. For Grealy's problem was, even more than she seems to have acknowledged, not hers alone, and this may in fact be why her book had such broad appeal. For one thing, it was not so much cancer as its treatment that disfigured her; the face she wanted fixed was the face that state-of-the-art biomedicine gave her. For another, her predicament was merely an extreme version of a common one, especially among women: feeling that a great deal, perhaps literally one's life, depends on presenting an acceptable, normal—symmetrical, if not beautiful—face to the world. One of the book's crucial revelations is that young Lucy first became aware of the anomaly of her appearance not spontaneously, by regarding herself in the mirror, but by picking up on others' responses to her, including her mother's attempt to normalize her postchemotherapy appearance by providing her with a wig (chapter 6). It was thus the metaphorical mirror of others' responses to her that first alerted her to the problem of her appearance, which a look in a literal mirror merely confirmed (111–12).

Her book may thus be regarded as in part an attempt to deflect the stares to which she was subjected. One of its great virtues is to demonstrate, albeit not programmatically and perhaps not entirely intentionally, how indeterminate her face was, how differently it signified at successive stages of her life and in various institutional settings: in primary, secondary, and postsecondary school; at home, at the hospital, at work. The testimony of her book is not that she considered herself finally a heroine or a victim but rather that she was continually renegotiating her "face value" in changing circumstances. A crucial and saving epiphany was, "Perhaps my face was a gift to be used toward understanding and enlightenment" (180). Using her face in that way was an endeavor that was not, and could not have been, concluded by the completion of her memoir, yet it is perhaps the foundation of its value. To come to terms with her face was to contest others' view(s) of it, to stare back, however modestly and indirectly.

To suggest otherwise is to deny the role of culture in what was undoubtedly an ordeal, but one that made her not only a writer but a life writer. What is wrong with the obituary—and the particular way it harms her—is the way it misreads her life, despite her having "willed" it to us in death-defying print. This is not a matter of ruining her reputation—apparently, the obituary deliberately withheld what it felt was a scandalous fact about her death—but rather of overwriting and oversimplifying her complex self-representation. So while I do not hold that memoirists have a "right" to control their own posthumous images or deserve a privileged status as subjects of obituaries, I think that the fact that such a well-meaning obituary as Grealy's can so subtly but drastically controvert her self-representation—setting back, I would say, her interest in getting her message out—suggests that life writers are particularly prone to posthumous harm by their obituaries.

And that is partly because the obituary tends to review the life—particularly when death is early and unexpected—in terms of the circumstances of the death. Perhaps not surprisingly, but nevertheless problematically, death writing tends to privilege death, a single event rarely in control of the subject, giving it a disproportionate and often misleading significance.[3] This can be particularly insidious in the case

---

3. This may not be so true in Britain; according to Elaine Showalter, whereas "American newspapers describe the causes of death, . . . British newspapers omit the medical details" (para. 4).

of people with disabilities. Disability conventionally plays a role in obituary either when it is a major factor in the subject's life (as with Helen Keller or, very differently, Christopher Reeve) or when it is the cause of the subject's death (as was the case with Christopher Reeve). And in the case of disabled subjects of obituary, the emphasis on death as a retrospectively explanatory factor may encourage spurious linkage between the disability and the death; this is what I think happened in the case of Lucy Grealy. Whereas in fact her death by drug overdose was likely a function of a dependence on pain killers as a way of coping with postsurgical pain, the obituary suggested that it was a function of discomfort with her appearance (thus entirely suppressing any iatrogenic factor in her substance abuse).

The practice of interpreting the entire course of a subject's life in light of its ending is a convention presumably borrowed from literature that is fictive (i.e., the novel) and/or religious (i.e., hagiography); however, what makes sense in those genres, in which the ending is shaped intentionally and sometimes teleologically, does not necessarily make sense in secular life writing. An obituary's writing of the subject's death often bids to rewrite the life. This is most obvious when the circumstances of the death reveal a hidden dimension of the subject's life, as was the case with obituaries of closeted gay men who died of HIV/AIDS early in the epidemic. In the case of autobiographers, this may mean also rewriting the subject's life writing. Thus, Grealy's death—even if it had been a suicide—should not persuade us that her self-representation was false. But the situation of the obituary in the writing of a particular individual's life favors the overinterpretation of the ending. Unfortunately, it may thus tend to overwrite earlier self-representation and unduly shape later biographical representation. The misrepresentations inherent in obituaries and their unique significance in print cultures make them peculiarly likely to dis-figure the dead. And this is perhaps especially true of disabled persons, whether life writers or not, because, as suggested in chapter 3, so many of the conventional scripts and rhetorics of life narrative reinforce, rather than challenge, their marginalization.

9 § Life Writing and Disability Law

Undoing Hardship

Whether the ADA has the transformative effect that
its supporters predicted will ultimately not be
resolved in the courtroom.

—MATTHEW DILLER, "Judicial Backlash" (87)

The opening words of the introduction to Kay Schaffer and Sidonie Smith's recent book, *Human Rights and Narrated Lives: The Ethics of Recognition,* link human rights and life narrative in a way that is highly applicable to disability as a human rights (and civil rights) issue.

> The post–Cold War decade of the 1990s has been labeled the decade of human rights. . . . Not incidentally, it has also been described as the decade of life narratives, what commentators refer to as the time of the memoir. Many of these life narratives tell of human rights violations. Victims of abuse around the world have testified to their experience in an outpouring of oral and written narratives. . . . [These narratives] begin to voice, recognize, and bear witness to a diversity of values, experiences, and ways of imagining a just social world and of responding to injustice, inequality, and human suffering. Indeed, over the last twenty years, life narratives have become one of the most potent vehicles for advancing human rights claims. (1)

Progressive disability laws (the ADA, its American antecedents, and its international equivalents) are prime examples of contemporary civil rights legislation, and, as I suggested in chapter 1, the current burgeoning of disability memoir is related to these legal initiatives insofar as

146

both life narrative and disability law are constituents of a broad disability rights movement. To this extent, the story of disability rights activism and disability life writing can be subsumed in Schaffer and Smith's master narrative of the simultaneous worldwide emergence and convergence of life narrative and human rights campaigns.

Further, the aims of the disability rights movement are essentially those of the Universal Declaration of Human Rights (UDHR), which, according to Schaffer and Smith, "signaled . . . a collective moral commitment to just societies in which all people live lives characterized by dignity, equality, bodily inviolability, and freedom" (2). Nor is it incidental that the adoption of the Declaration in 1948 "was an aftereffect of the revelation of war crimes by Japanese and German war efforts and the war crime trials, especially the Nuremberg trials" (14). Like the Universal Declaration of Human Rights, the Nuremberg Code was engendered by the revelations of the Nuremberg Trials, especially the series of cases known collectively as the Nuremberg Medical Trial (1946), which addressed the brutal experiments carried out on the bodies of people with disabilities in Nazi Germany. Thus, there is a strong historical connection between disability history and the advocacy of human rights.

In their discussion of human rights violations, however, Schaffer and Smith concentrate on depredations against groups defined by ethnicity, race, gender, or religion. Their case studies involve apartheid in South Africa, oppression of indigenous people in Australia, the exploitation of sex prisoners ("military comfort women") in East and Southeast Asia during World War II, incarceration in the United States, and the democracy movement in China. So although their generalizations are just as relevant to disabled people, the pertinence of disability rights to the universal discourse of human rights goes almost without mention in their book. While they are entitled to define the scope of their project—which is impressively global and inclusive—it's unfortunate that, once again, disabled people appear only marginally on the radar of prominent cultural critics.

It appears, then, that although human rights discourse and disability narrative may have converged in the recent past as never before, that convergence has not been fully recognized. There are a number of reasons for this. One is that among marginalized groups, people with disabilities have been the most hidden from public view. Many have been sequestered in institutions, and although their institutionalization has typically been represented as humane, even benevolent, it has denied them voice as well as visibility. A case in point is John Tayman's new book, *The Colony*, about the former leper colony on Molokai. Despite the welcome attention this book brings to the colony, archival material apparently did not permit Tayman to give voice to the people who were quarantined there.[1] This is often the case, as the *New York Times* reviewer pointed out: "the archives of an institution . . . typically contain far more information about the people running it than the people confined in it" (Roach, 15). Despite the broad parallel between human rights advocacy and disability rights advocacy, then, the two causes have not been advanced in parallel ways. This may be in part because—in the West, at least—disability rights are now a matter of civil rights rather than of human rights; that is, disability rights are encoded in enforceable national legislation rather than unenforceable international declarations.

This is not to say that disability rights are always clear-cut and actually available, even in the United States. I hope to illuminate the complex status of disability rights by exploring a number of ways in which personal narrative, cultural narrative, and law may inform and shape each other. In particular, I will discuss personal and cultural narratives as (1) *anticipating* legal developments, (2) seeking *confirmation* in the law but simultaneously risking *disconfirmation,* (3) having a *hypothetical* relation to the law, and (4) *tacitly informed* by the law. In exploring these relations, I shall attend to ways in which personal and cultural narratives about disability may diverge as well as converge.

The first relation I have in mind is an anticipatory relation between personal narrative and disability law; I am thinking here of personal testimony that demonstrates the lack of, and need for, disability rights laws. These narrators are aggrieved and "*plaintive*" (in the etymological sense, the root of the legal term plaintiff: that is, not mournful, but rather com*plain*ing of perceived injustice). This set of narratives, then,

---

1. Archives are one resource; survivors are another. Former patients of Kalaupapa, the institution on Molokai, have taken issue with the well-reviewed book on various grounds, including the author's use of the terms *leper* and *colony* (M. Wilson).

anticipates and demands the enactment of disability rights legislation. Such narratives call for laws that will prevent the injustices of which they complain. These narratives are often short, sometimes oral rather than written, and, if written, may take utilitarian (nonliterary) form. A historical analogy with slave narrative is perhaps appropriate: this testimony, like slave narrative, calls for legislation that will make it obsolete as a genre.[2]

I am not an expert on the prehistory of the ADA, but Tony Coelho is, and his keynote address at the Moritz College of Law's "Disability, Narrative, and the Law" conference in 2006 contained and recontextualized his own anticipatory personal narrative of discrimination and oppression. Coelho developed epilepsy in his teens, and his experience with disability discrimination—notably, he was disqualified from the priesthood on the basis of his condition—informed his subsequent career, especially his work in the U.S. House of Representatives as an author and sponsor of the ADA. Coelho's personal narrative had traction in the House because he and other members recognized that his story was, as it were, representative of countless others. The larger point here is that such narratives have a proleptic relation to the law: they seek in effect to pre-scribe disability rights law. Their doing so at once depends on, and helps to advance, a change in the prevailing *cultural* narrative of disability. That is, discrimination against disabled people can be outlawed only when it is recognized *as such* (by analogy with other more patent forms of discrimination). And this is what distinguishes the new cultural understanding of disability: that disability is seen—indeed, it is *defined*—as a condition of exclusion and oppression. Once such legislation is passed, the new cultural conception is, or should be, reinforced, and new personal narratives become possible. (Thus, as Coelho was pleased to report, the Catholic Church eventually changed its stance on epilepsy and the priesthood.)

To my knowledge these anticipatory narratives have not been col-

---

2. Disability and slave narrative are also interestingly parallel in that both may require collaborative production—because of constraints imposed on narrators by slavery and by some impairments. On the ethics of such collaborative life writing, see chapter 3, "Making, Taking, and Faking Lives: Voice and Vulnerability in Collaborative Life Writing," in my *Vulnerable Subjects: Ethics and Life Writing*.

lected and published as numerously and prominently as narratives of other forms of human rights abuses.[3] I am, however, aware of one volume in this vein: Mary Grimley Mason's *Working Against Odds: Stories of Disabled Women's Work Lives*. Mason collects and presents stories, based on interviews, of women facing discrimination in the workplace. One of these stories, that of "Adrienne" (whose last name is withheld, but who is evidently Adrienne Asch), illustrates the best-case relation between personal narrative and disability law. Born blind in 1946, Adrienne did not benefit much from disability rights legislation until she was an adult. Interestingly, the workplace was much less receptive to her than the classroom had been, and as she ventured into the job market as a young adult, her personal narrative, which can be summed up in two words—"I can"—kept running into a powerful cultural narrative whose gist was, "You [i.e., blind people] can't." In response, like many people with disabilities, she made her condition— not her visual impairment, but the discrimination that effected her disablement—her cause. As an advocate for disabled people in the New York State Division of Human Rights in the early 1970s, she helped enact the sort of legislation that would enable her (and others) to have a career and thus a life (125–28). So Adrienne Asch helped inscribe laws that altered the cultural narrative in ways that would in turn allow her to tell her story to Mary Grimley Mason as the prominent bioethicist she has become.

The passage of disability rights legislation does not entirely obviate plaintive narratives, of course; on the contrary, violations of civil rights persist. Indeed, one of the ADA's effects, and presumed intentions, is to

---

3. I thought I had come across just such a book when, while browsing, I stumbled on *If It Weren't for the Honor—I'd Rather Have Walked: Previously Untold Tales of the Journey to the ADA*. The author, Jan Little, had polio as a teenager, was educated at the University of Illinois at Champaign-Urbana, and later competed as a swimmer on the United States International Wheelchair Team. Most of her memoir is an account of how she and others like her succeeded individually in advance of significant disability legislation through a combination of luck, pluck, and persistence. At times she seems almost nostalgic for the bad old days, and her attitude toward the ADA is expressed in a passage in which she boasts of how a disabled pressure group forced O'Hare Airport to make bathrooms wheelchair accessible before any legal mandate: "Maybe the ADA was the result of such ground work by individuals and groups of people who have disabilities. Maybe the legislation wouldn't have been needed if more friendly discussions had been held between authorities of both the public and private sector and people with disabilities. It could have even resulted in using common sense" (165–66). I think subsequent developments have exposed the naïveté of her trust in common sense and friendly discussion.

evoke such narratives. Once such legislation exists, these narratives may become literal grievances, grist for legal cases; their narrators, legal plaintiffs. The relation between personal narrative and law is then changed significantly. To be successful in court, plaintiffs' narratives must be adapted carefully and deliberately to the language of the law itself. Indeed, as Robert Dinerstein pointed out in his conference paper, plaintiffs' narratives are typically mediated by—in effect, turned over to—their legal advocates. Furthermore, they are contested in an adversarial process. Thus, the process of adjudication inevitably constrains personal narratives of disability.

The outcome of adjudication may be to confirm the narratives by judgment in their favor or to disconfirm them by judgment against them. It is by now well documented, by Ruth Colker and the ABA itself, that the vast majority (upward of 90%) of Title I (Employment) plaintiffs have lost their cases. Indeed, according to Colker's research, "over 80% of the cases are dismissed by federal judges on summary judgment" (O'Brien, *Voices,* 100). One of the peculiar distinguishing characteristics of disability legislation as civil rights law is the requirement that plaintiffs first establish their standing; that is, they must prove that they are members of the "protected class." (This is not required in the same way of victims of discrimination on the basis of race or gender [O'Brien, 45].) In fact, most cases are dismissed because the plaintiffs are deemed not to have a disability (O'Brien, *Voices,* 100). In cases notorious among disability rights advocates, plaintiffs have been legally adjudged to be nondisabled under the law, which is to say that not only their narratives but, in some cases, their claimed *identities* have been discounted.

In cases that proceed to the issue of discrimination, personal narratives may be construed in a way that affects the interpretation of the law as precedent for future cases (and thus in some sense rewrites the law). This may be particularly true of the ADA, one of whose notable characteristics is its deliberate use of vague terms like "reasonable accommodation" and "undue hardship." Without such ambiguous terms, there would have been much stronger opposition to its passage; with it, however, once enacted, the law seems designed, or at least destined, to invite legal challenge. The effect, if not the intention, has been that the ADA's precise implications have been left to the courts to determine. Linda Hamilton Krieger has shown that over the short history of the ADA the trend of cases heard has been to narrow significantly the scope of the law's protections ("Introduction," 5–6). This is in large part a function of the power and resilience of the prevailing cultural narratives of disability. The narratives of unsuccessful plaintiffs, then, may inadvertently serve as bookends to the first set of stories I mentioned. The anticipatory stories suggested the need for a law; they evoked and justified the legislation that was to address and obviate their complaints. The latter set sometimes serves to restrict the law's application—in effect, to amend the law. Thus, while they are submitted as narratives of injustices perpetrated despite the law, they may end up serving as cautionary tales to others seeking their rights under the law. A kind of double jeopardy obtains: plaintiffs' individual losses can disqualify a whole category of individuals.

In the introduction to her edited volume, *Backlash Against the ADA,* Krieger discusses the parameters of the law.

> The act's definition of disability had been drawn broadly, to cover not only the "traditional disabled," such as individuals who were blind, deaf, or used wheelchairs, but also people who had stigmatizing medical conditions such as diabetes, epilepsy, or morbid obesity. It covered not only people who were actually disabled, but those who had a record of a disability, such as cancer survivors, whom employers might be unwilling to hire for fear of increased medical insurance costs or future incapacity. The statute covered people who were not disabled at all, but were perceived as such, like people with asymptomatic HIV or a genetic predisposition toward a particular illness. It covered not only physical disabilities, but mental disabilities as well, arguably the most stigmatizing medical conditions in American society. (3)

Whereas the drafters' intention was to define the protected class in the broadest terms, the tendency of judges has been to circumscribe the class very narrowly, limiting it to individuals who have an impairment that, in the words of the ADA, "substantially limits one or more of the major life activities of such [individuals]" (42 U.S.C. 12102, Sec.

3, [2] [a]). As a result, in cases heard under Title I, Employment, there has emerged a pattern described as follows by Matthew Diller.

> Typically, the ADA defendant argues that the plaintiff's impairments preclude him or her from performing the job at issue, but that the individual is not generally precluded from work, or any other "major life activity." When fully accepted by a court, this line of argument results in a ruling that the plaintiff is not a person with a disability, despite medical impairments that render him or her supposedly unqualified for the job. The import of these cases is that many people are precluded from performing their past jobs because of their employer's reaction to their medical impairments, yet are not viewed as having disabilities within the meaning of the ADA. (68)

Such results have created the notorious Title I Catch-22: many plaintiffs are deemed too impaired to do their jobs but not sufficiently disabled to be protected by the ADA. Ironically, as Tony Coelho noted in his speech, people with his condition, epilepsy, are sometimes victims of Catch-22. If their medication successfully prevents seizures, they are deemed not really disabled and thus not members of the protected class. As Diller goes on to point out,

> this restrictive interpretation has a number of perverse effects. [For example,] the likelihood that an individual plaintiff will be deemed "disabled" within the meaning of the ADA is directly inverse to the chances that he or she would actually be able to win on the merits. (70)

That is, those who meet the court's definition of "disabled" are unlikely to be able to establish that they are able to perform their jobs, even with "reasonable accommodation."

The crux of the issue, it seems to me, is that the distinction at the very heart of disability studies, that between impairment and disability, has been lost on jurists. This is the distinction between the way in which a particular condition resides in and affects the function (or form) of an individual's body, on the one hand, and the way in which social and cultural contexts exclude or penalize people with particular conditions, on the other. A standard way of conveying this distinction is to differentiate between the inability of people with various conditions, such as quadriplegia, to walk (their impairment) and their inability to travel where the absence of ramps, curb cuts, and elevators excludes their wheelchairs (their disability). Thus, one could question Krieger's use of the qualifier *actually* in the passage quoted earlier; one could argue that, according to the language of the ADA, people with a record of, or perceived as having, a qualifying impairment are *actually* disabled—that is, they are disabled, literally, by definition.

In chapter 1, I provided a long list of conditions, from aphasia and Alzheimer's to stroke and Tourette's syndrome, that have been the subject of recent disability memoirs—often more than one; indeed, as I noted there, some of these conditions, such as breast cancer and HIV/AIDS, have generated their own substantial bodies of narrative. I was struck, then, to come across this passage in Diller's essay.

> Courts [have] found [that] individuals with breast cancer, multiple sclerosis, and stroke did not have disabilities[;] courts have also found individuals with lymphoma, brain tumors, heart disease, diabetes, hemophilia, epilepsy, ulcerative colitis, carpal tunnel syndrome, incontinence, depression, bipolar disorder, and paranoia excluded from the definition of disability. (67–68)

Clearly, there is a disjunction between the trend of personal memoir, in which more and more disabling conditions are being publicly claimed, and the trend of judicial decisions on the provisions of the ADA, in which fewer and fewer conditions are deemed disabling. Although the ADA language about who qualifies as disabled may be somewhat unfortunate, the problem does not lie exclusively in the wording of the law's definitions. Part of the problem is that the law is interpreted in a society whose prevailing cultural narrative is one in which "disability" is assumed to be an individual problem (which is to say that disability is conflated with impairment), to which the traditional governmental response has been the provision of entitlement to services or subsidy, rather than the requirement or provision of accommodation and access.

After all, that cultural narrative is inscribed in a whole set of disability laws that seek to determine who shall qualify for public assistance on the basis that their impairments render them incapable of working. As I shall argue later, disability memoirs have generally not displayed much concern with the legal aspects of disability. Thus, the disjunction between personal narratives and judicial decisions is not a matter of individuals clamoring for entitlements or accommodations that courts are unwilling to grant on grounds of undue expense or inconvenience. Rather, the issue is that the prevailing cultural narrative is primarily about impairment, not disability. Entitlements (such as Supplementary Security Income) are (rightly) granted only to individuals whose *impairments* prevent them from supporting themselves. But the ADA was written to address *disability:* gratuitous and harmful discrimination against and exclusion of people with impairments. Many of the personal narratives that make up the current wave of disability narrative aim to heighten public awareness of the broad scope and diverse nature of disability: that is, of the manifold subtle ways in which people with impairments are disadvantaged by social and political arrangements—and by a cultural narrative that focuses mainly on impairment. So while the upsurge and dissemination of personal narratives of disability are, at some level, functions of the same disability rights movement that produced the ADA, the three phenomena—personal narrative, cultural narrative, and disability legislation—are not always in sync.

A third significant relation between personal narrative and disability law is the one that characterizes the narratives in Ruth O'Brien's *Voices from the Edge.* When I first came across this volume, I inferred from its subtitle, "Narratives about the Americans with Disabilities Act," that the stories in it would concern people whose rights under the ADA had been violated. But this is not necessarily the case. Instead, disabled writers were invited to tell stories—not necessarily true, not necessarily about themselves—that raise issues pertinent to the ADA, and they typically tell their stories without explicit reference to the law. The ADA is not the text, but the subtext, of their stories. O'Brien groups the stories according to the title (section) of the ADA that seems to pertain, and in her commentary on these narratives, she draws out the implications of the law for each. In this volume, then, people with various impairments write about their lives—just telling it like it is, so to speak; then O'Brien suggests how the courts would likely apply the law to the scenarios the writers have described. While the interpretations are hypothetical and may have no real-world consequences for the narrators, they can be very illuminating precisely because the narratives are not written with legal claims in mind but rather out of autobiographical and expressive impulses.

In some ways the most interesting of these stories is the first, Joan Aleshire's "Eye of the Beholder," which anchors the section called "What Is a Disability?" Aleshire was born with significant and highly visible birth defects, malformed lower arms, and although she does not, in her narrative, "claim" disability, it would seem that she would clearly qualify as legally disabled. According to O'Brien, however, it is far from clear whether Aleshire would qualify as a member of the "protected class" under the ADA's definition of disability.

Part of the conundrum here lies in the fact that the law was deliberately written so that *particular* diagnoses or conditions would not necessarily entail disability status; disability was not linked to a set of enumerated conditions but rather defined in the abstract. This leaves the determination of disability status to be made on a case-by-case basis, taking into account the effect of an impairment on the individual's life. Born in the late 1930s, Aleshire graduated from college before the advent of section 504 of the Rehabilitation Act of 1973 (she got an MFA in 1980), and she married and had children before the passage of the ADA, so she was not in a position to benefit much, if at all, from the provisions of these important laws. But she had the good fortune of being born into an affluent family that treated her as much as possible as a normal child. It was not her parents' style to advocate on her behalf; rather, she describes them as having been in a state of "benevolent denial" (38) about her impairment, by which she seems to mean that they generally minimized or ignored it and did not allow it to hold her back. Still, it will come as something of a surprise to most readers of *Voices* that O'Brien does not offer a definite affirmative answer to the question, is Aleshire legally disabled?

Although Aleshire's primary profession is that of self-employed poet, she has taught creative writing, and one would think that she would be legally entitled to certain accommodations (such as voice-recognition software) to help her do her job. But like many others, Aleshire might be subject to the ADA's Title I Catch-22. In the language of the ADA,

> the term disability means, with respect to an individual
> (A) a physical or mental impairment that substantially limits one or more of the major life activities of such individual;
> (B) a record of such an impairment; or
> (C) being regarded as having such an impairment. ([42 U.S.C. 12102] Sec. 3—Definitions)

According to O'Brien,

> relief would depend on the type of position [Aleshire] sought. If the major life activity being asserted was working at any job, however, then Aleshire would have to show that she is substantially limited in a class or broad range of jobs. (51)

Once Aleshire had established a work history, that very history might count against her on criteria A and B. Ironically, according to O'Brien, Aleshire's best legal claim to disability status might come under criterion C, "being regarded as having such an impairment": even though Aleshire's deformity evidently has not prevented her from having a successful career as poet and teacher, her impairment is so obvious that it might prejudice potential employers against her. Indeed, according to her narrative, she is sometimes literally regarded and labeled as disabled by others (33). Such are the ironies and contradictions of the way the ADA has been interpreted. Interpretations like O'Brien's may help readers understand how the seemingly open-and-shut question of an individual's disability status can be both vexed and vexing.

A fourth kind of relation between disability narrative and law is found in personal narratives that recount lives significantly shaped by disability laws such as the ADA. Published book-length narratives of the sort I study are, of course, only a small fraction of all personal narratives of disability and not necessarily typical of the larger class. They are more likely to be literary in manner and to take the form of memoir; these narratives typically lack the hard edge of testimony and advocacy. For various reasons, they tend not to be single-issue narratives, and, as it happens, few, if any, of the texts I have studied have a very close or explicit relation to disability law. Such narratives may not even mention the legislation that has subtly shaped the lives they recount. Thus, the relation between the law and the narrative has to be intuited or discovered by the reader (or the professional critic of narrative).

As I suggested in the introduction, one of the most significant developments in late twentieth-century life writing has been the emergence of the some body memoir—the memoir that explores what it means to be embodied, what it is to have, or to be, a particular kind of body. Not all, but a great deal, of this life writing is disability memoir. And much of this in some way or other reflects the effect of disability legislation, even if it goes without explicit mention.[4] Narratives by those in my generation, like Simi Linton's 2005 memoir *My Body Politic,* tend to recount lives changed in midcourse by the passage of disability laws in the 1970s and after (Linton's memoir is discussed at some length in the final chapter). Narratives by younger authors may recount lives shaped from the beginning by the way such laws have expanded rights and access. And increasingly, such narrators may take such legislation for granted.

The least direct, but not the least important, way in which personal narrative is shaped by legislation may be just the sense in which stories of being, or becoming, "disabled" reflect the sense of "disability" that is inscribed in current disability law, such that the condition referred to is a social construct rather than a physical condition. Such narratives will increasingly have a retrospective relation to disability law; they will be stories by beneficiaries of the law rather than plaintiffs. This we might characterize as an *existential* relation; the lives and the identities of these life writers have been defined and made possible, in part, by disability law. Here disability law may generate new sorts of personal narrative, even when the narrators are not fully aware of it.

---

4. Indeed, until I came to write this essay, it had not occurred to me how rarely the ADA, or any other disability rights law, is mentioned in disability memoir. Notable exceptions, however, are parental narratives of disabled children, which form a significant subgenre. As advocates for their children, parental narrators tend to be well versed in the provisions and limitations of disability legislation.

Take, for example, *Rescuing Jeffrey,* a father's story of the aftermath of a diving accident in which his teenaged son Jeffrey was paralyzed from the neck down.[5] At the scene, the author, Richard Galli, jumped into the pool to rescue his son from drowning. He did not realize at the time that Jeffrey was drowning because a spinal cord injury was preventing him from swimming and, for that matter, from breathing. Learning of the extent of Jeffrey's paralysis in the aftermath of his life-saving intervention, Richard Galli and his wife Toby decided that, if the hospital would allow it, they would pull the plug on their son in order to save him from a life of dependency on a ventilator and a wheelchair—a life, as they saw it, without privacy and without dignity.

When I summarize this story for people who haven't read the book, they often interrupt at about this point to say, "So Jeffrey was in a coma, right?" To their shock, my response is, "No, Jeffrey was conscious, alert, and oriented." His parents decided to disconnect his ventilator without asking—or telling—him in order to spare him the ordeal of having to decide his own fate and presumably choose to end his own life. A powerful cultural narrative is in play, according to which meaningful life is not possible for someone with a high spinal cord injury. Jeffrey's parents had never had to think about what living with such an injury would be like, and when they were forced to, they did so in terms of very negative preconceptions they had absorbed from the culture around them. Such preconceptions have been powerfully and influentially dramatized in two Oscar-winning films, both released in 2004: the American film *Million Dollar Baby* (Best Picture, discussed in chapter 2) and the Spanish film *The Sea Inside* (Best Foreign Language Film). The Gallis quite literally could not imagine their son living as a quadriplegic. And since they could not cure his quadriplegia, they decided that they would end his life.

Not incidentally, Jeffrey's father is a lawyer. And, though never cited explicitly, law plays an important role in this scenario. That Jeffrey's parents could choose to "kill" him (their word) was a function of two legal artifacts. First, the Federal Patient Self-Determination Act of 1990 had established that competent patients have the right to refuse any

---

5. I discuss *Rescuing Jeffrey* more fully in chapter 6 of *Vulnerable Subjects,* "When Life Writing Becomes Death Writing: Disability and Euthanography."

and all medical procedures; under this law, no one can be forced to accept medical treatment, even if refusal of it will result in death. Second, at the time of his accident, Jeffrey was legally a minor, several months shy of his eighteenth birthday. As a result, his parents were legally empowered to make health-care decisions on his behalf. The hospital in question exercised oversight on this, but it generally endorsed parents' decisions. The Gallis realized that the case they made to the hospital's ethics board needed to be more about the quality of their parenting than about the quality of their son's life; what the Gallis needed to do—and succeeded in doing—was to present themselves as acting in good faith with Jeffrey's interests at heart (and not, for example, out of financial considerations).

In the end, the Gallis decided not to disconnect Jeffrey's life support. The reasons for this are not clear—the narrative declines to answer this question simply and directly—but a number of considerations come into play. A significant one is Jeffrey's developing sense of his future. And one crucial determinant of that, as I read the narrative, is his father's answer to a poignant question that Jeffrey asks as he comes to grips with the ramifications of his injury: "Will I have to go to a school for cripples?" (159). Had the answer to Jeffrey's question been, "Yes, you *will* have to go to a special school for cripples," Jeffrey might have evinced less of a desire to live, and his parents might have been more inclined to end his life prematurely. But the reassuring answer was no. And the answer was no in large part because disability rights legislation had determined that schools must be accessible to students in wheelchairs: with disability segregation, as with racial segregation, the courts had determined that "separate but equal" schools were inherently *un*equal.

That Jeffrey could (and did) eventually resume his education at his old school was a function not of the medical technology on which his survival depended but of disability legislation on which, I would say, his *life* depended. The legal mandate to include students with disabilities, and the concomitant change in expectations about the presence of disabled people in the public sphere (a cultural narrative), may also have been a factor in the upwelling of sentiment among the Galli family's friends in favor of Jeffrey's living. Against what Richard Galli refers to as this "wave," the Gallis eventually felt powerless. So Jeffrey's life narrative—as told by his father (in one sense) and as allowed to continue by his father (in another sense)—is a story in which disability legislation may have been a decisive factor, even though it is never mentioned. (And, although Jeffrey's death would not have been a case of assisted suicide if Jeffrey had been disconnected from his ventilator, his story suggests how disability narrative illuminates the role of disability prejudice in so-called end-of-life scenarios.)

Cultural narrative is never monolithic, of course, and the cultural narrative of disability is currently very much in flux. But personal narrative is not necessarily progressive, either. Until recently, the standard scripts of disability memoir have been fairly regressive. As I argued in chapter 3, a number of rhetorics still common in disability memoir— for example, the rhetorics of triumph, of horror, of spiritual compensation, and of nostalgia for lost abilities (in the case of acquired disabilities)—are in fact inimical to the best interests of persons with disabilities. Those of us who are advocates for disability rights as human rights need, then, not just more disability narratives but more *progressive* disability narratives—narratives whose authors "claim disability" in the new sense.

Personal and cultural narrative and law may interact in a number of distinct ways, and there is no single mode of mediation, no single direction in which influence flows among the three phenomena under discussion. As Diller suggests, the narrowing of the ADA may be seen as a function of its having been too far ahead of the popular understanding of disability. Linda Hamilton Krieger sheds helpful light on the phenomenon of backlash when she distinguishes between "laws designed to enforce existing social norms and laws enacted to displace or transform them" ("Sociolegal Backlash," 341). Not surprisingly, transformative laws are more likely to generate backlash.

> Backlash tends to emerge when the application of a transformative legal regime generates outcomes that diverge too sharply from entrenched norms and institutions to which influential segments of the relevant population retain a strong conscious allegiance. ("Sociolegal Backlash," 341)

Another way of saying this is to say that law cannot be too far in advance of cultural narrative.[6] Personal narratives have much more leeway—and I tend to favor those in the vanguard, for obvious reasons—but *published* narratives, like the law, cannot be too far ahead of the cultural narrative for the same reasons. Personal narrative can push the envelope, but, to mix the metaphor, it alone cannot deliver the message.

The interaction between narrative—cultural or personal—and law is multidimensional and multidirectional, then. Disability narratives—long or short, written or oral, formal or informal, individual or communal—may first stimulate legislation by highlighting areas in which protection from discrimination is lacking; those laws in turn evoke narratives of their violation. Personal narrative may call for legislation, which in turn may call forth personal narrative. But the relation between disability narrative and disability rights law is double-edged: postlegislation narration can retroactively rewrite the law (either more broadly or, as has been the actual trend, more narrowly).

Toward the conclusion of his essay in *Backlash,* Matthew Diller offers this reminder.

> Judges construing and applying statutes are inevitably affected by the broader social and political environment, even as they disclaim any such influence. Only broad-based social understanding of and support for the principles undergirding the ADA will make the statute's promise a reality. Although enactment of the law and efforts to enforce it can play an important role in helping to create such understanding and support, neither ringing statutory language, nor seemingly tough provisions for judicial enforcement are sufficient to carry the day. (87)

There is cause for hope. Ideally, the next generation of jurists will come to the bench with a greater degree of "disability literacy" than the cur-

---

6. Although the ADA is obviously in some sense a "rights" law, it is also, as Ruth O'Brien has pointed out, a "needs law" insofar as it requires employers to "accommodate employees on the basis of their individual needs. Rather than creating a rationalized workplace that is staffed by standardized bodies, the individual peculiarities of all people could be addressed" (*Voices,* 21). For O'Brien this gives the law a kind of utopian potential because it can serve as a model for adjusting the workplace to the individual needs of *all* employees, nondisabled as well as disabled.

rent one,[7] thanks in part to the emergence and spread of disability studies in American higher education. And the proliferation and consumption of disability narrative can help to expand the general public's sense of what counts as disability. More immediately and most encouragingly, however, legislators disappointed by the federal courts' restrictive interpretations of the ADA have decided to amend the ADA to bring it back into conformity with their original intentions. In the summer of 2008, both the House and the Senate passed versions of such a law, the ADA Amendments Act of 2008, and on 25 September 2008, with little fanfare, President George W. Bush signed the act into law (Lewis). This revision, obviously impelled by a host of disability narratives, should ensure that the hard-won rights of disabled people will be preserved—or, rather, restored.

---

7. Of perhaps ironic significance is the little-known fact that the current Supreme Court chief justice, John Roberts, suffered a seizure while on vacation in the summer of 2007 (Park, "Does Justice Robert Have Epilepsy?"). This was his second seizure, and by some diagnostic criteria, this makes him an epileptic.

10 ❦ Epilogue

The New Disability Memoir

On the planet of the blind, no one needs to be cured.
On the planet of the blind self-contempt is
a museum.

—STEPHEN KUUSISTO, *Planet of the Blind,* 148

When bigotry is the dominant view, it sounds like
self-evident truth.

—HARRIET MCBRYDE JOHNSON, 54

I began this book by observing that the late twentieth century witnessed an upsurge in auto/somatography, life writing devoted to exploring *bodily* experience. Such writing often depicts lives distinctively shaped by anomalous bodies or unusual somatic conditions. In concluding, I wish to highlight several autosomatographies that are sufficiently novel to warrant the label "new disability memoir": Stephen Kuusisto's *Planet of the Blind* (1997), Georgina Kleege's *Sight Unseen* (1999), Anne Finger's *Elegy for a Disease* (2006), Harriet McBryde Johnson's *Too Late to Die Young* (2005), and Simi Linton's *My Body Politic* (2005). All of them were published within the decade spanning the turn of the twenty-first century, and their emergence at this time (the turn of the millennium as well) is an auspicious development in disability life writing—even though, interestingly, the words *disability* and *disabled* do not appear in their titles or subtitles. Their novelty is found primarily not in their form: though several of them are by creative writers, they are not innovative, much less experimental. Rather, their novelty lies in an aspect of their content: their disability consciousness. These are some body memoirs with (an) attitude.

To revert to the distinction between impairment and disability, established and elaborated in chapter 2, the novelty in this new species of disability memoir is in large part a function of their focus on disability rather than impairment. As I suggested earlier, this distinction is foundational to disability studies, and it is no accident it informs these memoirs, as all of their authors have been professionally involved in disability studies, in one way or another. It would not be inaccurate to call these memoirs "disability *studies* memoirs," but it might give the misleading impression that they are theoretical in approach or academic in manner. This is not at all the case; all of them are informal in tone. But they are characterized, as their authors' lives have come to be, by a sharp awareness of how disability is socially and culturally constructed. These memoirs may read at times like advocates' or activists' autobiographies, but rarely like academics'.[1]

The first two memoirs are by blind writers, Stephen Kuusisto and Georgina Kleege. Neither was born blind; both gradually lost their vision, owing to quite different conditions (retinopathy of prematurity for Kuusisto, macular degeneration for Kleege). Both grew up with enough sight to function and, at least as important, to *pass* as seeing, at least while young. Their memoirs, then, portray them as crossing gradually from one status to the other during adolescence and early adulthood. However, the emphasis in both texts is not on the loss of *vision*—though that is critical and undeniable—but on a shifting sense of *identity*. For both, the meaning of blindness changes with its progression, and both come around to the position that blindness is less a matter of the function of their eyes than of the constitution of their I's.

The prologue of Kuusisto's *Planet of the Blind*—a very brief vignette of the writer negotiating New York's Grand Central Station with his first guide dog, Corky—foreshadows two important dimensions of his memoir. It ends like this.

---

1. Disclosure: through my work in disability studies, I met (and came to admire) all of the writers discussed in this chapter before they published these memoirs.

This blindness of mine still allows me to see colors and shapes that seem windblown; the great terminal is supremely lovely in its swaying hemlock darknesses and sudden pools of rose-colored electric light. We don't know where we are, and though the world is dangerous, it's also haunting in its beauty. Even to a lost man with a speck of something like seeing, this minute here, just standing, taking in the air as a living circus, this is what tears of joy are for.

A railway employee has offered to guide me to my train. I hold his elbow gently, Corky heeling beside us, and we descend through the tunnels under the building. I've decided to trust a stranger.

Welcome to the planet of the blind. (2)

Kuusisto has an MFA from the Iowa Writers' Workshop, he is a teacher of creative writing, and he is a published poet as well as a memoirist. Like its prologue, *Planet of the Blind* is notably lyrical in style; it is chronological but not continuously so, and its mode is more descriptive than narrative or expository. Its lyricism is not decorative, however; rather, it serves to foreground the fact that, despite the danger and inconvenience entailed by his condition, Kuusisto experiences his blindness as a constant source of visual stimulation and aesthetic gratification: "I am blind in a bittersweet way: I see like a person who looks through a kaleidoscope; my impressions of the world are at once beautiful and largely useless" (13). Part of his charge as a memoirist is to convey that as a blind man he does not suffer from visual deprivation, as one might expect; rather, he experiences a very rich visual sensorium—perhaps all the richer for being unstable ("windblown").[2]

The other significant feature of his memoir illustrated in this brief passage is less obvious: the emancipating presence of his guide dog, which is expressed partly in the pronoun *we*. Note that the verb governed by this first-person plural subject has to do with cognition, rather than mere locomotion, which the two are also involved in, and that at this moment the two are *not* knowing. The passage represents Corky and Kuusisto as engaged in a kind of transhuman symbiosis and yet still dependent on the kindness of strangers in the person of the

---

2. In a later volume (not a sequel), *Eavesdropping* (2006), he focuses on the way in which his limited vision forced (or enabled) him to live a rich aural life, as well. He thus privileges sight in one volume, hearing in the other.

railway employee.[3] In addition, then, to insisting that his blindness is a source of "haunting beauty," Kuusisto presents himself here as venturing into the world at large only with help—the constant assistance of his personal guide dog and the contingent assistance of human others. It is a tale of autonomy (Kuusisto chooses his destinations) but not of individual independence (he can't get far alone). This is a story, then, not of triumph over impairment but rather of circulation in public made possible by an accessible environment, a cooperative community, and a kind of canine prosthesis.

In recounting the early years of his life (he was born in 1955), Kuusisto focuses on two consequences of his poor vision. The first is his attempt to pass as sighted; neither he nor his parents restricted his play in response to his impairment. Indeed, he not only walked without a cane; he ran headlong, drove his family's powerboat (under his father's watchful eye), and even rode a bike (not without mishap).

> Blind though I am, my mother is hell-bent on emphasizing my small window of vision. I am going to be dimly sighted and "normal." According to her, I will damn well ride a bike and go sledding, and do whatever the hell else ordinary children do. To her the prospect of the white cane denotes the world of the invalid. (14–15)

The second is related to his passing as sighted; well before the advent of disability legislation mandating inclusion of children with disabilities, Stephen's mother managed to pass him off as sufficiently sighted to function in public schools with normal kids.

Although the book is composed primarily of vignettes, its underlying plot line emerges in its second half, when he learns to take advantage of new disability resources in the form of technology, support, and accommodation. The plot, then, is that of the coming-out narrative. As conventionally understood (with regard to sexual orientation), the coming-out narrative has been described by Ken Plummer as follows.

---

3. A notable disability memoir is entirely devoted to the extension of selfhood that can accompany the use of a guide dog. See Rod Michalko, *The Two in One: Walking with Smokie, Walking with Blindness.*

[It] tells initially of a frustrated, thwarted and stigmatized desire for someone of one's own sex—of a love that dares not speak its name; it stumbles around childhood longing and youthful secrets; it interrogates itself, seeking "causes" and "histories" that might bring "motive" and "memories" into focus; it finds a crisis, a turning point, an epiphany; and then it enters a new world—a new identity, born again, metamorphosis, coming out. It is a story that has been told in fiction, in film, in research, and of course in the daily lives of many. (52)

Of course being blind is very different from being gay. Being blind may carry a stigma but not in the way, to the degree, or for the reasons that obtain for homosexuality. Kuusisto does, however, depict his impairment as subjecting him to a good deal of ridicule when he was young and as constricting the scope of his experience. The fundamental connection between narratives of coming out as gay and those of coming out as disabled is that both depend on, and recount, the private acceptance and public acknowledgment of a stigmatized identity that is somatic in its basis. Both *conditions* (homosexuality and blindness) are initially given, not chosen; coming out, however, requires that both *identities* be consciously affirmed and freely elected.

Coming-out narratives resemble conversion narratives in structure; they are usually dominated by a retrospective viewpoint shaped by a sharp, if not sudden, change in perspective, a transvaluation of the condition in question. In Kuusisto's prologue, the retrospective viewpoint is implicit in the reference to Corky, for Kuusisto's adoption of a guide dog was not merely strategic and pragmatic but also symbolic; it publicly proclaimed his identity as a blind person and thus his membership in the blind community. It is only then that he fully became a resident of the planet of the blind (where, his Web site announces, "It's not as dark as you think!").

Narratives of coming out as gay, like Paul Monette's *Becoming a Man,* are sometimes characterized by corrosive criticism of the closeted self. Kuusisto is kinder to his former self. (After all, while Kuusisto may have vigorously denied his status as a blind man—with the encouragement of his family, who were in on his secret—he was all too obviously visually impaired. He was better at denial than at passing.)

As the narrative approaches the time of his coming out, however, he highlights his evasiveness. Here he pictures himself (using the objectifying third person) trying vainly (in both senses of that word) to conceal his blindness in a university library.

> He sits with a thick magnifying lens under an oval of lamplight, struggling to read for twenty minutes at a time. He is ashamed to be seen reading this way. He reads defensively lifting his head whenever he thinks someone might be looking. He'd rather be thought of as one who naps over a book than one who cannot read it. (124)

After a frightening injury to an eye forces him to seek assistance (medical and otherwise), he realizes that his coping and compensatory skills have not been empowering and heroic but limiting and perhaps cowardly. In trying to master his impairment, he had inadvertently given it inordinate and unnecessary power over him: "My blindness was turning into a subject, and in a sense, I was its object" (133). However, rather than a sudden epiphany, his awakening takes the form of a series of discrete steps toward disclosing his impairment. The steps are a matter of public admission of his status—owning it (as with sexual orientation)—and also a matter of claiming accommodation (as is less the case with sexual orientation). Since the latter is largely a function of what is legally required, Kuusisto's narrative takes note of milestones in disability rights legislation. (This is in fact a distinguishing characteristic of the new disability memoir.) It is only when he is in graduate school in Iowa in the 1970s (after having majored in English, improbably and with considerable difficulty) that he first uses assistive reading devices. Coming out as disabled is represented as a personal decision but one that is far more appealing when there is cultural acceptance and legal protection for the hitherto stigmatized identity.

The major steps in Kuusisto's coming out, then, are (1) his adoption of the stigmatic white cane (which greatly increases his safety in public), (2) the adoption of a guide dog (which increases his mobility), and (3) his acceptance of public assistance (i.e., money) and accommodative devices in his education and profession. As reasonable and inevitable as these steps seem in retrospect, each is daunting in its turn. Thus when he is first urged to use a cane by an advocate for blind people, Kuusisto regards it as a visible marker of his blindness, rather than as an assistive device, and initially demurs: "he's directing me into the open, the cane is an invitation to be nude in public. I'll have to take this under advisement" (100–101). If the narrative has a decisive turning point, it comes after a dark night of the soul that involves painful introspection. He wonders, "Why should it take so long for me to like the blind self? I resist it, admit it, then resist again, as though blindness were a fetish, a perverse weakness, a thing I could overcome with the force of will power" (142). But then,

> I call the telephone operator and ask for the number for the New York State Commission for the Blind. I need help walking.
> I've needed help all my life.
> It's that simple. (143)

Although Kuusisto's "planet of the blind" is, as his epigraphs suggest, more metaphor than reality, more a place of the spirit than of the body, Kuusisto most closely approaches its earthly manifestation during a sojourn at a Guiding Eyes facility, where he is introduced to his first guide dog. Like guide dogs themselves, their masters also require careful and expensive training. The account of Kuusisto's initiation into the world of the guided provides the core of the very brief latter part of his memoir ("Walking"). Of the facility, he realizes, "This is in fact my first experience with a place that has been built for blind people" (161). This is not only a matter of its physical design. Its clients are all blind, so the person who had been mainstreamed as a boy at his mother's insistence is now, as a young man, sequestered for the first time with other blind individuals and equipped to reenter the outside world with an enabling canine companion. One of the early payoffs of this experience comes in sharing a blind perspective with others like him and reveling in blind humor.

Kuusisto's life is profoundly changed by his acquisition of Corky— mostly, but not entirely, for the better. On the positive side, his mobility is greatly improved, and "my first two years with Corky create dotted lines all over the United States" (176). On the negative side, as an openly blind person he becomes a target of public attention, not all of it welcome or benign (like many visibly disabled people, he repeatedly encounters others who feel he needs "healing"; such encounters form a leitmotif in the new disability memoir). So the upshot is mixed.

> There's power that comes with admitting how little I can see because the world is more open and admits me far more graciously than it did when I was in the closet. But it's hard in a different way. You are watched wherever you go, and sometimes I feel buried beneath the graffiti of other people's superstitions. (184–85)

And yet Kuusisto has no regrets, unless that he had not come out much sooner. As is typical of all coming-out narratives, time in the closet is seen as time wasted, or at least not fully lived. Kuusisto's election to live as an openly disabled person, to claim his identity and his rights, is characteristic of the new disability memoir, even when it does not overtly assume the form of the coming-out narrative.

Published the same year as *Planet of the Blind* (1998), Georgina Kleege's *Sight Unseen* offers a very different voice and mode.[4] Kleege is a novelist and essayist as well as memoirist, and *Sight Unseen* is not strictly speaking a narrative at all but rather a collection of personal essays unified by their concern with how her limited vision has shaped her— as a daughter, as a wife, as a writer, as a teacher: as a person. Her mode is less confessional than Kuusisto's, her style less lyrical. Like him, however, despite her impairment—or perhaps because of it—she is intensely visual. The child of artists, she acquired an abiding interest in visual art early in life, and she has traveled widely in part to see the same aesthetic monuments that attract sighted tourists. As with Kuusisto, for Kleege being blind is in the end, however, not a matter of visual acuity but of identity and posture in the world.

She opens her brief introduction with an arresting claim: "Writing this book made me blind" (1). She hastens to assure the reader that this was not a function of eyestrain leading to blindness (which in any case it doesn't). Rather it has to do with her perception of herself and the term she uses to label her condition. Thus, through the introspective and retrospective process of writing her memoir, she came to think of

---

4. For an extensive discussion of *Sight Unseen*, see Susannah B. Mintz, *Unruly Bodies*, chapter 2.

SIGNIFYING BODIES

herself as "blind" rather than, say, "partially sighted" or "visually impaired" (1), as she once would have described herself. The process of reviewing her life was one of surprised discovery—of how blind she is (how abnormal her vision is), of how sighted she is (how much she enjoys art and other visual media), and of what a sighted world she inhabits (how much it has been created by and for people who can see and thus how much it disadvantages her).

A highly self-aware writer, she goes on to explain and justify her choice of the essay as her form. She is leery of the traps into which so much blind autobiography falls: the implication that one can triumph over or, worse, be defeated by, one's blindness; the danger of performing a private freak show for the entertainment of voyeuristic normals—especially acute, perhaps, for a person whose impairment impedes the returning of an appraising or curious gaze. This sensitivity to the problems of representing disability is another distinctive characteristic of the new disability memoir. While, as noted earlier, none of the memoirs under discussion here is experimental in form, all are composed very deliberately by writers who are well aware of the limitations of disability memoir and who deviate consciously from what they perceive as failed or counterproductive formulas.

Kleege describes her book as a coming-out narrative with a difference: it lacks "fanfare or a specific time line" (5). As she is at pains to note, its mode is not really narrative at all; though the book comprises personal essays, the parts, like the whole, are discursive or expository—anecdotal at most. Kleege is wary of the messages implicit in the medium of plotted narrative. So the book is not so much a *narrative* of coming out (it doesn't rehearse the steps, as Kuusisto's memoir does) as a declaration (an enactment as well as an announcement) of her new status.

Rather than attempt to survey the book's diverse contents, I will concentrate on the first chapter, "Call It Blindness," which anchors the first section, "Blindness and Culture." Her main concern here is with how what is intensely personal to her (blindness as an idiosyncratic somatic condition) is also (and perhaps ultimately) cultural. Thus, in this chapter, she traverses back and forth between shards of personal narrative and more broadly cultural concerns. One of the latter is the way metaphors of blindness color our collective vision. She follows a long list of dead metaphors with this observation.

> Writers and speakers seem so attached to these meanings for *blind* they don't even find them clichéd. Deny them the use of the word and they feel gagged, stymied. If you want to talk about stupidity, prejudice, weakness, or narrow-mindedness, no other word will do. (22)

In an autobiographical segment, she tells of being "pronounced legally blind" when she was eleven (after having successfully disguised a significant impairment from her parents for about a year). But she also notes that her diagnosis was not accompanied by the provision of any adaptive materials. Like Kuusisto, Kleege was born too early (in 1956) to benefit from disability legislation during her school years. Like him, she coped on her own, sitting in the front of the class and ingeniously reading the blackboard by following her teachers' hand motions rather than by decoding the marks produced. Passing was not hard, she boasts.

> Looking sighted is so easy. For one thing, the sighted are not all that observant. And most blind people are better at appearing sighted than the sighted are at appearing blind. Compare the bug-eyed zombie stares that most actors use to represent blindness with the facial expression of real blind people, and you'll see what I mean. (19)

Thus, the personal (her ability to pass) is inseparable from the cultural (the inept impersonation of blind people by sighted actors). And vice versa: the lack of accommodation encourages her to attempt to pass.

Perhaps the most original part of this essay, as memoir, is a long passage written in the second person. This passage addresses the likelihood that most of her readers will experience significant vision loss if they live long enough. The point of the passage is not to deflect their pity for her, much less to turn the tables on them, but rather to reassure them about what it's like to be blind. Fear of blindness is very common, but, she argues, it is usually excessive and built on misconceptions—a form of hysteria. Here she attempts to demystify the reality of blindness by involving her readers in a thought experiment—a kind of mental disability simulation. She reminds them that everyone experiences blindness routinely and periodically—when they blink or in darkness—and she asks them to imagine doing their daily tasks without the aid of eyesight.

> In fact you discover that you can accomplish most of your routine tasks with your eyes closed. That may be how you define them as routine. . . .
>
> You turn on the TV. You have probably already observed that it is not really necessary to watch the TV—it's aimed at people who are not as smart as you. You know what's going on even with your eyes closed. (34)

And so on, through a reassuring survey of common everyday actions, which concludes, "You have faced one of your more debilitating fears and seen it for what it is. . . . blindness does not in itself constitute help-lessness. You will be as resourceful, capable, and intelligent as you ever were" (35).

And then the essay takes a clever turn, as Kleege diverts the readers' attention from the condition itself (the *impairment*) to some of its so-cial consequences (the *disability*): "It occurs to you slowly that you will not be alone in this. Your blindness will affect other people—family, friends, coworkers, strangers—and you are afraid that they will not adapt as well as you" (35). Which brings her back again, but with new force, to the notion that the personal is the cultural: "Face it. What you fear is not your inability to adapt to the loss of sight, it is the inability of people around you to see you the same way. It's not you, it's them" (35). Such emphasis on the context of impairment, rather than impair-ment in vacuo, is distinctive of the new disability memoir.

Like Kuusisto and Kleege, Anne Finger was disabled at an early age; when she was three, polio deprived her of control over her right leg. As a result, she could walk only with great effort or with crutches; for much of her adult life she has used a wheelchair. Born in 1951, Finger got polio in 1954, at the very end of the epidemic—just months before a vaccine became available in the United States. She opens her memoir with a familiar episode—a "what happened to you?" scene—with a twist. When she is asked by a young boy who helps her load groceries into her car, "What happened to your leg?" and she replies, "I had polio," he asks a second question: "What's that?" (3). The book is motivated in part by her sense of having become a kind of living anachronism, a survivor of a bygone and largely forgotten plague. Hence her provocative title: *Elegy for a Disease.*[5] It's unconventional as well as counterintuitive to compose an elegy for a disease: the *American Heritage Dictionary*'s example of an appropriate subject for an elegy is "youthful ideals." Finger is not nostalgic for the epidemic; rather, her point is that, like conventional elegiac topoi, polio is in danger of becoming irrecoverably lost.

Finger intends the title to be ironic, of course, and she continues her narrative with a mock-indignant lament.

> Polio was as famous as AIDS. Those of us who had it were *figures.* We limped around under its metaphoric weight. Polio had such cachet that occasionally people lied and said they had it when they hadn't. Having "overcome" polio was something you could put on life's résumé. (3)

While never indulging in nostalgia for this phase of her polio, she later expands on the unusual, perhaps unique, valence of polio among twentieth-century disabilities.

> As a disabled girl I was allowed to have dreams and ambitions that were denied to nearly all other girls in the 1950s. . . . When you had polio it didn't matter if you were a boy or a girl: You were always being told about President Roosevelt. You were expected to be smart, to be accomplished, to make something of your life, maybe even grow up to be President. (169)

One of her points is that, since polio was eradicated in North America, its survivors are an aging population and easy to ignore; her mem-

---

5. Finger had published an earlier memoir, *Past Due: A Story of Disability, Pregnancy, and Birth.* For a discussion of that memoir, see Mintz, chapter 4.

oir is part of an effort to provide testimony from that dwindling cohort. But there's another irony to the early vignette; as later becomes
evident, polio is not "over" for Finger—or any of its survivors. Its initial effects still shape her daily life, and the onset of postpolio syndrome exacerbates those effects. So her memoir, though seemingly
oriented to a dim receding past, is firmly grounded in present and even
future concerns. It does not merely recover and record the experience
of her generation of polio survivors; it also attests to their continuing
presence in the world, to the ways they have benefitted from, and contributed to, progress on disability rights.

Of the memoirs discussed here, Finger's is the most confessional.
The backbone of the book is a chronological and highly detailed account of her life, carrying her from early childhood through polio and
rehabilitation into early adulthood, when she is briefly and unhappily
married, hospitalized for depression, divorced, and then has a son
with a new partner. Polio is not the only disability she experienced,
then. (For that matter, it was not so much her bout with the virus as
the subsequent therapies and surgeries that were punishing.) Her depression is actually more immobilizing. Nor was polio her only childhood trauma: although (according to an interview distributed with
complimentary copies) she was initially disinclined to divulge this, her
father was a frustrated, angry, depressed, alcoholic, and abusive man.
Among his five children (one son, four daughters), it was Anne who
bore the brunt of his physical abuse. She believes that she may have
been the target because her broken body was a daily reminder of a
kind of failure or disappointment. If this is so, her depression may
have been connected to her polio through the resulting abuse. This ex-
ploration, tentative as it is, of the complex interrelation of disease (polio), resulting physical disability, child abuse, and mental illness is unusual in memoir.

Intimate and detailed as is her account of her childhood, the book
is not *primarily* confessional. For one thing, while the engrossing narrative of her life serves as a unifying through-line, her experience of
the *virus* is one of the vaguest episodes in the narrative: she simply
doesn't remember it very clearly. She has a mental image of gowned
figures hovering around her and of being in a ward with others, but "of
what happened to my body, of that I have no memories" (55). Return-

ing as an adult to her childhood hometown, she scans the local news-paper, in vain, for some documentary evidence of her illness. But more important in shaping her book than the black hole of this key episode is her desire to place her *illness* (her experience of polio) in the context of the postwar polio epidemic and, indeed, the larger history of the *disease* of polio. Hence her subtitle, *A Personal and Cultural History of Polio.*

As it happens, a fine scholarly history of modern American polio, *Living with Polio: The Epidemic and Its Survivors,* by Daniel J. Wilson, was published the year before Finger's memoir. But Wilson does not preempt Finger; their accounts nicely complement one another. Not a professional historian, she does not attempt a comprehensive histori-cal analysis; rather, she seeks to understand her place in a larger popu-lation, and to illuminate what it meant to have polio in a particular place and time, using the tools of a memoirist: memory and literary skill. Her memoir is densely detailed in the manner of some fiction; in a sense, then, it is novelistic. And the degree of description of her per-sonal world may seem excessive to some readers. But as a member of her generation, I appreciate the skill and thoroughness with which she evokes period details of food, clothing, schooling, and speech. In any case, the personal narrative is only one thread in a rich weave. And what some might dismiss as "novelistic" also provides historical detail, a thick description of the world in which she existed and which shaped her. In any case, among the memoirs discussed here, hers alone is the product of considerable research; in that way, it is historical in method.

As a whole the book is quite miscellaneous—at times collagelike—because of its comprehensive attempt to supplement the personal with the collective. (On some level, of course, they are inseparable.) Thus, the book flashes back to the epidemic of 1916 and to earlier ones, even in antiquity; it includes a long excursus on "Sister Kenny," an Aus-tralian nurse associated with controversially aggressive "therapies," and much more. So the book embeds her story in a diachronic sam-pling of polio through the ages. It also opens up her story synchroni-cally to include her contemporaries. Like Wilson, she calls on other survivors for their testimony, whether it reinforces or conflicts with her own. This collective testimony comes in two forms; she quotes from other survivors' memoirs (e.g., Charles Mee's, Lorenzo Milam's), and she interviews other survivors and folds their oral testimony into her text. Thus, as is typical of the new disability memoir, this narrative avoids the trap of autobiographical solipsism by manifesting an identification with others who share her condition.

Like other new disability memoirists, Finger is willing to share her story only on her own terms. In her case, she supplies an explanation of her stance within the first ten pages of her book, in a brief chapter entitled "The Stories I'm Not Going to Tell."

> I'm not going to tell the story of the plucky little cripple stepping gamely forward on two crutches. . . .
>
> This won't be the elegiac story with its expected arc beginning with normalcy . . . then ascending into crisis . . . And then the hard-won ending, with its return to the empire of the normal . . . ; the final chapters of the narrative, when not just the body but the self has been chastened, and from that chastening, grown. . . . I do not want to give you just my story. . . . I also want to write about the social experience of disability. (7–8)

She recognizes, and wants to write against, the social and cultural isolation of disabled people, their being singled out and set aside. Her epidemic, she realizes, is privileged historically for contingent reasons: "The combination of expecting children to survive childhood, a mass media that could spread the word of an outbreak, and a medical system that was geared to surveillance of childhood illnesses 'created' epidemic polio" (46). (The fact that in the United States it struck children of the baby boom, born in a period of peace, prosperity, and optimism, also contributed to its stature—not to mention its association with the heroic FDR, although, as she notes, he may have been disabled by Guillain-Barré syndrome, not polio [126].)

Finger is also attentive to ways in which the cultural construction of diseases conditions individuals' lives and identities. For example, despite—or in contradistinction to—her sense of the privilege accorded to children with polio, she cites Daniel Wilson on the corrosive effect of polio on boys' sense of their masculinity and discusses Leonard

Kriegel as an example of a hypermasculine overcompensator (171–74). For people with polio there was a sharp downside to the prevailing belief that hard work would maximize recovery. It may have been simply wrong: aggressive physical therapy may have led to eventual muscle damage, some of which became apparent only long afterward. Indeed, she reveals that postpolio syndrome was not unknown but rather had been forgotten.

> We don't think of medical knowledge as simply being forgotten, as having been stuffed in closets and then lost. But that is what happened with awareness of what has now come to be known as postpolio syndrome. . . . Knowledge of postpolio syndrome disappeared because it no longer fitted with the story of the disease. (155–56)

Narratives of triumph over impairment through perseverance, then, were often doomed to be reversed. However misleading, the myth of overcoming shaped Finger's character: the cultural becomes the personal by internalization. She speculates at the very end of the memoir that even as her polio may have provoked her father to abuse her, it may have made her determined and resilient in a way that enabled her to survive it.

Finger's early awareness of being one of a large cohort of people with polio is not the same as identifying as disabled, which she came to do only as a mature adult. Thus, while her narrative is not organized as a story of coming out, her acknowledgment of being a member of an often oppressed minority is an important element in her book. She is candid in admitting that, despite being impaired while very young, she came late to disability consciousness. One of the obstacles was her sense of shame, which tended to diminish her sense of being unfairly discriminated against. And her shame led her to shun others with disabilities.

> I had a sense that my problem was a social one, not an individual one—but, having cut myself off from other disabled people, and knowing nothing of what those who had gone before me had experienced, I was unable to translate that vague sensibility into anything else. In short, I lacked both a history and a community. (236)

She laments the fact that she never had a sudden epiphany (and thus cannot write a conversion narrative): "I wish there had been a moment when, like Saul on the road to Damascus, the scales fell from my eyes and I saw the truth in a blinding light. My journey toward the disability-rights movement had few dramatic moments" (262).

Various forces combined to move her toward solidarity with disabled people; feminism, along with involvement in the Women Writers Union, prepared the way. The HIV/AIDS epidemic (she was living in the Bay Area in its early years) raised her awareness of how stigma was attributed to disease. But the climactic moment came when she attended a conference on postpolio syndrome: "I felt like an adoptee meeting her birth family for the first time at an enormous family reunion. Here I was surrounded by people who shared my personality quirks—my tough sense of humor, my drive, my big smile, my anger" (264). Clearly, she had adopted a disability identity before undertaking to research and write her memoir; but there's a sense in which the composing of her memoir, like others here, is not merely a retroactive statement but also a willful creation of the disability "history and community" that she once had lacked.

Of all the memoirists under consideration here, the only one with a congenital disability is Harriet McBryde Johnson, and it may be no accident that hers is the only memoir that takes disability identity and consciousness for granted. While both concepts take time and self-awareness to develop and mature—they are not innate—Johnson knew from a very early age that she was in a class apart. Born in 1957, she was literally in a class(room) apart in her first school years. In a throwaway line, she refers to having been "the biggest little dog in crip school and then . . . the culture-shocked lone crip in nondisabled high school and nearly lone crip in college" (20–21). Thus does she sum up her changing status as a disabled student before and during the disability rights movement. Rather than being organized as a narrative of coming out, then, *Too Late to Die Young* (2005) is composed of a series of discrete autobiographical episodes, as indicated by its subtitle, *Nearly True Tales from a Life*. (Sadly, Johnson died suddenly and unexpectedly in June 2008, at the age of fifty—if not young, far too soon.)

With a degree in public administration and a law degree, Johnson worked in Charleston as an attorney emphasizing disability issues, and she was involved in Democratic politics in South Carolina; on the side, she was an enthusiastic protestor of telethons. All but one of her tales come from her active adult life—her career—rather than her growing up. The tales are organized in chronological order, but they do not form a continuous, linear narrative; there is no overarching plot. And the episodes themselves are not firmly plotted.

In addition to her personal history of activism and advocacy, Johnson brings to the new subgenre a distinctive Southern voice, a sly sense of humor, and a love of, and talent for, storytelling—which she says in her prologue is a kind of currency she offers in partial payment for being driven places like to the state capital, Columbia. Johnson is the only one of these memoirists who required the use of personal assistants, and one of the other distinctive elements of her memoir is that it gives a matter-of-fact account of what it's like to live with that kind of help. The following snippet about a job candidate reveals both Johnson's sense of humor and the economy with which she can write about her life and the lives of others in her situation: "Her résumé gave no indications of any desire to serve humanity or help people and she had no hospital or nursing home experience. I thought she might be exactly what I was looking for" (21).

Not surprisingly, given her profession, Johnson's memoir focuses on advocacy more than the others'. "Hail to the Chief!" has to do with her protesting a visit by Ronald Reagan to her campus, the University of South Carolina—in two ways. First, Johnson objects to the Secret Service plan to search rooms and evacuate her dorm so the president can address a crowd in front of it. The disability angle here is that, despite needing a personal assistant to help with bathing and toileting, Johnson values her privacy intensely: "Even though I share my private space with a lot of people, it's still private" (41). Not only that, as a disabled young woman desiring to fulfill her ample potential, she had learned to insist on her rights in a way that her nondisabled contemporaries had not. So while she agreed to have her room swept by dogs and agents, she insisted on being there during the process.

The second element of her resistance was that she took advantage of her disability to smuggle protest signs past security to the wheelchair section in front, where she hoped to get them displayed on television. Here she compares herself to a Miltonic tragic hero.

> Once again, it seems I'm just a disabled person, inherently harmless, with my nice helper girl. No threat. It's a scene that had been acted throughout the centuries, at least since that big festival day when newly blind Samson, escorted by a nice helper boy, was directed to his special place, all the way in front, in the Temple at Gaza. (42–43)

In her chapter on going to the 1996 Democratic National Convention in Chicago as a South Carolina delegate ("Unconventional Acts"), the disability angle again has two elements. The first is the sense it gives of how, even six years after the passage of the ADA, accommodation and access were more often promised than delivered: "You never know what you'll get" (113). The onus is always on the disabled person to think ahead, plan ahead, and then be prepared for failures. She understands, nevertheless, that "the existence of rights—rights on paper— implies a duty to assert them" (113).

The second is her dismayed response to Christopher Reeve's speech, which predictably galvanizes the crowd. She finds herself regarding him as a "ventriloquist's dummy," not because of the stillness of his body but because of what she perceives as the inauthenticity of his views: "He's being used . . . This is a new role for him. He has no script" (119). A local activist gets her an appearance on local television, and she succinctly states her case: "He's still learning. He still wants to be cured, but for us it's more important to live our lives, the way we are. He doesn't speak for us" (122). Partly because his disability was so severe and suddenly acquired in midlife, he was on one side of the impairment/ disability divide; like so many with congenital disabilities, Johnson was on the other. She had no pre-disabled life to be nostalgic for, and she accepted that her condition was incurable. (Significantly, her only expression of nostalgia has to do with "the crip world of my childhood . . . a place where I felt at home and valued; leaving it was a wrench" [75].)

I said in the previous chapter that surprisingly few disability memoirs refer directly to disability legislation. As is evident by now, this is not true of the new disability memoir. Not surprisingly, given her legal specialty, Johnson's is no exception. In fact, one of its tales, "Trial and Error," concerns her arguing a case under the ADA. This gives her an opportunity to enlighten a broader audience of readers about the nature of the act and why it should be interpreted as applying to people who can work (and who thus may not seem "disabled").

> Many people—regular working people—have disabilities but don't become disabled so long as their disabilities are accommodated. . . . When I . . . called myself disabled, was I saying I'm unable to work? Of course not. Was I giving up my rights to fair treatment under the ADA? I hope not. (147–48)

For me the best chapters come at the beginning and end of the book. The first chapter, "Too Late to Die Young," focuses on the expectation she formed when very young that she would never grow up. As she grew older and older, defying her own expectations, she realized that this sense of her own mortality was shaped by telethons; for her this is one of the subtle ways in which they damage children with congenital disabilities.

> I reconsider my childhood death sentence and decide I have been the victim of a fraud. . . . I have never been terminally ill the way I was led to believe. I study the telethon and try to understand its peculiar power. It spews out the same old messages—"killer disease," "life ebbing away," "before it's too late." As I hear the death sentence being pronounced on another generation of children, I wonder how many have actually been killed by the predictions. . . . Worst of all, how many have lived and died without learning to value their own lives? (13)

As a critic of disability life writing, I particularly value that which responds creatively and preemptively to some of the prejudicial conventions of disability representation. Johnson begins her book by describing herself in deliberately unflattering ways, thus thrusting herself in the reader's face, figuratively speaking: "I'm Karen Carpenter–thin, flesh mostly vanished, a jumble of bones in a floppy bag of skin." But the focus of this preface is really on the viewer: "I have come to expect it. The glassy smile. The concerned gaze. The double take . . . when I show up someplace where someone like me is not expected" (1). Similarly, she offers a brief catalog of the insulting verbal responses she can evoke, such as "I'll pray for you" and "If I had to live like you, . . . I'd kill myself" (2). What she does through this self-exposure (verbal rather than visual, virtual rather than actual) is negotiate the terms of her autobiographical pact, so to speak. Even as she presents her body for inspection, she scrutinizes the standard reactions to that body. This is not only about what her body "signifies" to others but about what their response reveals about them and their assumptions.

Like the other memoirists discussed in this chapter, Johnson scorns the usual generic formulas.

> The world wants our lives to fit into a few rigid narrative templates: how I conquered disability (and others can conquer their Bad Things!), how I adjusted to disability (and a positive attitude can move mountains!), how disability made me wise (you can only marvel and hope it never happens to you!), how disability brought me to Jesus (but redemption is waiting for you if only you pray). (2–3)

As she ends her preface, she acknowledges the special risk of self-revelation in print, no matter how carefully gauged: "Despite my fine talk, I am offering parts of me and of my life as objects for sale and consumption. As much as I resist, those dominant narrative templates may be imposed from without. . . . In this medium I can't adjust the tale as I go along, based on individual reactions" (5). Despite this danger, she concludes with the hope that "what follows will expand perspectives. . . . If so, I will count it as an adventure worth the undertaking" (5).

As it happens, her burgeoning career as a writer leads to an episode that returns her (and her memoir) to the theme of disability representation. When the *New York Times Magazine* picks up her account of meeting and debating Peter Singer, the Princeton philosopher, on the subject of killing disabled infants (first published in *New Mobility*), the editors decide it warrants lavish photographic illustration. Her account of the process of negotiating self-exposure in this medium provides one of the book's most rewarding chapters, "An Art Object." Briefly, the struggle is between photographers and editors who want more (and more invasive) exposure of her—in her home, in her bath, and in the nude—and Johnson, who prefers to be photographed at work or in public. There are two significant factors on the side of the editors. First, the fee she is to be paid for the story is, by her modest standards, a windfall. Second, the photos, taken by a New York portrait photographer, are very flattering—including those she permits to be taken of her unclothed body.

Johnson is not opposed to having powerful and aesthetically pleasing photos illustrate her essay, and she is intrigued by the fact that her body can be presented as beautiful, the "art object" of the title. Rather, the crux of the disagreement seems to be what counts as "powerful." The editors' view is that she looks frail in her chair, powerful out of it. She vehemently disagrees: "They are nuts if they think I look more 'powerful' in bed, when in fact I need my chair to do anything or go anywhere on my own. I do happen to be 'frail,' in or out of my chair" (245). To Johnson, her chair is the site and source of her power. And, as a disability rights lawyer, she is able to advocate for herself. The photographer tells her she is the most difficult subject she has ever worked with (246), and in the end Johnson gets her way; she feels the pictures are consistent with the thrust of her story (247). However, the subtext of this tale may be that, if a self-described prima donna has to exert so much energy to control her own representation in a presumably enlightened medium, ordinary disabled citizens have much to fear.

The book's final chapter, "Good Morning—An Ending," picks up themes of the preface. Having just shown herself protecting her privacy (she refuses to be photographed inside her home), Johnson now seems to let down her guard and admit her readers to her private life; for the first time she mentions her love life, offering a tantalizing glimpse of what seems to be a nascent love affair with an unnamed Valentine. She remains very circumspect, however, and the point is not to gratify her readers' curiosity about her sex life but to demonstrate that her life is not, as they may assume, one of unremitting physical suffering. So she enumerates some of her sources of gratification: "social engagement of all kinds: swapping stories, arguing hard, getting and giving a listening ear. A challenging professional life. Going to movies, concerts, and exhibits. Wearing a new pair of earrings. Savoring the afternoon hit of Dove dark chocolate" (253–54). In addition to these gratifications, shared with nondisabled people, she offers a list of pleasures uniquely enjoyed by disabled people. Her personal example is the luxury of being bathed by someone else. Thus, she concludes by attesting that her life is rich in many kinds of pleasure, including sensual pleasure.

While the other memoirists under consideration here were disabled either from birth (Johnson) or from childhood (Finger, Kuusisto, Kleege), Simi Linton was paralyzed in early adulthood in a highway accident (significantly, while en route to an antiwar demonstration in Washington, D.C., in 1971). Although her memoir, *My Body Politic,* proceeds in roughly chronological order, it is not a full life narrative; it does not begin with her birth but rather with the accident, which claimed the life of her husband and her best friend, leaving her bereaved as well as paralyzed. Rather than reviewing her whole life, then, Linton devotes nearly her entire memoir to her life after her accident. While later chapters fill in salient parts of the backstory—her pre-paraplegic life—the omission of a progressive narrative of that earlier life militates against the rhetoric of nostalgia. Moreover, this structure replaces her birth and development as a unique *individual* with her birth and development as a *disabled* person; her memoir becomes a kind of disability bildungsroman. Like the other memoirists, she shapes her "life" in conscious deviation from dominant narrative and rhetorical models.

Another sign of her self-consciousness about disability narrative is that Linton deliberately avoids equating impairment with disability. She uses the term *disabled,* then, not as synonymous with *impaired* (and not as synonymous with *disadvantaged*) but to signify a positive identity that puts her in solidarity with a large category (if not a "community") of people whose lives are shaped primarily by social and cultural restrictions on them. This is *her* body politic.

The new shape and formation of my body were set on that April day; the meaning this new body would have for me took years to know.

For it wasn't until some time after I sustained the injury to my spine that immobilized my legs, after I learned to use a wheelchair, and after I had reckoned with myself and the world for a while in this new state—it wasn't until then that I gained the vantage point of the atypical, the out-of-step, the underfooted. . . . The injury was a sudden cataclysmic event, and the paralysis in my legs was instant. Becoming disabled took much longer. (3)

So one thread in the memoir is devoted to narrating (and explaining) how, after suddenly becoming severely impaired, she slowly became disabled. A key episode in this sequence is devoted to a summer she spent in Berkeley, California, after she had completed her rehab and was beginning to resume a more active life. Berkeley was a revelation to her because, in 1975, it was so far advanced (compared to New York, where she had been living) in things like the provision of curb cuts, so crucial to mobility for wheelchair users. With no further rehab or improvement in her ability to control her lower body, Linton found herself significantly less disadvantaged on the West Coast than on the East. As a result, she began to identify with a distinct interest group, whose concentrated presence in the Berkeley area had forced the community to accommodate it. Although she went there with the intention of taking courses, she dropped out early; as she tells it, her Berkeley education was entirely extracurricular, and it had everything to do with the radical politics for which Berkeley had become famous, or notorious. Gradually, she began to see the connection between the politics of the antiwar protest that she never got to and the developing politics of the nascent disability rights movement, her body politics.

Like Johnson, Linton permits a moderate degree of intimacy in her memoir. While she avoids dwelling on her physical condition, she does briefly describe the nature and extent of her sensation in the paralyzed part of her body (7–8). Similarly, she gives a matter-of-fact account of how she transfers from her wheelchair to any other seat (19). Unlike the others, she does discuss how her impairment affects her sex life. But the impulse here is more didactic and demystifying than confessional: she is at pains to establish that her paralysis changed but did not end her sex life (25). In any case, she gets all this out of the way early on; as with the other new disability memoirs, her focus is largely on the interface between her newly impaired body and the context in which it dwells.

It is only when she is disadvantaged by her impairment that she understands how privileged she had been previously—and how a whole category of people, once largely invisible to her, had been denied access to supposedly public institutions and spaces. Thus, a good deal of her memoir is about negotiating life with minimal restrictions. Returning to New York from Berkeley and enrolling at Columbia, she is much more aware of how the design and structure of the campus limit her movement. Grand outdoor stairs that she once would have admired for their monumentality she now views as impediments from the vantage of her wheelchair (56–57). She asserts, or claims, her rights, and the authorities seem to pay attention, but little changes; she realizes later that their receptiveness—such as it was—probably resulted from new legislation (the Rehabilitation Act, section 504). Aided by her sense of the parallels between discrimination against women and that against people with disabilities, she begins to develop a disability consciousness, though still pretty much in isolation.

For Linton, unlike Kuusisto and Kleege, passing was not an option; her impairment was too visible. There is no closet for her, so her memoir is not cast as a coming-out narrative. Still, when first injured, she tended to distance herself from disabled people generally, whom her culture characterized as unfortunates. So it takes her a while to identify herself as disabled. But in the end, her book is probably the most political of those discussed here. Her growing sense of being part of a collective determined her title. The accident to her particular body endowed her, eventually, with a distinctive politics because she came to understand how it threatened to place her, along with myriad diverse others, on the margin of what is usually understood as the "body politic."

A whole chapter, then, is devoted to her adoption of a motorized chair, which she names Rufus (after the sort of city dog that loves to go for walks). Like moving from using a white cane to using to a guide dog, this move is fraught. While it promises greater mobility, ironically it seems to signify a greater degree of dependency (read: helplessness). As it happens, of course, Rufus is a boon, and Linton regrets not having adopted a motorized chair sooner. To illustrate Rufus's empowerment of her, she offers a matter-of-fact account of how she gets around her hometown, New York, with the help of kneeling buses (178). Late in the book, after earning a doctorate in psychology and entering, tentatively at first, the new field of disability studies, she engages in open advocacy. Here she adopts the first-person plural, but its referent is not her distinct community of disabled people but the entire citizenry, who stand to benefit from maximal inclusion, universal design, especially in education.

> Let's erase the line between disabled and nondisabled children, drawn at a very early age, imprinting each group with indelible ink. Let's identify the supports and accommodations that every child needs, rather than catalog the "special" kids' deficits and incapacities. (162)

And she comes out strongly against legalizing physician-assisted suicide.

Indeed, Linton ends her memoir not on a personal note (how far I've come!) but rather with a sober, balanced assessment of the historical moment, which she sees as characterized by, on one hand, a good deal of progress since the moment of her entry into the category of the disabled (her first chapter is entitled "Conscripts to the Cavalry") and, on the other, the dangers of complacency. Her very final note is in fact cautionary, if not pessimistic.

> I fear that in the present century, the disability-line could wreak more havoc. It could increasingly determine who, based on their outward appearance or functioning and, significantly, on their genetic makeup, gets to do what, and under what circumstances. (245)

This sharp sense of historicity is also a feature of the new disability memoir. Throughout, there is a new (usually retroactive) understanding of how the lives of disabled people have changed, and are changing, because of their own activism and agency. This is not merely the memoir of a disability educator and advocate, then; it is a memoir that *performs* advocacy and education, in a markedly explicit way.

As much as I like all of these memoirs and want to regard them as the beginning of a new wave of disability life writing, I have to acknowledge that their authors, and the scenarios the memoirs depict, are hardly representative of the population of disabled Americans. Like most first-person narratives of disability, these memoirs issue from positions of considerable class and race privilege: all of the authors are white, and they are not merely gainfully employed (unlike so many disabled Americans) but working as professionals (teachers, lawyers, advocates, and writers). Jobs in professions are typically easier to manage for individuals with disabilities than most other kinds of employment. So the demographic traits of this small sample of new disability memoirists are quite different from those of the disabled population as a whole, which is disproportionately elderly and poor.

But of course part of what these individuals have discovered as disabled people is that their other statuses (of race, ethnicity, and class) carry them only so far; in some ways, disability trumps these other privileges. For them, the disadvantage of disability is so at odds with inborn advantages that their disability has sensitized them to other causes of marginalization. So to acknowledge their relative privilege is not to discount their authority to write from a position of disability. And while we can acknowledge that their class standing is a great help in getting their stories published and read, it should not detract from their memoirs' value. For all of them demonstrate qualities and features that have been slow to be fully expressed in disability life writing: a proud sense of disability identity, a sharp sense of disability history, and a sophisticated sense of the poetics and politics, the ethics and aesthetics, of disability memoir. For these, we should be grateful.

Works Cited

Adams, Lorraine. "Almost Famous: The Rise of the 'Nobody' Memoir." *Washington Monthly,* Apr. 2002. Accessed online at http://www.washingtonmonthly.com/features/2001/0204.adams.html on 24 Oct. 2008.

Ainslee, Ricardo. *The Psychology of Twinship.* Lincoln: University of Nebraska Press, 1985.

Aleshire, Joan. "Eye of the Beholder." In *Voices from the Edge: Narratives about the Americans with Disabilities Act,* ed. Ruth O'Brien, 29–39. New York: Oxford University Press, 2004.

Als, Hilton. "We Two Made One." *New Yorker,* 4 Dec. 2000: 72–78, 80–83.

Americans with Disabilities Act of 1990. Accessed online at www.ada.gov/pubs/ada.htm on 27 Sept. 2008.

Angier, Natalie. "Joined for Life, and Living to the Full." *New York Times,* 23 Dec. 1997: B15.

B., David. *Epileptic.* New York: Pantheon, 2005.

Bacon, Francis. "Of Deformity." In *The Essayes or Counsels, Civill and Morall,* ed. Michael Kiernan, 133–34. Cambridge: Harvard University Press, 1985.

Baggs, A. M. "In My Language." Video. Accessed online at http://www.youtube.com/watch?v=JnylM1hI2jc on 22 Oct. 2008.

Bauby, Jean-Dominique. *The Diving Bell and the Butterfly.* Trans. Jeremy Leggatt. New York: Knopf, 1997.

Bayley, John. *Elegy for Iris.* New York: St. Martin's, 1999.

Beauchamp, Tom L., and James F. Childress. *Principles of Biomedical Ethics.* 5th ed. New York: Oxford University Press, 2001.

Beverley, John. "The Margin at the Center: On *Testimonio* (Testimonial Narrative)." In *De/Colonizing the Subject: The Politics of Gender in Women's Autobiography,* ed. Sidonie Smith and Julia Watson, 91–114. Minneapolis: University of Minnesota Press, 1992.

Brookes, Timothy. *Catching My Breath: An Asthmatic Explores His Illness.* New York: Vintage, 1995.

Brown, Claude. *Manchild in the Promised Land.* New York: Macmillan, 1965.

Callahan, John. *Don't Worry, He Won't Get Far on Foot.* New York: Random House, 1989.

Canby, Vincent. "Bob Hope, Master of One-liners and Friend to G.I.'s, Dies at

100." *New York Times*, 29 July 2003. Accessed online at http://nytimes.com/ 2003/07/29/obituaries/29HOPE.html?pagewanted=1 on 11 December 2003.

Charlton, James I. *Nothing About Us Without Us: Disability Oppression and Empowerment*. Berkeley: University of California Press, 1998.

Cheney, Terri. *Manic: A Memoir*. New York: William Morrow, 2008.

Clare, Anthony. "Discord in Unison." Review of *The Silent Twins*, by Marjorie Wallace. *Times Literary Supplement*, 28 Feb. 1986: 212.

Clark, David L., and Catherine Myser. "Being Humaned: Medical Documentaries and the Hyperrealization of Conjoined Twins." In *Freakery: Cultural Spectacles of the Extraordinary Bodies*, ed. Rosemarie Garland-Thomson, 338–55. New York: New York University Press, 1996.

Cleaver, Eldridge. *Soul on Ice*. New York: Delta, 1968.

Clifford, James. *The Predicament of Culture: Twentieth-century Ethnography, Literature, and Art*. Cambridge: Harvard University Press, 1988.

Clifford, James, and G. E. Marcus, eds. *Writing Culture: The Poetics and Politics of Ethnography*. Berkeley: University of California Press, 1986.

Clinton, Hillary Rodham. *Living History*. New York: Simon and Schuster, 2003.

Cohen, Elizabeth. *The House on Beartown Road: A Memoir of Learning and Forgetting*. New York: Random House, 2003.

Conjoined Twins. BBC. BBC2, London. 19 October 2000. Accessed online at http://www.bbc.co.uk/science/Horizon/2000/conjoined_twins_transcript .shtml on 16 Aug. 2003.

Couser, G. Thomas. *Recovering Bodies: Illness, Disability, and Life Writing*. Madison: University of Wisconsin Press, 1997.

Couser, G. Thomas. *Vulnerable Subjects: Ethics and Life Writing*. Ithaca: Cornell University Press, 2004.

Daniels, A. M. "Sick Notes." Review of *Recovering Bodies*. *Times Literary Supplement*, 24 Apr. 1998: 31.

Davis, Angela. *Angela Davis: An Autobiography*. New York: Random House, 1974.

Davis, Lennard J. "Crips Strike Back: The Rise of Disability Studies." In *Bending over Backwards: Disability, Dismodernism, and Other Difficult Positions*, 33–46. New York: New York University Press, 2002.

Davis, Lennard J. *Enforcing Normalcy: Disability, Deafness, and the Body*. London: Verso, 1995.

Davis, Lennard J., ed. Introduction. In *The Disability Studies Reader*, ed. Lennard J. Davis, 1–6. New York: Routledge, 1997.

Davis, Lennard J. "The Rule of Normalcy: Politics and Disability in the U.S.A. (United States of Ability)." In *Bending over Backwards: Disability, Dismodernism, and Other Difficult Positions*, 102–18. New York: New York University Press, 2002.

Davison, Al. *The Spiral Cage*. Los Angeles: Active Images, 2003.

DeBaggio, Thomas. *Losing My Mind*. New York: Touchstone, 2003.

Diller, Matthew. "Judicial Backlash, the ADA, and the Civil Rights Model of Disability." In *Backlash against the ADA: Reinterpreting Disability Rights*, ed. Linda Hamilton Krieger, 62–97. Ann Arbor: University of Michigan Press, 2003.

The Diving Bell and the Butterfly. Dir. Julian Schnabel. In French. Miramax, 2007.

Dubus, Andre. *Meditations from a Movable Chair.* New York: Knopf, 1998.

Eadie, Mervyn J., and Peter F. Bladin. *A Disease Once Sacred: A History of the Medical Understanding of Epilepsy.* Eastleigh, England: John Libbey, 2001.

Eakin, Paul John. "Relational Selves, Relational Lives: The Story of the Story." In *True Relations: Essays on Autobiography and the Postmodern,* ed. G. Thomas Couser and Joseph Fichtelberg, 63–81. Westport: Greenwood, 1998.

Egan, Susanna. *Mirror Talk: Genres of Crisis in Contemporary Autobiography.* Chapel Hill: University of North Carolina Press, 1999.

Ells, Carolyn. "Lessons about Autonomy from the Experience of Disability." *Social Theory* 27, no. 4 (October 2001): 599–615.

Face to Face: The Schappell Twins. Dir. Ellen Weissbrod. A&E, 2000.

Feinberg, Joel. *The Moral Limits of the Criminal Law.* Vol. 1, *Harm to Others.* New York: Oxford University Press, 1984.

Finger, Anne. *Elegy for a Disease: A Personal and Cultural History of Polio.* New York: St. Martin's, 2006.

Finger, Anne. *Past Due: A Story of Disability, Pregnancy, and Birth.* Seattle: Seal Press, 1990.

Fox, Michael J. *Lucky Man: A Memoir.* New York: Hyperion, 2002.

Frank, Arthur W. *The Wounded Storyteller: Body, Illness, and Ethics.* Chicago: University of Chicago Press, 1995.

Frank, Gelya. *Venus on Wheels: Two Decades of Dialogue on Disability, Biography, and Being Female in America.* Berkeley: University of California Press, 2000.

Frankel, Max. "News of a Lifetime." *New York Times Magazine,* 11 June 1995: 28.

Frey, James. *A Million Little Pieces.* New York: Doubleday, 2003.

Fries, Kenny. *Body, Remember: A Memoir.* New York: Dutton, 1997.

Galli, Richard. *Rescuing Jeffrey.* Chapel Hill: Algonquin, 2000.

Garland-Thomson, Rosemarie. "Ways of Staring." *Journal of Visual Culture* 5, no. 2 (2006): 173–92.

Gibaldi, Joseph. *The MLA Style Manual and Guide to Scholarly Publishing.* 2d ed. New York: Modern Language Association, 1988.

Goffman, Erving. *Asylums: Essays on the Social Situation of Mental Patients and Other Inmates.* Chicago: Aldine, 1961.

Goffman, Erving. *Stigma: Notes on the Management of Spoiled Identity.* Englewood Cliffs: Prentice-Hall, 1963.

Goffman, Erving. "The Underlife of a Public Institution: A Study of Ways of Making Out in a Mental Hospital." In *Asylums: Essays on the Social Situation of Mental Patients and Other Inmates,* 171–320. Chicago: Aldine, 1961.

Goleman, Daniel. "'Sweetness the World Would Not Believe.'" *New York Times Book Review,* 19 Oct. 1986: 3.

Gould, Stephen Jay. "Living with Connections." *Natural History* (Oct. 1982): 18, 20, 22.

Grealy, Lucy. *Autobiography of a Face.* Boston: Houghton Mifflin, 1994.

Grealy, Suellen. "Hijacked by Grief." *The Guardian,* 7 Aug. 2004. Accessed online at http://www.guardian.co.uk/books/aug/07/biography. Feature on 23 Mar. 2009.

Gregory, Julie. *Sickened: The Memoir of a Munchausen by Proxy Childhood.* New York: Bantam, 2003.

Handler, Lowell. *Twitch and Shout.* New York: Dutton, 1998.

Hefferman, Virginia. "The Many Tribes of YouTube." *New York Times,* 27 May 2007. http://www.nytimes.com/2007/05/27/arts/television/27heff.html. Accessed on 21 Mar. 2009.

Hornbacher, Marya. *Wasted: A Memoir of Anorexia and Bulimia.* New York: Little, Brown, 1998.

Howells, William Dean. "Autobiography, A New Form of Literature." *Harper's Monthly* 119 (1909): 795–98.

Hume, Janice. *Obituaries in American Culture.* Jackson: University Press of Mississippi, 2000.

Hurston, Zora Neale. *Dust Tracks on a Road: An Autobiography.* Philadelphia: J. B. Lippincott, 1942.

Jezer, Marty. *Stuttering: A Life Bound Up in Words.* New York: Basic, 1997.

Johnson, Harriet McBryde. *Too Late to Die Young: Nearly True Tales from a Life.* New York: Holt, 2005.

Johnson, Kirk. "Fred Sandback, Sculptor of Minimalist Installations, Dies at 59." *New York Times,* 26 June 2003. Accessed online at http://www.nytimes.com/2003/06/26/0 . . . / 26SAND.html on 11 Dec. 2003.

Jones, Margaret B. *Love and Consequences: A Memoir of Hope and Survival.* New York: Riverhood, 2008.

Juska, Jane. *A Round-Heeled Woman: My Late Life Adventures in Sex and Romance.* New York: Villard, 2003.

Karasik, Paul, and Judy Karasik. *The Ride Together: A Brother and Sister's Memoir of Autism in the Family.* New York: Washington Square, 2003.

Kaysen, Susanna. *Girl, Interrupted.* New York: Turtle Bay Books, 1993.

Keith, Lois, ed. *"What Happened to You?": Writing by Disabled Women.* New York: New Press, 1996.

King Gimp. Dir. Susan Hannah Hadary and William A. Whiteford. Tapestry International, 1999.

Kingsley, Jason, and Mitchell Levitz. *Count Us In: Growing Up with Down Syndrome.* New York: Harcourt, 1994.

Kingston, Maxine Hong. *The Woman Warrior: Memoirs of a Girlhood among Ghosts.* New York: Knopf, 1976.

Kisor, Henry. *What's That Pig Outdoors? A Memoir of Deafness.* New York: Hill and Wang, 1990.

Kleege, Georgina. *Sight Unseen.* New Haven: Yale University Press, 1999.

Kolata, Gina. "Still Counting on Calorie Counting." *New York Times on the Web,* 29 Apr. 2005. Accessed online at http://www.nytimes.com/gst/health/article-page.html?res=9804EEDB1131F93AA15757C0A9639C8B63 on 7 May 2005.

Krieger, Linda Hamilton, ed. *Backlash against the ADA: Reinterpreting Disability Rights.* Ann Arbor: University of Michigan Press, 2003.

Krieger, Linda Hamilton. Introduction. In *Backlash against the ADA: Reinterpreting Disability Rights,* 1–25. Ann Arbor: University of Michigan Press, 2003.

Krieger, Linda Hamilton. "Sociolegal Backlash." In *Backlash against the ADA: Reinterpreting Disability Rights,* 340–93. Ann Arbor: University of Michigan Press, 2003.

Kuusisto, Stephen. *Eavesdropping: A Memoir of Blindness and Listening*. New York: Norton, 2006.

Kuusisto, Stephen. *Planet of the Blind*. New York: Dial, 1997.

Lakoff, George, and Mark Johnson. *Metaphors We Live By*. Chicago: University of Chicago Press, 1980.

Lane, Harlan. *The Mask of Benevolence: Bio-power and the Deaf Community*. New York: Knopf, 1992.

Lehmann-Haupt, Christopher. "Lucy Grealy, 39, Who Wrote a Memoir on Her Disfigurement." *New York Times*, 21 December 2002: B7.

Lejeune, Philippe. "The Autobiographical Pact." In *On Autobiography*, ed. Paul John Eakin, trans. Katherine Leary, 3–30. Minneapolis: University of Minnesota Press, 1988.

Lewis, Tyler. "Senate Passes the ADA Amendments Act." Civilrights.org. 11 Sept. 2008. Accessed online at http://www.civilrights.org/library/features/024-senate-adaaa.html on 18 Sept. 2008.

Linton, Simi. *My Body Politic*. Ann Arbor: University of Michigan Press, 2005.

The Lion King. Dir. Roger Allers and Rob Minkoff. Disney, 1994.

Lionnet, Françoise. *Autobiographical Voices: Race, Gender, Self-portraiture*. Ithaca: Cornell University Press, 1989.

Little, Jan. *If It Weren't for the Honor—I'd Rather Have Walked: Previously Untold Tales of the Journey to the ADA*. Cambridge: Brookline Books, 1996.

Mairs, Nancy. *Waist-High in the World: A Life Among the Nondisabled*. Boston: Beacon, 1996.

Malcolm X. *The Autobiography of Malcolm X*. With Alex Haley. New York: Grove, 1965.

Mason, Mary Grimley. *Working Against Odds: Stories of Disabled Women's Work Lives*. Boston: Northeastern University Press, 2004.

McCrum, Robert. *My Year Off*. New York: Norton, 1998.

McGowin, Diane Friel. *Living in the Labyrinth*. New York: Delacorte, 1993.

McLean, Teresa. *Seized: My Life with Epilepsy*. London: Richard Cohen, 1996.

Michalko, Rod. *The Two in One: Walking with Smokie, Walking with Blindness*. Philadelphia: Temple University Press, 1999.

Miller, Sue. *The Story of My Father: A Memoir*. New York: Knopf, 2003.

Million Dollar Baby. Dir. Clint Eastwood. Warner Brothers, 2004.

Mintz, Susannah B. *Unruly Bodies: Life Writing by Women with Disabilities*. Chapel Hill: University of North Carolina Press, 2007.

Mitchell, David T., and Sharon L. Snyder. *Narrative Prosthesis: Disability and the Dependencies of Discourse*. Ann Arbor: University of Michigan Press, 2000.

Monette, Paul. *Becoming a Man: Half a Life Story*. Boston: Houghton Mifflin, 1992.

Montaigne, Michel de. "On a Monster-child." In *The Essays of Michel de Montaigne*, trans. and ed. M. A. Screech, 807–8. London: Allen Lane, 1991.

Moore, Judith. *Fat Girl: A True Story*. New York: Hudson Street, 2005.

Murphy, Robert. *The Body Silent*. New York: Holt, 1987.

Myser, Catherine, and David L. Clark. "Fixing Katie and Eilish: Medical Documentaries and the Subjection of Conjoined Twins." *Literature and Medicine* 17, no. 1 (1998): 45–67.

O'Brien, Ruth. *Bodies in Revolt: Gender, Disability, and a Workplace Ethic of Care.* New York: Routledge, 2005.

O'Brien, Ruth, ed. *Voices from the Edge: Narratives about the Americans with Disabilities Act.* New York: Oxford University Press, 2004.

"Outpouring of Grief as Twins Die." CNN.com. 7 July 2003. Accessed online at http://www.cnn.com/2003/HEALTH/07/08/conjoined.twins/ on 16 Aug. 2003.

Park, Alice. "Does Justice Roberts Have Epilepsy?" *Time,* 31 July 2007. Accessed online at http://www.time.com/time/nation/article/0,8599,1648384,00.html on 14 Jan. 2008.

Park, Clara Claiborne. *The Siege: The First Eight Years of an Autistic Child.* Rev. ed. Boston: Little, Brown, 1982.

Patchett, Ann. "The Face of Pain." *New York,* March 2003: 30–37.

Patchett, Ann. *Truth and Beauty: A Friendship.* New York: HarperCollins, 2004.

Paterson, Heather. "Separated Conjoined Twins Going Home." AP. Accessed online at http://www.salon.com/mwt/wire/2001/11/16/ twins/index.html on 16 Nov. 2001.

Plummer, Ken. *Telling Sexual Stories: Power, Change, and Social Worlds.* New York: Routledge, 1995.

Pratt, Mary Louise. *Imperial Eyes: Travel Writing and Transculturation.* London: Routledge, 1992.

Price, Reynolds. *A Whole New Life: An Illness and a Healing.* New York: Atheneum, 1994.

Queller, Jessica. *Pretty Is What Changes: Impossible Choices, The Breast Cancer Gene, and How I Defied My Destiny.* New York: Spiegel and Grau, 2008.

Reed-Danahay, Deborah E. Introduction. In *Auto/ethnography: Rewriting the Self and the Social,* ed. Deborah Reed-Danahay, 1–17. New York: Berg, 1997.

Riding the Bus with My Sister. Dir. Anjelica Huston. Hallmark Hall of Fame, 2005.

Roach, Mary. "Exiles of Molokai." Review of John Tayman, *The Colony. New York Times Book Review,* 22 Jan. 2006: 12.

Robillard, Albert B. *Meaning of a Disability.* Philadelphia: Temple University Press, 1999.

Robinson, Jill. *Past Forgetting: My Memory Lost and Found.* New York: HarperCollins, 1999.

Rollins, Betty. *First, You Cry.* Philadelphia: J. B. Lippincott, 1976.

Roney, Lisa. *Sweet Invisible Body.* New York: Holt, 1999.

Rothenberg, Laura. *Breathing for a Living.* New York: Dimensions, 2003.

Sacks, Oliver. *An Anthropologist on Mars: Seven Paradoxical Tales.* New York: Knopf, 1995.

Sacks, Oliver. *A Leg to Stand On.* New York: Summit Books, 1984.

Sacks, Oliver. *The Man Who Mistook His Wife for a Hat, and Other Clinical Tales.* New York: Summit, 1985.

Sacks, Oliver. *Migraine: Understanding a Common Disorder.* Berkeley: University of California Press, 1985.

Sacks, Oliver. *Seeing Voices: A Journey into the World of the Deaf.* Berkeley: University of California Press, 1989.

Sandbank, Audrey C. "Personality, Identity, and Family Relationships." In Sandbank, ed., *Twin and Triplet Psychology: A Professional Guide to Working with Multiples,* 167–85. London: Routledge, 1999.

Sarton, May. *After the Stroke: A Journal.* New York: Norton, 1988.

Scarface. Dir. Brian DiPalma. Universal, 1983.

Scarface. Dir. Howard Hawks. Caddo, 1932.

Schaffer, Kay, and Sidonie Smith. *Human Rights and Narrated Lives: The Ethics of Recognition.* New York: Palgrave Macmillan, 2004.

Schneider, Joseph W., and Peter Conrad. *Having Epilepsy: The Experience and Control of Illness.* Philadelphia: Temple University Press, 1983.

Schwartz, Hillel. *The Culture of the Copy: Striking Likenesses, Unreasonable Facsimiles.* New York: Zone Books, 1996.

The Sea Inside. Dir. Alejandro Amenabar. New Line, 2004.

Segal, Nancy L. *Entwined Lives: Twins and What They Tell Us about Human Behavior.* New York: Dutton, 1999.

Seligson, Susan. *Stacked: A 32DDD Reports from the Front.* New York: Bloomsbury, 2007.

Shakespeare, Tom. *Disability Rights and Wrongs.* London: Routledge, 2006.

Shapiro, Harriet, and Dianna Wagonner. "A British Journalist Unravels the Tale of the Twins Who Wouldn't Talk." *People,* 27 October 1986: 61ff.

Showalter, Elaine. "Way to Go: On Why Obituaries Are a Business in the U.S. and Art in the U.K." *Guardian,* Saturday Review section, 2 Sept. 2000: 7.

Sienkiewicz-Mercer, Ruth, and Steven B. Kaplan. *I Raise My Eyes to Say Yes.* Boston: Houghton Mifflin, 1989.

The Silent Twin—Without My Shadow. Dir. Olivia Lichtenstein. BBC, 1994.

The Silent Twins. Dir. Jon Amiel. Written by Marjorie Wallace. BBC, 1985.

Simon, Rachel. *Riding the Bus with My Sister: A True Life Journey.* New York: Plume, 2003.

Skloot, Floyd. *The Night-Side: Chronic Fatigue Syndrome and the Illness Experience.* Brownsville: Story Line, 1996.

Slater, Lauren. *Love Works Like This: Moving from One Kind of a Life to Another.* New York: Random House, 2002.

Slater, Lauren. *Lying: A Metaphorical Memoir.* New York: Random House, 2000.

Slater, Lauren. *Prozac Diary.* New York: Random House, 1998.

Slater, Lauren. *Welcome to My Country.* New York: Random House, 1996.

Smith, Sidonie, and Julia Watson. *Reading Autobiography: A Guide to Interpreting Life Narratives.* Minneapolis: University of Minnesota Press, 2001.

Spiegelman, Art. *Maus I: A Survivor's Tale: My Father Bleeds History.* New York: Pantheon, 1986.

Spiegelman, Art. *Maus II: A Survivor's Tale: And Here My Troubles Began.* New York: Pantheon, 1991.

"Strom Thurmond Finally, Finally Dies." *The Onion,* 2 July 2003. Accessed online at http://www.theonion.com/onion3925/index. html on 10 July 2003.

Styron, William. *Darkness Visible: A Memoir of Madness.* New York: Knopf, 1989.

Tavalaro, Julia, and Richard Tayson. *Look Up for "Yes."* New York: Kodansha, 1997.

Taylor, Debra. "Obituaries." In *Encyclopedia of Life Writing,* ed. Margaretta Jolly, 2:667–68. London: Fitzroy Dearborn, 2001.

Tayman, John. *The Colony: The Harrowing True Story of the Exiles of Molokai.* New York: Scribner, 2006.

Temkin, Owsei. *The Falling Sickness: A History of Epilepsy from the Greeks to the Beginnings of Modern Neurology.* 2d rev. ed. Baltimore: Johns Hopkins University Press, 1971 [1945].

Thomas, Carol. *Female Forms: Experiencing and Understanding Disability.* Philadelphia: Open University Press, 1999.

Twitch and Shout. Dir. Laurel Chiten. 1994.

United Nations Population Fund. Accessed online at http://www.unfpa.org/swp/2005/english/ch1/index.htm on 1 Sept. 2008.

U.S. Census Bureau. Disability Status: 2000. 1–2. Accessed online at http://www.census.gov/hhes/www/disable/disabstat2k/disabstat2ktxt.html on 21 Mar. 2009.

Van Dijck, José. "Medical Documentary: Conjoined Twins as a Mediated Spectacle." *Media, Culture, and Society* 24, no. 4 (Sept. 2002): 537–56.

Wallace, Marjorie. *The Silent Twins.* 1986. New York: Penguin, 1987.

Webb, Ruth Cameron. *A Journey into Personhood.* Iowa City: Iowa University Press, 1994.

Weber, Bruce. "Barbara Warren, Winner of Endurance Competitions, Dies at 65." *New York Times,* 30 Aug. 2008. Accessed online at http://www.nytimes.com/2008/08/30/sports/othersports/30warren.html?ref=obituaries&pagewanted=print on 9 Sept. 2008.

Wexler, Alice. *Mapping Fate: A Memoir of Family, Risk, and Genetic Research.* New York: Times Books, 1995.

Whitman, Alden. "The Art of the Obituary." In *The Obituary Book,* 7–13. New York: Stein and Day, 1971.

Wilensky, Amy S. *Passing for Normal.* New York: Broadway, 2000.

Wilkomirski, Binjamin. *Fragments: Memories of a Wartime Childhood.* Trans. Carol Brown Janeway. New York: Schocken, 1996.

Willey, Liane Holliday. *Pretending to be Normal.* London: Jessica Kingsley, 1999.

Wilson, Daniel J. *Living with Polio: The Epidemic and Its Survivors.* Chicago: University of Chicago Press, 2005.

Wilson, Michael. "Book on Leprosy Draws Fire." *New York Times,* 27 March 2006. Accessed online at http://www.nytimes.com/2006/03/27/books/27wils.html on 24 Oct. 2008.

Wire, Nicky. "Tsunami." *This Is My Truth Tell Me Yours.* CD. Virgin, 1999.

Wolf, Helen Harker. *Aphasia: My World Alone.* Detroit: Wayne State University Press, 1979.

Zola, Irving. *Missing Pieces: A Chronicle of Living with a Disability.* Philadelphia: Temple University Press, 1982.

Index